EXPLOSIVES
and
HOMEMADE BOMBS

EXPLOSIVES
and
HOMEMADE BOMBS

Second Edition

By

MAJOR JOSEPH STOFFEL, AUS (Ret)

CHARLES C THOMAS · PUBLISHER
Springfield · *Illinois* · *U.S.A.*

Published and Distributed Throughout the World by

CHARLES C THOMAS • PUBLISHER

BANNERSTONE HOUSE

301-327 East Lawrence Avenue, Springfield, Illinois, U.S.A.

NATCHEZ PLANTATION HOUSE

735 North Atlantic Boulevard, Fort Lauderdale, Florida, U.S.A.

© *1962 & 1972 by* CHARLES C THOMAS • PUBLISHER

ISBN 0-398-02424-3

Library of Congress Catalog Card Number 75-180822

First Edition, First Printing, 1962
First Edition, Second Printing, 1968
First Edition, Third Printing, 1969
First Edition, Fourth Printing, 1970
Second Edition, 1972

With THOMAS BOOKS *careful attention is given to all details of manufacturing and design. It is the Publisher's desire to present books that are satisfactory as to their physical qualities and artistic possibilities and appropriate for their particular use.* THOMAS BOOKS *will be true to those laws of quality that assure a good name and good will.*

Printed in the United States of America
N-1

DEDICATION

T<small>HIS BOOK</small> is respectfully dedicated to the American Federation of Police, who were the first to recognize that explosive and bomb incidents were a national hazard to law enforcement personnel and therefore sponsored regional training seminars in this vital subject; to the Institute Makers of Explosives, who have provided inert explosive training aids to law enforcement training agencies without cost to the agency; and to all law enforcement and firefighting personnel who in the course of their many duties may be called upon to deal with explosives in their many varied forms.

Last but not least to my family, Kay, Joe, Anne and Stephen, for their assistance and patience.

PREFACE

MAJOR CITIES such as New York, Chicago and Los Angeles require the full-time service of police officers specially trained and equipped to handle and dispose of homemade bombs. It is not feasible for smaller municipalities, county and state law enforcement agencies to maintain full-time bomb squads; nor can the agency justify the cost or use of special handling equipment for this purpose. However, it is a recognized fact that these agencies have to contend with homemade bomb incidents and are at a decided disadvantage.

The basic edition of *Explosives and Homemade Bombs,* the first book devoted exclusively to the subject, was written to acquaint inexperienced law enforcement personnel with the techniques of coping with explosive incidents and has become the basic text for training officers in this vital subject.

Since the introduction of the basic text, both the number of explosive incidents and the types and complexity of explosives and homemade bombs have increased. This completely revised text constitutes an advanced training manual that serves to bring the officer up-to-date with the latest advances and techniques of handling explosive incidents. Maximum attention is given to the methods of the bomber, the construction and employment of homemade bombs and the techniques of homemade bomb disposal. The simplicity of layout and practicality of the first edition have been retained.

Nontechnical language has been used deliberately to facilitate the understanding and retention of the subject matter by law enforcement and fire service personnel who would not normally perform full-time bomb disposal duties, but who may have to deal with explosives or homemade bombs at any moment.

No attempt has been made to identify all commercial explosives by their trade names except in instances where the explosive or device is unique to the manufacturer. Several explosives and devices peculiar to the military forces have been included, since these items have turned up on the civilian economy in the form of war souvenirs or for illegal purposes. Information on Civil War munitions has been included for the benefit of law enforcement personnel in the central and southeastern United States.

No book can hope to offset the value of practical experience, but practical experience alone is the slow, hard and dangerous path to bomb disposal expertise. This textbook is unique in that a large number of questions, examples, problems, and practical exercises are included that are intended to provide the next best training; a combination of text and practical exercises that are based on actual incidents that have confronted disposal personnel. The practical exercise chapter combined with the questions asked at the end of each chapter in the text are designed to lead the officers in a step-by-step learning procedure and to stimulate the decision-making ability of the officer; they are intended to develop his knowledge, confidence, and competency to handle explosive incidents of any type.

This textbook is not only written for the individual student, but for employment by training officer and student in a formal classroom teaching situation. The questions at the end of the chapters constitute a review of the important teaching points of each chapter, or a method for the officer-instructor to measure student comprehension. Chapter 12 consists of fifteen practical exercise problems that combine photographs of explosives and homemade bombs and questions on the illustrated bomb or explosive. To further assist the training officer, a chapter is included on the materials and construction of representative homemade bombs which may be used in the classroom to enhance instruction.

There are many gray areas in the handling of explosive incidents, such as decisions that must be made at the site concerning evacuation, search, rendering safe and final disposal of explosive components. These gray areas are identified in the text and options, i.e. alternate methods and/or suggestions, are given.

The officer who combines the information attained from the

text with common sense application at the scene of an incident will enjoy the greatest success in his mission of protection of the public and himself.

This textbook has three major objectives:

1. To provide the officer with a working knowledge of explosives and homemade bombs, and practical safeing, transport, and disposal techniques that he may employ when confronted with an explosive incident.

2. To present situations by means of questions and practical exercise problems that will provide for individual application of this working knowledge.

3. To instil confidence in the officer in his ability to make on-the-job, practical, safe, judgmental decisions concerning any explosive incident that may arise.

JOSEPH F. STOFFEL

ACKNOWLEDGMENTS

Mr. J. S. Stoffel, Beloit, Wisconsin; Mr. M. M. Batzer, Philadelphia, Pennsylvania; Mrs. B. Picket, Oneonta, Alabama; Mrs. J. Street, Arab, Alabama; Mrs. C. Umphrey, Redstone Arsenal, Alabama; Mr. J. Hays, FBI, La Grange, Georgia; PIO & 89th Ord Det (ED), Fort Benning, Georgia; J. Arenberg, American Federation of Police, Miami, Florida; Institute Makers of Explosives, New York, New York; Mr. W. Berchtold and Mr. F. Sawyer, E. I. Du Pont de Nemours & Co. Inc., Wilmington, Delaware; Mr. V. Estes, Estes Industry, Penrose, California; Mr. T. Keller, Model Missiles Inc., Denver, Colorado; Vashon Industries, Vashon, Washington; Mr. G. Weaver, Explosive Technology, Fairfield, California; Mr. C. Lauve, Explosive Corporation of America, Issaquah, Washington; Mr. D. Lucas, Center for Forensic Sciences, Toronto, Canada; Mr. P. Tabor, Colt-Tabor, Colt Industries, Hartford, Connecticut; Federal-Spooner Laboratories, Saltzburg, Pennsylvania.

E. I. Du Pont de Nemours & Co. Inc., Figure 19; Explosive Technology, Figure 22; Explosive Corporation of America, Figure 23; St. Louis *Post Dispatch,* Figure 45; Colt-Tabor, Colt Industries, Figures 57-62; D. M. Lucas, Center for Forensic Sciences, Figure 63.

J.F.S.

CONTENTS

xiii

EXPLOSIVES
and
HOMEMADE BOMBS

TRAINING MATERIALS AVAILABLE

Training materials, 35MM color slides that duplicate most of the illustrations in this text and that are especially useful in police training programs may be ordered through the author. Appendix E lists by number the illustrations for which color slides are available. These may be ordered by writing to Maj. Joseph F. Stoffel, AUS, (Ret), 6008 Cowin Drive, N.W., Huntsville, Alabama 35810.

Chapter 1

THE EXPLOSIVE PROBLEM

BOMBERS AND BOMBINGS

In 1969 A STUDY WAS MADE of known bombers in an attempt to determine if there were certain characteristics that were peculiar to the bomber and which would assist law enforcement agencies in identifying a potential bomber. The resultant report proved to be of value in one sense only. It was determined that a potential bomber could not be identified by any detailed characteristics, but the composit characteristics indicated a young white male of upper middle class or wealthy background.

A potential bomber can be loosely identified through his activities and association in an organization that is known to employ violence and explosives to gain their ends. The Ku Klux Klan (KKK) and the Students for a Democratic Society (SDS) are examples of this type of organizations. Surveillance of known violent groups by police intelligence units and the infiltration and use of informers within the groups are still the best methods of identifying potential bombers and preventing bombings in any area.

During hearings that were conducted in 1970 by the Senate Investigatory Subcommittee on Explosives, the Justice Department reported on the results of a survey on bombings covering the period of January 1, 1969, through April 15, 1970. The resultant statistics were admittedly not complete, but did much to indicate the extent of the bombings and opened the eyes of many to the major scope of the explosive problem. The report indicated that during the fifteen and one-half months that were surveyed, a total of four thousand three hundred thirty explosive and incendiary bombings had occurred, one thousand of which involved explosives. Bombings had resulted in forty deaths, and three hundred eighty-four citizens were injured. Property damage was estimated at twenty-two million dollars. In addition, there were one thousand four hundred seventy-five attempted bombings, and thirty-five thousand bomb threats throughout the country.

In testimony before the subcommittee, Eugene T. Rossides, Assistant Secretary of the Treasury, testified that only about one-third of recent bombings could be attributed to any one cause or group and provided the following percentages:

Campus disturbances and student unrest	56%
Black extremists	19%
White extremists	14%
Criminal pursuits	8%
Labor disputes	2%
Religious motives	1%

Schools for bombers have been and are being conducted by various groups. In the mid-sixties, a House investigator testified that the Georgia Ku Klux Klan ran a how-to-do-it school for its members on time bombs, booby traps, judo and karate. A three-hour demonstration included:

—How to make a booby trap using a mercury switch from a washing machine.

—How to make an explosive charge using dynamite, blasting cap and fuse.

—How to make a time bomb by taping dynamite to a board and using a cigarette and book of matches as a timing device to allow the bombers to get away before the explosion.

—How to construct an incendiary bomb using a bottle, powdered sugar and potassium chlorate, to be set off by a capsule of acid. It was to be used against department stores that integrated, by having a klansman deposit the bottle in the pocket of a suit.

—How to set a car on fire by taping a firecracker to a bottle of gasoline. The explosion would spray the interior with burning gas. This was actually demonstrated on a derelict automobile.

—How to make a bomb using a common fertilizer and sodium phosphate.

In 1969, Students for a Democratic Society (SDS) distributed a pamphlet called *Your Manual* to many of the universities throughout the country. The initial issue of *Your Manual* promises in future issues to highlight a revolutionary leader of the month, publish an assasination list and new instructions on firebombs, napalm bombs and time bombs.

The manual advocates the gathering of rocks and bottles by students, bringing them on campus by filling purses, book bags and attaché cases, and placing them in strategic locations. "An empty bottle or rock can disable a pig for the whole campaign. Throw first at pig cameramen on top of buildings."

Red pepper, darts, water guns with ammonia solution, cherry bombs, ice picks, leather punches, can openers and sling shots are recommended for use against "mounted pigs."

Heavy duty picket signs and axe handles are recommended as clubs along with steel and lead pipes, black jacks, chains and VC Mace (Fig. 1).

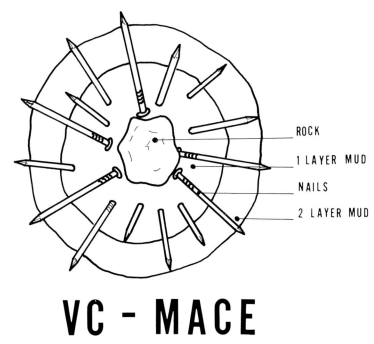

ROCK

1 LAYER MUD

NAILS

2 LAYER MUD

VC - MACE

Figure 1. Construction of the *VC Mace.*

The Zippo cigarette lighter is recommended for igniting curtains, waste baskets, bulletin boards, or paper towels in washrooms.

Oven cleaner in aerosol cans is to be used aginst "exposed skin area of the enemy."

Cherry bombs dipped in glue, then into tacks and BB's several times to form layers are to be "thrown into the middle of advancing pigs." (Fig. 2)

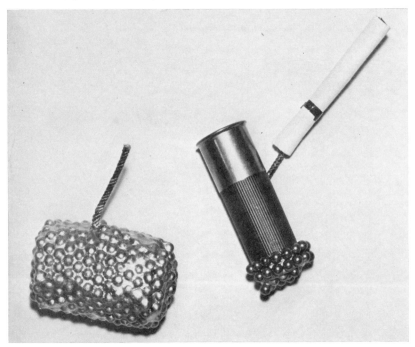

Figure 2. M-80 firecracker with liquid solder and BB surround. 12 ga. shotgun shell with fuse and BB surround.

The following is extracted from the manual and details the manufacture of a *pipe bomb:*

1. Buy a piece of pipe at any hardware store and buy cap-ends for the pipe at a second hardware store.
2. Buy gunpowder at a gun shop. If any questions are asked, tell them you are learning to reload your shells "for hunting deer on the coast range."

3. You can buy fuse at another gun store.
4. Now you are ready to construct a bomb.
5. BE CAREFUL.
6. First, drill a one-eighth hole in the pipe at the middle.
7. Second, screw one cap on pipe.
8. Now insert a three-inch length of fuse into the hole in pipe.
9. Fill the pipe with black powder; don't spill it on the threads of the exposed pipe. Now screw on the other cap.
10. For a simple time fuse, take a long cigarette and tape the fuse along the bottom of the cigarette. Now leave quickly. You have five to ten minutes until it goes off. Make sure that the cigarette burns freely to insure detonation.

SDS literature indicates American industry is to be attacked using disruptive tactics similar to those used against the nation's schools. SDS instructional material is filled with violent techniques that are used to gain their ends: destruction of the capitalist system.

The FBI has charged that the SDS has sponsored workshops to teach sabotage and how to manufacture explosives for possible use against government agencies. The 1969 annual report of agency activities said a workshop on sabotage and explosives was conducted during the national SDS convention. "It was only a short time after this national convention that a wave of bombings and arson occurred throughout the country."

Armed Forces schools have taught the largest number of individuals the functioning and use of explosives. In many instances, this training has been put to use upon the return of servicemen to civilian life. Military manuals on explosives, booby traps, demolitions, and field manufacture of bombs and other explosive devices were easily obtained from government sources.

Bomb factories have figured prominently in the news accounts across the country; most generally they concern the explosion of a bomb factory. In 1970, explosions destroyed a town house in Greenwich Village, New York. The basement was apparently being used to manufacture bombs, and one had exploded. Bomb components retrieved from the wreckage included fifty-seven sticks of dynamite, thirty blasting caps, doorbell wire, clock timing devices and plumbing pipe with dynamite and nails. Members of the SDS Weatherman faction were involved.

The explosion in Greenwich Village seemingly triggered a rash of bombs and threats from the radical left and kooks. There were five hundred ninety bomb threats in New York in three days; twenty-eight in Washington in one day; bombs exploded at the Manhattan headquarters of IBM, Mobile Oil, and General Telephone and Electronics. Bombs exploded in a Pittsburg shopping center, a Washington night club, Michigan State University's School for Police Administration, the Dorchester County courthouse in Cambridge, Maryland, and two black militants were killed when their car blew up on a highway near Bel Air, Maryland.

In Chicago, after a bomb factory explosion, fifty-seven sticks of dynamite, explosive liquid, and communist literature on bomb making were recovered.

Recovered after a bomb factory explosion that killed one Black Panther and injured another in New York were chemicals used in explosive manufacture: potassium nitrate, ammonium nitrate, sulphuric acid and gasoline, smokeless powder, lead pipes for bombs, and a map pinpointing sites of police and fire stations.

In November of 1970, police arrested six persons in New York. They uncovered a variety of explosive materials for making bombs. Material seized included explosives, over nineteen books plus other instructional material on bomb making, building plans for fifty buildings in Chicago and New York, and metal pipes and fuses.

Bombings Are Up

In the 1950's, New York experienced no more than fifty bombings a year; however, by 1969 the number of bombings had almost doubled. In 1969 there were ninety-three bombs that exploded and nineteen that did not explode in New York City. In 1969, the San Francisco bay area had an estimated sixty-two bombings and in Seattle, Washington, there were sixty. Communities that have never experienced bomb problems in the past are now involved. Bomb threats and explosive incidents are particularly threatening to communities that have a war-related industry, a college or university, or a government facility.

The year 1970 could be titled the "year of the bomb." In October, concurrent with the school year, the radical revolutionary faction of the SDS announced a "fall offensive" during which "all institutions of American injustice will be attacked." A tape recording of a voice identified as that of a radical Weatherman leader said: "Now we are everywhere and next week families and tribes will attack the enemy around the country. We intend to disarm, disable and destroy the military and pig might of America, wherever we are, however we can. We have no B-52's; our bombs are lovingly constructed by hand." The statement was also made that the "fall offensive" would spread from "Santa Barbara, to Boston and back to Kent and Kansas." In rapid succession there were bombings in California, Illinois, Washington and New York.

Airports, industry, universities, government buildings, R.O.T.C. and recruiting facilities, police and fire stations are all prime targets of the revolutionary radical. Police, government, and airport facilities were placed on special alert. A House internal subcommittee heard testimony that the Black Panthers actually supported foreign revolutionary movements. The ties of other radical groups to foreign training and influence were documented. The author, as well as the Attorney General of California, the American Federation of Police and the Fraternal Order of Police made statements to the effect that "there is a war on in this country—the police are in the forefront."

Bombing incidents went up from 1.6 per day in 1969 to 3.1 per day in the first six months of 1970. The General Services Administration reported a sharp increase in the number of bomb threats against federal buildings. There were three hundred eighty-three bomb threats directed against federal buildings in fiscal year 1970. This was an increase of three hundred thirty-seven over the previous fiscal year. Actual bombing and arson incidents in federal buildings went up from thirteen in the twelve-month period ending June 30, 1969, to thirty-eight in the corresponding period of 1970. Property damage rose from seven thousand five hundred fifty dollars to six hundred twelve thousand five hundred sixty-nine dollars. In 1970 federal buildings under GSA experienced an 800 percent increase in bomb threats and 4.4 million dollars loss in man-hours. The first two months of

1971 saw six bombings, one death, and forty-eight thousand dollars in damages to federal buildings, excluding the bombing of the Capitol.

An ominous trend developed in 1970. Many bombs were set off without warning threats being received. This was a reflection of the revolutionary thought that the killing and injuring of people, including the innocent bystander who happened to be at the scene, would emphasize their protest. Bombs were exploded that incorporated a *surround* of fence staples, nails, or BB's for increased fragmentation injuries, or used ammonium nitrate fertilizer, along with a small quantity of high explosive, to increase the explosive effects with little added cost to the bomber. An increasing number of bombs were used against police officers and police stations.

Bombs in general were more complex and more skillfully constructed than in the past. The use of small wristwatches to activate time bombs, the employment of mercury switches as triggers, and the use of small mercury and transistor batteries as power sources reflected the increased knowledge and skill of the bomb constructor. Dynamite was the favored explosive.

Extremist groups started consolidation of activities in 1970 at a midyear strategy meeting that included representatives of seventeen new-left organizations. They announced that they would initiate year-round actions at regional and local levels, and major national actions. Staff headquarters were set up in many major metropolitan centers across the country. A secret memorandum listed cities, corporations, and government buildings as targets.

During the first five months of 1970, dynamite thefts amounted to eighteen thousand nine hundred eighty-nine pounds. In Omaha, Nebraska, a suitcase bomb exploded killing one police officer and injuring seven. Black Panthers were charged. One man was killed at the University of Wisconsin when a huge bomb, consisting primarily of fuel oil and ammonium nitrate, exploded next to a research center. Student leftists were suspected. In Philadelphia, Black Panthers were charged after they threw hand grenades into a city parking lot.

During December, 1970, and January, 1971, the International Association of Chiefs of Police recorded ninety-three explosive and incendiary incidents; fifty involved explosives, forty of which exploded. Eleven of these fifty were against government facilities, thirty involved commercial and manufacturing facilities. Protest was the suspected motive for nineteen of the bombings.

MOTIVES OF THE BOMBER

As previously mentioned, a bomber cannot be identified by his appearance or characteristics prior to his committing the bombing act, but police intelligence can identify potential bombers through surveillance of groups known to employ violence.

Bombers can roughly be divided into two groups, professional and amateur. The professional bomber presents only a minor disposal problem as his bombs explode. In contrast to the professional, the amateur, who is responsible for most bombings in the United States, presents a very real and deadly threat to the disposal officer, the public and himself. While the amateur does become more proficient with time, his bombs are quite basic straight bombs; they are visually identifiable as bombs for the most part and may or may not explode. Most of the triggering methods used have been quite crude and in a great many instances they have proven deadly to the bomber. During one six-month period in the late sixties, over one-half of the persons killed by bombs were the bombers themselves.

There are many similarities between bombers and arsonists. If a person does not possess the necessary knowledge to construct a bomb or if explosives are not available, he thinks of arson as the means of accomplishing his objective. Both bombers and arsonists have the same motives; the difference is one of method. There is one exception. Despite such newspaper terms as "The Mad Bomber," there is apparently no bomber counterpart to the pyromaniac, who derives physical pleasure from the fire itself. The crazed bomber attempts to satisfy a motive such as revenge, and his satisfaction is derived from the accomplishment of the motive rather than from the fulfillment of a compulsive urge. However, when we compare the motives of the arsonist and bombers, we find a great similarity. The following is a list of the motives that were behind actual bombings that have occurred:

Political   Anti-establishment
Religious   Extortion
Nationalistic   Business rivalry
Prank   Insurance
Attempt to cause gang war   Terrorist-anarchist
Labor strife   Concealment of a crime
Organized crime activities   Attempt to gain notoriety
Racial   Jealousy
Revenge   Hate-Love
Suicide

The above motives should sound familiar to the investigator, as the same motives apply to crimes other than bombings. Law enforcement and fire service investigators with training in explosives and homemade bombs need only apply normal investigative procedures to bombing incidents.

EXPLOSIVE PROBLEMS

While bombs used by radical elements dominate the news, there are many other explosive incidents that occur with regularity: accidents involving explosives and munitions shipments; accidents and explosions involving war souvenirs and explosives stolen from military installations; bombings with labor, political, religious and other similar motives; all occur with regularity throughout the United States and constitute part of the total explosive problem.

The police departments of our larger metropolitan cities, such as New York and Chicago, have had to cope with the problem of explosive devices for a number of years. Due to the frequency of explosive incidents in these communities, police bomb squads operate on a full-time basis. Within the last few years, explosive problems confronting the police have become more numerous and are no longer confined to our larger cities. The fact is that the majority of explosive incidents occur outside of our larger metropolitan cities, and incidents involving the use of incendiary and explosive materials have occurred in all areas of the country and in small communities that cannot afford the luxury of one or more officers whose primary duty would be to cope with explosive incidents.

The abundance of dangerous explosive-loaded war souvenirs brought home by returning servicemen has created serious problems for all police agencies who are called upon to remove these explosive munitions from attics, basements and the like. This will be a continuous problem because of the necessity for our country to maintain large standing armed forces and the fact that death or movement of ex-service personnel many times confronts others with explosive souvenirs left behind, the condition of which is unknown.

Police departments, whether consisting of one or one hundred officers, have the identical problems associated with explosive incidents. A frequent occurrence throughout the United States is the bomb threat, to schools in particular. The telephoned bomb threat is a fearful problem for the unprepared agency to cope with.

Most of the explosive incidents that confront police agencies involve one of the following sources:

1. Homemade bombs
2. Transportation accidents involving explosives
3. Bomb threats
4. War souvenirs and military munitions
5. Commercial explosives
6. Sabotage devices
7. Military aircraft accidents

Certain advice can be given that will remove some of the uncertainty and place the explosive problem in its proper perspective. The explosive problem is just another of the many diversified duties of a police agency and not a very hazardous one at that. This is not meant to belittle the bomb squads of our larger communities. As a full-time job with a large number of explosive incidents occurring, the percentage of risk goes up and certainly becomes more hazardous. For the greater part, the police officer who is not a member of a bomb squad has more to fear from pursuit driving and normal police activities than from explosives. Explosives are a hazard and must be treated with respect and common sense, yet a stick of dynamite, for example, is not the awesome threat television programs would lead us to believe.

What primarily dictates the police officer's actions when he is confronted with an explosive problem? *Common sense.* The police officer at the scene of an incident is faced with the decision of what to do. In most instances, doing nothing immediately except to safeguard the area (keep others away) and to inform his superiors is the correct common sense procedure. For example, an explosive item that has been stored in an attic for a number of years has harmed no one. Disturbing the item unnecessarily, transporting it to the police station and depositing it in a desk drawer, can result in a number of complications. The number of times that the author has removed dynamite, hand grenades, even a rocket from station houses is innumerable. Certainly a police firing range or even a large field is available for placement until the item can be disposed of.

Homemade Bombs

A homemade bomb may range from a single stick of dynamite with blasting cap and fuse to a complicated time-delay type of homemade bomb, perhaps concealed in a package or suitcase. It is recommended that a department that does not have an individual trained in explosives and bombs confine its actions to security of the area and request advice and/or assistance from state police or military officials.

Transportation Accidents

An accident involving the transport of commercial or military explosives or munitions, can be a disaster of great magnitude. With the placement of missile sites throughout the United States, shipments of explosive warheads and propellants via railroad and truck are being made. In addition, shipments of atomic warheads and munitions over railroads and highways further complicate the problems facing police and fire departments of all communities.

Trucks and railroad cars transporting explosives will be placarded in accordance with regulations set forth by the Interstate

Commerce Commission (ICC). In the event of an accident involving a placarded carrier, protection to the public is the officer's first duty. Cordoning off the accident area to prevent all except competent personnel from approaching and to prevent injury or death should an explosion occur is a must. If a fire is involved, cordoning off an area is virtually all that can be done until the explosive has burned or detonated.

Certain munitions, after having been subjected to the shock of an accident and perhaps heat if there was a fire and/or explosion, may become extremely sensitive and detonate if disturbed. Accidents involving shipments of military munitions and explosives will be taken care of by military explosive disposal units upon request of the common carrier. If the accident is such as to constitute a public disaster or if the possibility of such disaster exists, police or civic officials should request immediate assistance from the nearest military installation. The Army maintains explosive disposal units on call in all Army areas and these would be immediately dispatched.

Accidents involving the shipment of explosives can occur at any time and any place in the United States. An example of a railroad accident involving a military munitions shipment took place in Southern Railroad's Norris Yards in Irondale, Alabama, and is shown in Figures 3, 4 and 5. The railroad derailment resulted in a fire and explosions that involved four cars of military high explosive artillery shells. Firemen from a nearby community were fighting the fire when an explosion occurred that killed one fireman and resulted in abandonment of firefighting activities. The fire continued to burn over twenty-four hours. State police and railroad security personnel cordoned off the area quickly and quite possibly prevented further loss of life by excluding a tremendous number of sightseers. High explosive artillery shells that had not exploded were thrown to a distance of three hundred yards. Since this incident involved military munitions, the Southern Railroad (carrier) requested the assistance of U.S. Army explosive disposal personnel, and several explosive disposal units from various locations were dispatched to the scene of the accident. Approximately four days were spent on cleanup and disposal

Figure 3. Unexploded 106MM high explosive artillery shells. Explosive is exposed inside the base end of some shells. Others are blackened and distorted due to the fire and the explosion of other shells. Irondale, Alabama.

operations. The Alabama State Police provided highway escort for trucks transporting unexploded munitions to a site where they could be disposed of by demolition.

Figure 4. General view of railroad derailment, fire and explosion of four boxcars of HE artillery shells. Note holes in the sides of some gondola cars. Live unexploded rounds were found inside and underneath other cars in the yard and out to a distance of several hundred feet. Irondale, Alabama.

The accident occurred inside the railroad yards. Had the accident taken place near a highway or an area less restricted to the general public, the loss of life and destruction could have assumed major proportions. The necessity for police to immediately establish a safety perimeter of at least 500 yards is demonstrated by this accident. Protection to the public and to the officers and firefighters is paramount. In any explosion that involves munitions or bulk explosives, red-hot metal fragments of the transport vehicle will be thrown some distance and will possibly cause secondary fires. The nearest firefighting facility should be notified and requested to stand by until the danger of an explosion is past. Always inform any fire-service personnel that the transport vehicle is explosive loaded.

Figure 5. Remnants of a steel boxcar that contained 40MM high explosive shells. Unexploded shells littered the area. Irondale, Alabama.

Bomb Threats

The statistics on bomb threats have been covered earlier in this chapter, and recommendations and suggestions for coping with the problem are covered in detail in a later chapter. It is to the communities' benefit to take an interest in the problem, as an ambulance, fire engine, or officers tied up at a school may easily cost the life of others elsewhere, lives that perhaps could have been saved had the equipment and men been available. School officials can play a leading educational role in informing students of the possible in-depth effects of a prank call.

War Souvenirs

The presence of war souvenirs and military munitions in civilian communities is definitely not restricted to our larger cities. This is and will continue to be a problem that confronts police in all sections of the United States. The proximity of a large military installation to a town presents a continuous danger insofar as explosive incidents are concerned. Military munitions are constantly used for training purposes, and some military personnel will retain some of these items. Certain military installations are so large that state and federal highways bisect the installation range areas. While these areas are posted as to the hazards and dangers of trespassing, inquisitive persons will enter these danger areas from the highway and remove many dangerous unexploded munitions (duds). That this does occur is attested to by the deaths of three children in Texas by the explosion of an artillery projectile they were playing with. In Pennsylvania, four children were killed by a rocket (dud) found on an artillery firing range.

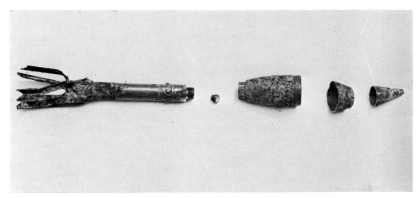

Figure 6. A World War II 2.36-inch rocket (bazooka) dud fired. This rocket was cut with a hacksaw and taken apart in a crowded machine shop. The individual attempted to remove the explosive with a screwdriver.

Upon being notified of the presence of a military munition, the police should safeguard the item only and notify the nearest military installation. The military will respond quickly and remove the munition. *Caution:* The police officer with prior military service should not assume that he knows the particular munition. The fuses and functioning of many items of ammunition such as rockets, grenades, motar rounds, etc., have undergone many changes since World War II and the Korean police action, and changes will continue to be made. The ammunition may appear familiar, but a police officer who assumes it is the same munition as he used in service may be responsible for the occurrence of an explosion.

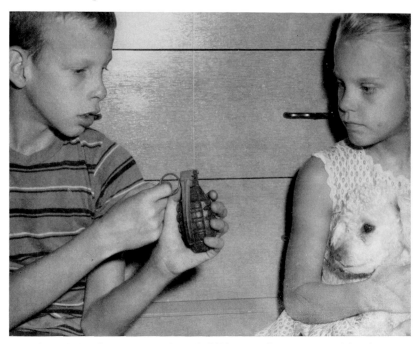

Figure 7. Dad's war souvenir and children—a dangerous combination.

Commercial Explosives

There are explosives in commercial use, such as blasting caps, black powder and dynamite, that may be pilfered by children or inadvertantly left behind after completion of a construction project. Children have an affinity for picking up bright copper or aluminum blasting caps when left unattended.

In this case also, untrained personnel should merely safeguard the item and request assistance from commercial explosive suppliers.

If nitroglycerine is suspected, safeguard and secure the services of a chemist from the nearest crime laboratory for disposal.

Sabotage Devices

The Federal Bureau of Investigation is responsible for the investigation and disarming of explosive sabotage devices unless the item is atomic. If atomic, the Army will disarm the device with the responsibility for investigation remaining with the Federal Bureau of Investigation.

All law enforcement officers, both federal and state, should promptly report all information relating to espionage, sabotage, subversive activities and related matters to the nearest representative of the Federal Bureau of Investigation.

Aircraft Accidents

Military aircraft accidents are few in number but present a potentially hazardous situation for police and fire officers to cope with. In many instances, aircraft are combat-loaded or contain explosive munitions for target practice firing on a range. Officers should confine their activities to assisting any personnel in the downed aircraft and imposing a strict guard to keep the curious away from the aircraft until military personnel arrive to take charge.

Officers should stay clear of pods, tanks, etc., and should not touch levers within the cockpit. Touching the wrong lever may fire the guns, release bombs, fire rockets, or eject the pilot seat explosively. Do not allow matches or flame in proximity to the aircraft. Confine activities to rendering assistance to aircraft personnel, reporting the location to the military, and guarding the site until military authorities arrive.

Atomic Weapon Accidents

Accidents involving atomic weapons being transported by air, truck or rail have occurred and can be expected to occur in the future. Nuclear warheads that are being transported to missile sites and nuclear weapons carried by military aircraft can be involved in an accident anywhere, in or over the United States.

What are the chances of a nuclear explosion as the result of an accident? The services agree—one in a million or more. Nuclear weapons have been transported for many years; yet a nuclear explosion has never occurred as the result of any accident. This is due to designed safety features being built into all atomic weapons to prevent nuclear yield except when intended by the user.

While a nuclear yield is remote if not impossible as the result of an accident, there is still a hazard due to conventional high explosives. There are two components that constitute a hazard: (1) high explosives and (2) plutonium.

The high explosives, which may amount to hundreds of pounds, constitute the main hazard and must be treated just as accidents involving high explosives. Plutonium may be dispensed as small alpha-emmitting particles as a result of the detonation of high explosives, or in fumes if involved in a fire. It may enter the body through cuts in the skin or through swallowing.

Officers should remain upwind from the immediate area of any fire and cordon off an area of five hundred yards radius— greater if possible. When reporting an accident to the nearest military installation, give details if possible, that is, aircraft type (fighter-bomber-transport), railroad, truck, etc. Special emergency teams will be dispatched immediately in the event of an accident involving a nuclear weapon. These teams possess their own transport and are made up of trained men using special equipment, men who can cope with the cleanup associated with this type of accident. The teams consist of medical, military police, radiological, explosive disposal, public information, communications, decontamination and other such personnel.

Additional information relative to the radiological hazards can be secured from civil defense offices.

Guerrilla Warfare Devices and Munitions

Guerrilla warfare munitions are used by the armies of all nations. However, the Vietnam conflict has been responsible for a massive education of our young men and civilians in the construction and use of these field-expedient munitions. In addition to the availability of government publications, many articles with detailed drawings of explosive devices and munitions used by the Viet Cong (VC) have been written and published by nationally distributed magazines. Fortunately, the percentage of individuals who have put this knowledge to use in the construction of home-made bombs has been small.

In addition to the large numbers of men that have been trained in explosives by the Armed Forces and the availability of United States publications, there have been large numbers of foreign publications and pamphlets circulated on explosive devices and their uses. These have been supplied by foreign subversive interests and reproduced and distributed by dissident groups in the United States. Testimony before Senate subcommittees has further indicated that many of the militants have received training in guerrilla warfare and in the construction of homemade explosive munitions outside of the United States.

For the most part, explosive devices used by guerrillas are substitutes for manufactured explosive munitions and triggering devices. Figure 8 depicts a substitute for the U.S. Army's *Claymore* mine. The Claymore is an antipersonnel mine that has a rectangular plastic body with one inner face being covered with BB's. Plastic explosive (C-4) is packed in the rest of the inner area and upon detonation many hundreds of BB's are propelled in the

Figure 8. The U. S. Army *Claymore* mine is shown on the left. The guerrilla's substitute is shown on the right.

direction toward which the mine is pointed. The substitute mine is a container with explosive packed into one end and with nuts, bolts, nails, stones, etc., packed into the other end.

Several police officers have been killed or injured due to booby-trapped automobiles and containers, and many officers search their cars for explosive devices before going to or from work. Bombs have been devised to be used specifically against police officers.

Fireworks

Fireworks are a part of the overall explosive problem. In 1970, the National Fire Protection Association estimated that fireworks used to celebrate Independence Day would cause five thousand injuries, four fatal, and one thousand four hundred fires. Most of the victims would be children and teenagers. This prediction was based on a study of over one thousand fireworks incidents in 1969. Counting unreported injuries, as many as ten thousand may have been injured. Among the 1969 injuries that were recorded were five fatalities, forty-three blindings and thirty-five serious maimings. In three hundred thirty-seven cases, the victims were holding the fireworks. About 72 percent of the victims were under twenty-one; 58 percent were fifteen or younger, and about 29 percent were aged one to eleven. About 42 percent of all injuries were caused by class "C" fireworks—firecrackers, sparklers, fountains and others generally regarded as safe. Sparklers reach a temperature of 1800 degrees and caused twenty-eight eye injuries.

Loopholes in the law combined with bootleg fireworks cause a rising toll of injuries, accidents and deaths. Over the last fifty years, fireworks accidents have killed approximately four thousand Americans—about as many as died in the Revolutionary War.

In Charleston, South Carolina, five persons were killed and fourteen injured in a fireworks explosion at a suburban grocery. The grocery was destroyed and the blast blew out windows in surrounding business firms within a radius of 200 feet. Fireworks powders are low explosives and very sensitive to heat, spark and friction. They must be treated with respect because of their extreme sensitivity.

In 1970, *merchants of death* in several midwest states were shipping explosive formulas in booklet form to youths via mail order, using advertisements that were deliberately devised to appeal to youth—*"Manufacture explosive fireworks in your own home, with homemade equipment."* Books of formulas are shipped throughout the United States, down to and including elementary school levels. One of dozens of these books that are indiscriminately sold states: "Pyrotechnics from sugar. Plans for making fireworks from ordinary table sugar. Make smoke powder, gunpowder, and rocket fuel." Formulas for black powder, ammonium picrate, a plastic explosive, fuse, rocket mixtures, nitroglycerine and hundreds of other explosive formulas are easily obtained from these sources. Manufactured fuse, the type used in M-80 firecrackers, is widely advertised and obtained at a cost of one dollar for 25 feet. While military manuals on explosives are obtainable from the Government Printing Office, these mail-order merchants of death were advertising government manuals for sale at an increased cost: "Explosives—$6.00; Demolition Materials—$3.50."

Basement Bombers

This is a term used to describe youths who mix rocket propellants (explosives) in their homes with predictable results, death or injury. In recent years, concurrent with the development of military and space rockets, youths have become increasingly involved in amateur rocketry. Virtually every state has recorded instances of deaths and injuries that have been caused by the explosion of home compounded rocket propellants. A teacher in Texas, a former employee of the A.E.C. research center at Los Alamos, was killed and seven students injured in a rocket blast. The students gave this account: "We mixed together carbon, potassium chlorate and sulfur, and placed it inside a one-foot long piece of pipe. The ends of the pipe were capped with a hole in one end. The rocket was fastened to a roller skate and we planned to hold it back with twine. Later the teacher said we would make a stronger fuel. He struck a match and held it to the end of the rocket. The rocket fizzed a second and then exploded."

Statistics on basement bombers are grim—a one-in-seven chance of being maimed or killed for each year a person engages in such activity. The combination of homemade propellants and metal rocket bodies produce, in a very high percentage of cases, *a bomb*. Many homemade propellant mixtures are so sensitive that they will explode when shaken, dropped, or compressed. Note the following accounts of injuries:

> . . . I was making a fuel of zinc dust, sulfur and potassium chlorate. When I finished putting the mixture in a jar and was about to put it up, I dropped it and it blew up.
> My friend was burned badly while firing a steel tube rocket with sulfur and gunpowder for fuel . . .
> Boy down the street blew his hand off packing zinc and sulfur.
> . . . he and some of his friends were making rockets out of pipes filled with match-heads. The pipe blew up and almost blew his stomach out . . .
> One was hurt and fingers blown off using an iron pipe stuffed with match heads, another hurt using black powder, still another when trying to preheat a CO_2 cartridge.

In a city in Georgia, local papers and television news carried a running account of a youth who constructed a homemade rocket and explosive propellant in his home. The very large metal rocket was taken to a nearby Army range and fired. Neither the news media, parents, neighbors, civil authorities, nor the Army bothered to question the fact that a dangerous explosive had been manufactured in a home; whether the steel rocket body was strong enough to contain the explosive forces without fragmenting; whether the explosive propellant was of a type that would burn, or detonate, and the fact that laws governing the manufacture and use of explosives and fireworks were ignored. This is typical of parental and official attitudes until something goes wrong. All forms of fireworks are prohibited in the Georgia city concerned.

Most rocket propellant mixtures compounded in homes by so called "basement bombers" are extremely sensitive to initiation from friction or spark.

There are several safe substitute motors used for legitimate model rocketry; these are propellants that are manufactured under safeguards and are sold in hobby shops. The most widely used rocket motor consists of a hard cardboard cylinder filled with highly compressed black powder that is not subject to accidental initiation (Fig. 9). In operation, this propellant motor throws no sparks or flame, but emits a fine grey-white powder (Fig. 10).

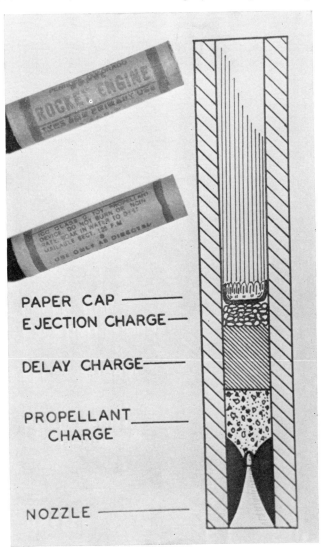

PAPER CAP ————

EJECTION CHARGE —

DELAY CHARGE———

PROPELLANT———
CHARGE

NOZZLE ————

Figure 9. Rocket propellant motors.

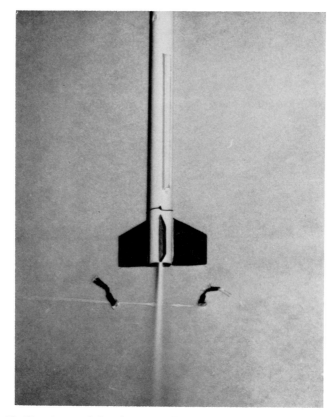

Figure 10. Burning model rocket propellant motor. There is no heat evidence, the expelling gasses are in the form of a gray-white powder.

A second safe substitute is a nonflammable, nontoxic, odorless mixture (Difloorodichloromethane) sold in aerosol cans.

It is recommended that police and fire service agencies recommend legislation to control basement bombers, but that approved propellant motors be excluded. This will direct youthful interest into safe channels and possibly eliminate a future bomb constructor. Chlorates and perchlorates have already been employed in bomb fillers. Appendix A lists many common ingredients used in explosive propellants by basement bombers.

TRENDS IN EXPLOSIVES AND HOMEMADE BOMBS

A study of individual bombings during recent years indicates a definite trend towards the construction and use of more sophisticated bombs and triggering devices.

Prior to 1968, most bombs employed were quite simple in construction and consisted of one or more sticks of dynamite with a nonelectric blasting cap and fuse or a fuse and black powder in a container. Percentage wise, automobile bombs, time bombs and release of pressure-triggered bombs were a rarity.

Since 1968, there has been a definite trend toward the construction and use of the more complex time bomb and in the use of other triggering devices such as anti-disturbance mercury switches. Small transistor batteries have been increasingly used as power sources for electrically initiated homemade bombs. More ominously, a bomb specifically designed to kill police officers was used during 1970.

While the majority of homemade bombs are still simple in their construction and functioning, the percentage of the more complex bombs employed has risen. The officer must now be prepared to cope with small wristwatch-triggered time bombs, release-of-pressure devices, pull devices, mercury switches, miniaturized bombs and booby-trapped bombs that will explode if cut into improperly or if disturbed slightly. Explosive fillers will appear in more variety than in the past, due in part to increased controls being placed on the storage and sale of commercial high-explosives. The bomber who is unable to obtain a high explosive such as dynamite will mix his own explosive which will be less powerful and less effective than dynamite. Further, the bomber will run more individual risk in the mixing of explosive and the assembly of the bomb. Explosive bombs using ammonium nitrate in combination with dynamite were used during 1970 and will probably be used in the future.

THE SOLUTION

The solution to the explosive problem is threefold: (1) Stringent control over the storage, sale, qualifications of personnel and use of explosives. (2) Increased police intelligence to prevent the bombing. (3) Provide at least basic explosive and homemade-bomb training to all police officers, and as a minimum, advanced training to personnel assigned to disposal duty.

The first part of the solution is being accomplished as a result of Senate hearings on the subject of explosives. This will not stop bombings, but will force the bomber to use less powerful explosives and increase his risk because of a reduction in safety. Damage and costs as a result of the explosion will be greatly reduced.

The second part of the solution, increased police intelligence, experienced a big jump in 1970 partially due to the increased use of drugs by youth. This stimulated the police and public to act. The results of police intelligence have been astounding and have prevented many planned bombing operations.

The third part of the solution involves police training in explosives and homemade bombs and has been the least supported in the past. This is partly due to the fact that the majority of communities cannot justify the full-time assignment of officers to bomb squad duties or the spending of necessary money to cope with what was then and is now an intermittent minor problem as far as frequency is concerned. This has further discouraged the research and development of special equipment by industry, as the available market does not justify the cost. In 1969 when campus unrest and the militant groups were most active, the small communities with a college or university in their midst were singularly unprepared to cope with the explosive problems that occurred. Many officers laid their lives on the line in dealing with explosive incidents that would have been fairly simple had the officer received even the most basic training.

Law enforcement personnel, fire department investigators and private security personnel, virtually on their own, have procured the small amount of training materials that are available on explosive and homemade bombs and conducted their own training on the subject. Many officers have financed their own training program for their department and paid their own way to attend training courses on the subject.

It is recommended that all law enforcement and fire service

personnel receive training in explosives and homemade bombs for the following reasons:

1. The first person at the scene of an explosion is the individual police officer and the fire department. Trained officers are more expert witnesses. If required, their testimony in court will be more valid for having received explosive training.

2. The officer's ability to protect himself, the public and property from the potential effects of an unexploded bomb will be greater.

3. In some circumstances the officer may be able to act immediately to prevent an unexploded bomb from exploding.

4. A trained officer may be able to identify an object as an explosive bomb, and conversely he may prevent a false alarm being given.

Several of the above advantages are dependent on the quality and the amount of training that the officer has received. Limitations should be specified in department procedures.

Those departments that do not have assigned, full-time bomb squad personnel should have at least two officers who are familiar with the advanced techniques of disposal and assign them this additional duty.

The combined training of law enforcement and fire service personnel is recommended since both are involved in many explosive incidents. In some areas, fire department personnel are assigned to and charged with bomb disposal. Many of the devices employed by arsonists are also used by homemade bomb constructors to trigger their bombs. Consideration should be given to inviting representatives from local, federal, state, county, and private security groups to attend combined explosive training. The resultant standardization, cooperation and teamwork should be invaluable in coping with bomb threats and explosive incidents.

Chapter 2

HISTORY OF EXPLOSIVES

THE ORIGIN of explosives has been lost to history, credit being given variously to the Chinese and Arabs, who used explosives primarily for rocket and pyrotechnic displays. The use of explosives has been noted in history as far back as 660 A.D. Mention is further made in the history of the 7th century of "Greek Fire," an explosive incendiary mixture consisting of salt, pitch, sulfur, rosin and oil, which was used in naval warfare of that period. In the latter half of the 12th century, Roger Bacon, an English monk writing a defense against a charge of witchcraft, outlined the ingredients of this mixture, which he called "black powder," as consisting of saltpeter, sulfur and hazel wood. Early in the 13th century, the powder monk, Berthold Schwartz, was credited with using black powder to propel stones from a gun that he invented. Black powder was rapidly developed for use as a propellant powder in warfare and was eventually used in commercial mining operations.

Three varieties of black powder have been used: black, brown, and smokeless. Black powder consisted of potassium nitrate, charcoal and sulfur. Varying the percentage of charcoal to sulfur to secure a slower burning powder resulted in a brown powder. Black powder was the principal military explosive until around 1880, when it was replaced by smokeless powder. Smokeless powder, called guncotton or nitrocellulose, was first discovered in 1838 and is produced by the action of strong nitric acid on ordinary cotton. Colloidal nitrocellulose was used in the manufacture of celluloid products and was responsible for a notorious record of fires and injuries. The celluloid collars worn by men in earlier years were a distinct fire hazard.

Nitroglycerin was first prepared in 1846-1847. The suitability of nitroglycerin as an explosive was severely limited, because it is a liquid of extreme sensitivity. In 1867, Nobel of Sweden effectively desensitized nitroglycerin by saturating porous earth called "Kieselguhr" with the liquid nitroglycerin. He called the resultant mixture *dynamite*. To initiate or explode this desensitized dynamite, Nobel invented a blasting cap filled with a small quantity of an extremely sensitive high explosive, mercury-fulminate. Nobel continued his experimentation and in 1875 invented the nitroglycerin-nitrocellulose mixtures called *blasting gelatin* or *gelatin dynamite*.

From the latter part of the 18th century through World War I and World War II, tremendous strides in the development of propellants and high explosives took place. Picric acid, trinitrotoluene (TNT) and the amatols are but a few of the many high explosives that were developed. Most of these explosives were suitable for military use only and will not be encountered by the law enforcement officer.

Tremendous strides have been made since World War II in the development of solid and liquid propellants, a fact that has not been overlooked by the homemade bomb constructor. Chlorates and perchlorates, powdered metals and other ingredients associated with rocket propellant mixtures have been used as homemade bomb explosive fillers.

Commercial explosive developments include solid and flexible explosives that may be cut into any desired shape; liquid explosives that consist of two ingredients that are completely safe (non-explosive) but when mixed together at the time of use become a powerful high explosive; and linear-shaped charge applications for cutting purposes.

Dynamite and black powder are the main explosives that are produced and used commercially, their annual production being measured in the millions of pounds. Dynamite black powder and smokeless powder are the explosives that are most widely used by homemade bomb constructors; however, TNT. and composition C-4 (plastic) explosives, attained through theft from military facilities, are also employed on an increasing scale. Crude ammonium nitrate has been employed as an explosive additive.

The history of explosives throughout the ages is replete with examples of their use by bombers, to gain their ends. As the bomber develops new techniques and applications, the police-fire officer must keep abreast of these developments in order to provide maximum protection to the public and to himself.

AUTHOR'S NOTE

The following chapters are unique in that questions are asked at the end of each chapter which constitute a review of the important teaching points of the chapter. They further assist the officer-instructor in measuring student comprehension and the success of his presentation.

Chapter 12 contains practical exercises that combine photographs and questions/problems. The written questions in the early chapters, combined with the practical exercises, constitute a complete written and practical examination on the subject of "explosives and homemade bombs." The instructor who uses this book as an individual student text may, if desired, reproduce any or all of the questions contained in the text for examination purposes.

Answers to all questions will be found immediately following individual *Questions* pages.

Chapter 3

EXPLOSIVES: CHARACTERISTICS AND EFFECTS

T HERE ARE three types of explosions: mechanical, chemical and atomic. A mechanical explosion is best illustrated by the explosion of a steam boiler, in which the pressure builds up to a point which exceeds the structural limits of the boiler. We are not concerned with the mechanical and atomic explosions in the homemade bomb sense, although it is possible that an atomic sabotage device might someday be encountered.

A chemical explosion involves the extremely rapid self-propagating (autocombustion) transformation of the unstable explosive into stable substances, accompanied by the formation of a large volume of gas and the liberation of heat. A more simplified description might be "a loud noise and the sudden going away of things from where they have been."

CLASSIFICATION OF EXPLOSIVES

The speed of the chemical reaction (autocombustion) or detonation of the explosive determines the classification of the explosive. Explosives are classified as follows:

1. Primary-initiating explosives.
2. Low explosives.
3. High explosives

Primary-initiating

These explosives are extremely sensitive to detonation by heat, shock, friction, impact, etc. The sensitivity, or ease with which they may be initiated, makes them an ideal explosive to initiate the detonation of less sensitive high explosives such as dynamite. An example of a primary-initiating explosive is "lead azide" used in blasting caps.

Low Explosives

These explosives explode rather slowly in comparison with high explosives and may be said to exert more of a pushing or heaving effect. They are used mainly as propellant powders with their burning rate being primarily determined by the size and shape of the powder grain. In general, the larger the caliber of the ammunition, the larger the grain, with the smaller grains burning faster than the larger grains. Examples of low explosives are smokeless powder used in small arms ammunition, and black powder.

High Explosives

These explosives have a very fast or high detonation rate and are relatively insensitive, requiring initiation by one of the primary initiating explosives. Examples of high explosives are dynamite, PETN and TNT. (trinitrotoluene).

Low explosives undergo autocombustion (deflagrate) at speeds of up to four hundred meters per second and produce pressures of approximately thirty thousand pounds per square inch, in comparison with high explosives that detonate from one thousand to eight thousand five hundred meters per second and up, and produce pressures up to a million pounds per square inch. When detonated, high explosives expand approximately ten thousand to fifteen thousand times their original volume.

Low explosives, including rocket propellants, burn progressively, that is, the burning action involves only the exposed outer surface of the explosive. High explosive action is not confined to the exterior surface, but progresses through the high explosive in the form of an explosive wave and in all directions from the point of initiation. Figure 11 depicts the shock wave passing through a stick of dynamite in a direction away from a blasting cap—the point of initiation. In the shock zone, the molecules of the unstable high explosive are being successively disrupted. Following the explosive wave (shock zone), chemical reaction (detonation) occurs with the liberation of heat and gas.

Note: The energy of an explosive is lower than that of many common substances such as coal. The difference in power is due to the speed of the transformation and liberation of energy.

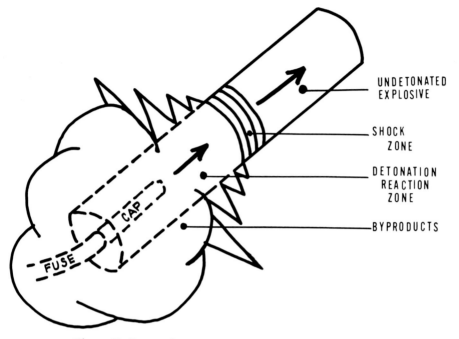

Figure 11. Detonation progress through a stick of dynamite.

EFFECTS OF AN EXPLOSION

The large volume of gas produced in a fraction of a second during an explosion occupies a much larger area than the original substance. We can readily see that certain effects are produced by an explosion, particularly if the explosive is confined in a container such as a section of pipe (pipe bomb), or confined by the walls of a room. The primary effects of an explosion may be classified as follows:

1. Fragmentation—debris.
2. Blast (pressure-concussion).
3. Incendiary (flame-heat).
4. Vacuum (suction).

The effects of a slow-burning low explosive encased in a section of pipe (pipe bomb) are the same as for a high explosive encased in an identical container. However, since low explosives burn slower (deflagrate) than high explosives which detonate, the effects will be less violent and damaging.

Fragmentation—Debris

The expanding gasses of an explosion cause any container in which the explosive is encased to expand, fragment, and propel the fragments through the air at high velocity. If we could observe the effects of the explosion of a pipe bomb in slow motion, we would first see the pipe stretch and balloon under pressures as high as seven hundred tons per square inch, then fragment. This stretching of the container is evident by heat-stress marks on the sharp edges of recovered metal fragments, and the steel fragment is noticeably thinner. (Fig. 12).

A fragmentation type of bomb is most effective when used against a group of people and where maximum death and injury is the objective of the bomber.

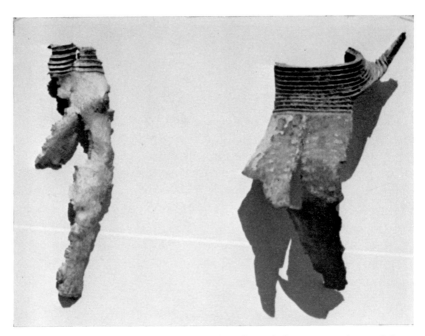

Figure 12. Note the stress marks and thinning of the recovered metal fragments of a pipe bomb.

Debris is included with the fragmentation effect, since an uncased (open) explosive that is located inside a steel baggage locker, a room, an aircraft, etc., is encased by its surroundings and parts of the enclosure may be propelled outward, away from the point of initiation. Parts of any timing or triggering device will be found imbedded in the materials that surround the bomb. An explosion that is on or below the surface of the earth will propel debris such as dirt and stones outward at high velocity.

In most instances the fragmentation hazard will extend outward to a greater distance than other effects of an explosion. On occasions the writer has had to dodge flying fragments at distances where the blast effect of the bomb was hardly noticeable.

Blast (Concussion)

Blast is the primary effect of a simple homemade bomb, which may consist of one or more sticks of dynamite taped together and fitted with a blasting cap and time fuse. Most homemade bombs are designed to produce blast damage in varying degrees dependent on the amount of explosive that is used.

Much of the energy produced by the explosion of a pipe bomb, for example, is used in the expansion of the case prior to rupture and in propelling fragments of the case. The remaining energy of the explosion is expended in compressing the surrounding air and producing a blast effect. When an explosion is initiated, the expanding gasses of the explosion reach maximum pressure in a fraction of a second and rush outward at a rate that may be as high as seven thousand miles per hour, gradually subsiding over a distance. This outward rush of gasses (blast) may damage anything in its path and sets up a compression wave in the surrounding medium. An artificial gale is set up in the air with the air acting similar to the outward radiating waves which form when a stone is thrown into water. Successive layers of air are compressed and expanded until the wave of air gradually subsides. This is generally called concussion and will sometimes be felt for a considerable distance. In one instance the writer set off a sizable high-explosive charge on an overcast day. A school eight miles away was severely shaken by the noise of the concussion because of a temperature inversion that focused the concussion noise in the school area. The writer, approximately a city block away from the explosion, felt little effects from the explosion.

When an explosion occurs below the surface of the earth or under water, this concussion effect is known as earth shock and water shock, respectively. Earth shock will damage building foundations, underground pipes, etc. Water shock travels faster, farther and with much higher pressure, and is of shorter duration. An explosion in water will rupture the plates of a ship or damage an underwater object a distance away from the explosion itself. The military services utilize the effects of an explosion by fuzing bombs, artillery shells, and such to obtain an air, surface, or an underground/underwater explosion, depending on the particular target.

Incendiary (Flame-Heat)

Observing an explosion, we would see a flash of flame, a cloud of smoke, and the surface material at the point of the explosion would be left blackened by the byproducts of combustion. This flash of flame may be of extremely high temperature and will cause fires in combustible materials at or near the point of the explosion. The incendiary effect can be classified as a secondary effect, since the use of explosives by a bomber indicates that the primary effect desired is explosive rather than incendiary action. The combustion temperatures of high explosives are in the magniture of 3,000° to 4,000° Centigrade.

Vacuum (Suction)

In the air a vacuum or suction effect is created behind the moving blast wave. In this area, pressure is reduced to a point below the atmospheric pressure. The vacuum effect is of longer duration than the blast phase, but is not as destructive. For example, the atmospheric pressure inside a building within the blast area suddenly becomes greater than the atmospheric pressure outside the building during the vacuum phase, and walls will bulge and collapse outward back towards the point of the explosion. Following air raids on cities in England during World War

II, bodies were found in doorways that fronted on city streets, with no exterior cause of death being discernible. The cause of death was internal rupturing of the lungs due to the sudden reduction in atmospheric pressure outside of the body.

Atmospheric pressure differences cause the damage during the vacuum phase. The vacuum phase is fluid and may cause damage around corners and behind barricades, whereas fragmentation and blast effects are produced only along a straight line from the point of the explosion and are deflected by barricades.

The winds of blast and vacuum may assume cyclone proportions and cause debris to be tossed around, further increasing the damage.

The vacuum effect is relatively unimportant as far as homemade bombs are concerned, since most homemade bombs contain small amounts of explosives and only a very large amount of explosive will have any appreciable vacuum effect.

Note: The effects of an atomic fission or fusion bomb are similar to the effects of a conventional high-explosive bomb, only more so. The additional effect of radioactivity can be added to the list of conventional results. It is interesting to note that the effects associated with a conventional explosion accounted for 85 percent of the casualties at Hiroshima and Nagasaki, Japan; radiation accounted for only 15 percent.

SENSITIVITY OF EXPLOSIVES

The sensitivity of explosives refers to the ease with which they may be initiated. Black powder is sensitive to spark or flame, yet is relatively insensitive to a blow or shock. TNT. (trinitrotoluene) is detonated by a powerful shock, and in small quantities will burn without detonating if the flame of a match is applied. Nitroglycerin and lead azide, an explosive used in blasting caps, are classified as being extremely sensitive, while dynamite is relatively insensitive and requires a blasting cap to set it off. Since many explosives become more sensitive with age or under long conditions of storage, the officer should treat all explosives as being extremely sensitive, for his own protection.

SHAPED CHARGE EFFECTS

In 1888, C. E. Munroe conducted experiments that made possible the development of shaped charges. He determined that if letters were cut into a block of nitrocellulose and the block placed letters down against a steel plate and detonated, that the letters were indented on the steel plate. Conversely, if the letters were raised on the nitrocellulose block, the letters appeared raised on the plate. Munroe found that deepening the cut in the nitrocellulose resulted in deeper penetration of the steel plate. Explosives that employ this effect are called shaped charges; they focus the heat and energy of an explosion against a small area.

World War II saw the first use of the shaped charge in the rocket-propelled "bazooka" and in rifle grenades that were used against armored targets. Following World War II, the shaped charge has been incorporated into many more military munitions and has found limited use in some specialized industrial work, such as the tapping of furnaces in steel mills.

The physics of a shaped charge involve a conical liner of metal or glass, explosive packed around and behind the conical liner, and a detonating source (Fig. 13). When the explosive is initiated, shock waves travel from the point of initiation through the explosive; the liner collapses and the collision of the shock waves results in a focusing of the wave. Small particles of the liner form a long narrow jet stream moving at speeds of twenty to thirty thousand feet per second. Pressures on a small area of the target of several hundred thousand atmospheres exceed the strength of the target and push the target material aside by plastic flow.

Note: Several applications of the shaped charge are shown in the next chapter under explosive developments.

FIRING OR EXPLOSIVE TRAINS

If we were to attempt to ignite a piece of coal using only a match, we would fail, since the ignition point of the coal requires a much higher temperature than the weak flame of the match can produce. The small, low temperature flame of the

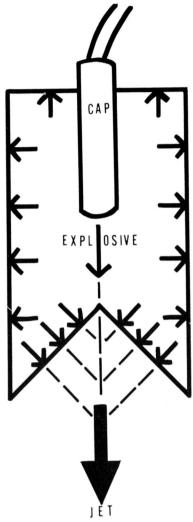

Figure 13. Construction and mechanics of a shaped charge.

match can be used to ignite paper, which has a relatively low ignition point, and the paper used to ignite wood. The wood in turn will produce the sustained high temperature necessary to ignite the coal. By using a fire train, the weak flame of the match was built up until the coal, which was insensitive to the flame of the match, ignited (Fig. 17).

Figure 14. Assorted military shaped charges.

Most commercial and military explosives have been desensitized and are relatively safe to handle and transport. Since these explosives are insensitive, a powerful shock is necessary to cause them to explode. We must apply the idea of the fire train, the flame of a match being built up until coal can be made to burn, to the problem of initiating an insensitive explosive such as dynamite or TNT, whose sensitivity to rifle bullet impact is only 4 percent. An insensitive explosive requires a powerful shock to cause it to detonate, and this shock is achieved through the use of an explosive firing train. A small quantity of very sensitive explosive called a detonator is used to explode a larger quantity of insensitive explosive called the main charge. The small detonating wave of the initiating explosive is transmitted and built up until the detonating wave is strong enough to explode the main charge (Fig. 17).

Figure 15. Metal plates penetrated by a shaped charge. The heat and plastic flow of the metal is evident.

All ammunition items, explosive demolition charges and homemade bombs utilize a firing train. As an example, a .38 caliber round of small arms ammunition has a primer in the base of the cartridge case that contains a small quantity of sensitive priming composition that will flash when struck by the firing pin of the weapon. This flash of flame ignites the less sensitive propellant powder in the cartridge case which explodes and produces a large volume of gas which in turn propels the bullet outward.

Large caliber high-explosive artillery rounds have a propellant firing train which utilizes a sensitive percussion primer, an igniter (booster) of black powder, and a large quantity of relatively less sensitive smokeless powder propellant in the cartridge case or powder bag. In addition to the propellant firing train, these artillery rounds have a high explosive firing train in the projectile.

Figure 16. A can or bottle with a curved indented base can be packed with explosives and will produce a shaped charge effect when detonated.

When functioned, a small detonator in the fuze containing sensitive explosive is initiated and detonates. The explosion of this initiating explosive in turn sets off a larger quantity of less sensitive explosive contained in the fuze and called a booster. The booster detonates, amplifying the detonating wave which sets off the main charge of high explosive in the projectile (Fig. 18).

The firing train of an aerial bomb is similar to that of an artillery projectile except that the aircraft takes the place of the propellant firing train. A bomb will generally incorporate more

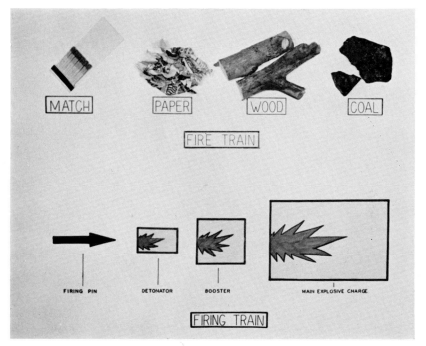

Figure 17. Fire train—firing train.

than one fuze; in case one fails, the second will detonate the bomb (Fig. 18).

Demolition firing trains and firing trains associated with home-made bombs are covered in a later chapter.

Questions

1. Explosives are classified as to the speed of their chemical reaction. What are these three classifications?

    a. _____

    b. _____

    c. _____

2. Dynamite is classified as a _____ explosive.

3. Low explosives burn progressively, involving only the exposed outer surface of the explosive; in contrast, high explosive action progresses through the explosive in the form of a _____ wave.

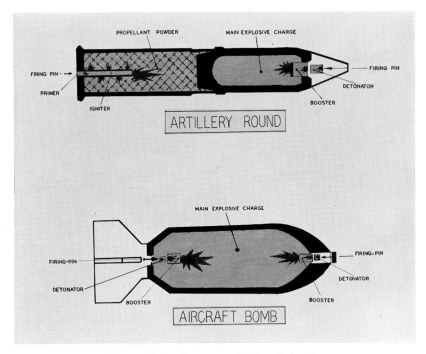

Figure 18. Artillery round—aircraft bomb.

4. What are the four primary effects of an explosion?
   a. _____
   b. _____
   c. _____
   d. _____

5. What is the primary effect produced by the detonation of an uncased stick of dynamite?

   _____

6. Is dynamite more, or less sensitive than lead azide?

   _____

7. The shock necessary to detonate a stick of dynamite is achieved through the use of a _____ _____.

Answers to Questions

1. Primary-initiating.
   Low explosive.
   High explosive.
2. High.
3. Detonation or shock.
4. Fragmentation.
   Blast.
   Incendiary.
   Vacuum.
5. Blast.
6. Less.
7. Firing train or explosive train.

Chapter 4

EXPLOSIVES WITH WHICH LAW ENFORCEMENT AND FIRE SERVICE OFFICERS MAY HAVE TO COPE

IT IS THE intent of this chapter to include only those explosives with which an officer may conceivably come into contact. Also included are military demolition explosives that are secured by the homemade bomb constructor through theft, and new commercial explosives that may be incorporated into a homemade bomb, or have a police-fire application.

The tabulation of all explosives, especially by their commercial trade names, would serve no useful purpose. If all known or suspected explosives are treated with practical common sense care, the particular type of explosive becomes of minor significance; further, there is no quick method for an officer dealing with a homemade bomb to identify the particular explosive by its chemical name. His prime worry and objective at the time is to stop the possible functioning of the bomb and safely transport the safed bomb to a final storage/disposal area. Except for well trained laboratory personnel, the officer is virtually restricted to visual identification only.

BLACK POWDER

Black powder is our oldest known explosive, originally consisting of a mixture of potassium nitrate (saltpeter), charcoal and sulfur. It is a low explosive, that is, it burns progressively in contrast to a high explosive which detonates by means of a shock wave that passes through the explosive with great speed. Until the latter part of the 18th century, black powder was identified with all blasting, propellant, and bursting charges. The formula for black powder has changed very little in the last four hundred years, remaining basically at approximately 75% potassium or sodium nitrate, 15% charcoal, and 10% sulfur. Bituminous coal has been substituted for charcoal and sodium nitrate for potassium nitrate in some commercial grades of black powder because it is less costly, but the burning rate of the black powder is reduced by the substitution. The potassium nitrate or sodium nitrate in the mixture act as oxidizers. For this reason black powder does not need air to ignite and burn. It absorbs moisture readily, a factor which reduces its effectiveness. The charcoal and sulfur in the mixtures are combustibles and the burning rate can be affected by varying the percentages of charcoal and sulfur slightly. Grain size influences the burning rate, with small grains burning faster than large grains. In form, black powder varies from fine powder to dense pellets. It is black in color except for some grains that have a grayish black color because of glazing with graphite to prevent caking in the container and the accumulation of static electricity. Commercial black powders are graded as to whether they contain potassium or sodium nitrate and are further graded as to grain size. Black powder is primarily used in fireworks, primer compositions, ignition charges for smokeless powder and rocket propellants, core-type safety fuse, pyrotechnics and mining.

Commercial black powder is packed in metal kegs containing two bags of twenty-five pounds of powder or in fifty-pound fiber cases containing two bags of twenty-five pounds of powder each. In addition to its being manufactured in various grain sizes, black powder is manufactured in a pressed pellet form. Compressed cylinders (pellets) of black powder, approximately 1 and $\frac{1}{4}$ to 2 inches in diameter, are wrapped in paper, four pellets to a cartridge which is paraffin-dipped. Each pellet has a $\frac{3}{8}$ inch center hole to allow fuse to be laced through the cartridge or an electric squib to be inserted. Pellet powders are designed primarily for blasting boreholes, whereas granular powders are bulk explosives for heavier blasting.

The ingredients for homemade black powder may be easily obtained by anyone. Drug stores maintain stocks of sulfur and potassium or sodium nitrate, and are not required to obtain a signature or to record sales. For this reason, black powder is one of the favored explosives of those individuals who construct homemade bombs. Adolescents of junior high and high school level, and adult bombers who do not have access to manufactured explosives such as dynamite, prefer black powder. Confined, such as in a section of steel pipe (pipe bomb), black powder does not need a blasting cap to explode it; the small flame from a simple homemade fuse is sufficient to cause detonation. Black powder is extremely sensitive to sparks, static electricity, heat and flame. Commercial black powder is approximately 50 percent as strong as TNT, which is a high explosive, but homemade black powder is much less powerful; the quality of the charcoal, inaccurate measuring, the inability to "weld" or secure a finely pulverized mixture of the ingredients accounts for the much slower burning and lesser power of the homemade mixtures. Strong laws governing the sale and use of high explosives such as dynamite, force the homemade bomb constructor to use less powerful explosives such as black powder, with a corresponding reduction in death, injury, and in the amount of destruction caused by the homemade bomb.

TRANSPORTATION. The law enforcement officer who may be required to transport a homemade bomb or container suspected to contain black powder must treat the bomb with a great deal of respect. Black powder is a very dangerous explosive because of its extreme sensitivity to flame and spark. The following precautions should be observed:

1. No smoking or flame should be permitted around exposed black powder.
2. If an opening in a container exists, wet the black powder prior to handling and transport.
3. If it becomes necessary to handle exposed black powder, ground your body by touching a pipe, auto body, etc., prior to handling the powder to elimate static electricity. A static discharge from your body can set off this explosive.
4. Do not allow any metal object to touch the explosive or use a metal container to transport the explosive. Use wood, plastic, cardboard or glass. Do not shake the container.
5. If the black powder is not in a tightly sealed container, tape the container to seal all openings and prevent accidental spillage.

6. If a pipe bomb or sealed bomb suspected to contain black powder must be opened, do so remotely. See Chapter 8.
7. Do not transport any explosive in the trunk of a police car in which radio components are installed. The seat is probably the safest location.
8. *Use Your Head.* A liberal application of plain common sense is the officer's best protection when dealing with explosives.

SOLVENT. Water is the solvent which dissolves the potassium or sodium nitrate.

DISPOSAL. The disposal of black powder may be accomplished by the following methods:

1. Small amounts of black powder may be disposed of by dumping the powder in a fast flowing body of water, providing that dumping is not prohibited by state law. It may also be disposed of by *leaching* with water, which will dissolve the saltpeter. The water containing the saltpeter must be disposed of separately from the charcoal and sulfur which is not explosive. Black powder which is wet is not explosive, but if allowed to dry out it may retain some of its explosive properties.
2. Black powder may also be disposed of by burning or demolition. See Chapter 9.

SMOKELESS POWDER

Smokeless powder was first discovered in 1838; however, it was not until the latter part of the 18th century that it replaced black powder as the propellant for most weapons in the United States. It is a low explosive that burns progressively and is manufactured in many shapes and sizes of grain by various nations. A graphite coating is added to the grains to facilitate loading into cartridge cases and to reduce static electricity that may be generated in manufacture. Oxygen from the air is not necessary for the combustion of smokeless powders, as they contain sufficient oxygen to burn completely even in an enclosed container such as a sealed pipe bomb.

From the practical standpoint of the officer, flame and heat are the prime hazards associated with smokeless powder. Normally, unconfined smokeless powders will burn; however, they may detonate if burned in large quantities or when under confinement.

Smokeless powders are more powerful than black powder and produce a larger volume of gasses. The burning rate is also controlled by the size and shape of the powder grains. The powders have a high degree of stability over long periods of time and are very resistant to moisture.

Two types of smokeless powder are predominately used as small arms propellants, and they are known as single-base or double-base propellants.

Single-base

This propellant is used in the majority of small arms cartridges and consists primarily of nitrocellulose. It is manufactured in various forms as flakes, pellets, and cylindrical grains. The grains may be solid or have a perforation designed to increase the surface burning area and control the burning speed. Single-base propellants ignite at approximately 315°C, and are relatively insensitive. Depending on the manufacture, the color may be amber, gray or black. It is stronger than black powder, safer, and produces pressures up to 60,000 pounds per square inch. Single-base propellants produce up to 900 cubic centimeters of gas per gram compared with approximately 300 cubic centimeters per gram for black powder.

Double-base

This propellant is essentially single-base propellant to which 30 to 40 percent nitroglycerin has been added. The nitrocellulose-nitroglycerin mixture is more sensitive, burns faster, produces more heat and gasses, and has a lower ignition temperature (150°C) than single-base powder. However, double-base propellant has a disadvantage in that the residue in the gun barrel after firing is very corrosive when compared with single-base, and for this reason is only used when the gain in power is considered sufficient to offset the disadvantages of corrosion and cleaning problems. Double-base propellant powder is used in .45 caliber, carbine cartridges, 12-gauge shotgun shells, and by the military as a rocket propellant.

The law enforcement officer will encounter smokeless powders in flake, ball, or cylindrical small grains. Like black powder, it is easily obtained for illegal purposes by anyone desiring an explosive for use in a homemade bomb, and would be used by individuals who do not have access to a high explosive such as dynamite. Many individuals handload their own ammunition and therefore have access to bulk smokeless powder, but the easiest method for the average individual to use to obtain smokeless powder is to purchase shotgun shells at various retail outlets and extract the powder from the shells. Some homemade bombs have been constructed and used that contained a large quantity of smokeless powder and were functioned through the use of a homemade percussion device (firing pin) that utilized a shotgun shell with primer intact as a percussion igniter. Smokeless powder that is confined in a good steel container, such as a section of pipe that is capped on each end and ignited by a length of fuse, will explode with great force, propelling fragments of the container outward at high velocity. Low explosives such as black and smokeless powders do not require a blasting cap to set them off.

TRANSPORTATION. Smokeless powder is a great deal less sensitive than black powder, heat and flame being the primary hazards. In general, transporting smokeless powder in a sealed container on the seat of a car and taking smoking-flame precautions will suffice.

SOLVENT. Acetone.

DISPOSAL. Smokeless powder is best disposed of by burning. *Caution:* Smokeless powder burns very rapidly and produces a great deal of heat. Follow exactly the burning method described in Chapter 9.

P E T N
(Pentaerythrite tetranitrate)

PETN, the practical abbreviation for its chemical name, was first produced in 1901. Today it is used as the explosive core in detonating cord, as the explosive in new flexible explosive sheets, and as a boosting explosive in blasting caps. Its color is white or light buff. While PETN is quite sensitive, it is classed as a non-initiating explosive, that is, it requires a blasting cap to set it off.

TRANSPORTATION. The officer will encounter PETN in other than its raw explosive form, that is, as a sheet explosive, as the boosting explosive in blasting caps and in the form of detonating cord. All forms are quite safe, and normal precautions for the transportation of blasting caps or high explosives will suffice.

Caution: Do not transport blasting caps and any high explosive in close proximity to one another. See Chapter 5 for precautions associated with the transportation of blasting caps. Detonating cord may be transported in an automobile with relative safety with smoking and flame precautions observed.

SOLVENT. PETN is not completely soluble in any medium but the best solvent is acetone.

DISPOSAL. Burning or detonation in all forms.

SHEET EXPLOSIVE
(DETASHEET)

Detasheet® is a flexible high explosive developed by E. I. Du-Pont de Nemours & Co., Inc. Detasheet is a flexible high explosive that has both military and commercial applications. It is composed of an integral mixture of PETN and a binder. This explosive is flexible over a wide range of temperatures (0° to 130° F.), may be easily cut with a fixed-blade knife and is safe to use and handle, yet it retains the high explosive properties of PETN alone. It is waterproof and available in a variety of extruded shapes and in sheets and cords (Fig. 19).

Two types of Detasheet are provided: Detasheet "A" (85% PETN), the commercial form, and Detasheet "C" (63% PETN), used by the Armed Forces. The "A" variety is colored red and the military "C" variety is colored olive green for identification. A blasting cap is required for detonation.

TRANSPORTATION. This is a very safe explosive to transport. Flame and heat precautions are most important.

SOLVENT. Acetone.

DISPOSAL. Detonation or burning.

Figure 19. "Detasheet" is available in a variety of forms. It may easily be cut to any pattern. (Courtesy E. I. Du Pont de Nemours & Co. Inc.)

NITROGLYCERIN

Nitroglycerin was first prepared in 1846 or 1847; however, it was so sensitive that little use could be made of this powerful explosive until 1904 when Nobel of Sweden discovered a method that effectively desensitized nitroglycerin. Nobel desensitized the explosive by mixing it with an absorbent material that so effectively cushioned it from shock that blasting caps had to be devised to set it off. Nobel called this mixture dynamite.

Nitroglycerin is an extremely powerful explosive, having a detonating velocity of 7,700 meters per second as compared to black powder with a burning rate of 400 meters per second.

Nitroglycerin is a clear liquid in the pure state, but yellow to brown when containing impurities, and may spontaneously decompose explosively. It is not soluble in water.

Because of its sensitivity to shock, nitroglycerin is not transported by common carrier. It is very sensitive to impact, shock, friction and flame, and an increase in temperature will increase its sensitivity greatly. Frozen nitroglycerin is less sensitive than the liquid, but accidents involving the jarring of nitroglycerin during thawing operations have occurred.

Nitroglycerin is not toxic but is readily absorbed through the skin and into the blood stream. The handling of raw dynamite may cause severe headaches, from which strong black coffee may provide some relief.

While the criminal may manufacture his own nitroglycerin, it is most easily obtained by "cooking," that is, placing the dynamite in boiling water and skimming the nitroglycerin off of the top or by "milking" the dynamite through a silk stocking in hot water, and again skimming off the nitroglycerin. Both methods are hazardous, as many criminals have found out, and the resultant "soup" from skimming is impure, highly sensitive and dangerous as a result.

TRANSPORTATION. Transportation of small amounts of nitroglycerin from an interrupted safe burglary, for instance, is not recommended. Neutralization on-the-spot by chemical means is suggested. If the liquid must be moved as such, then use an absorbent material such as sawdust, pulverized dry earth, or cotton to soak up the liquid nitroglycerin, as extreme care must be taken to protect the explosive from shock during movement.

DISPOSAL-SOLVENT. It is recommended in all instances that the services of a chemist from the police laboratory be secured, prior to movement of nitroglycerin. The disposal of nitroglycerin by neutralization is recommended. In an emergency, mixing nitroglycerin with acetone, 70 to 30 percent respectively, will desensitize the mixture which should then be soaked into an absorbent material.

If nitroglycerin has separated from old dynamite (exuded) and stained the floor of the storage location, the following mixture is recommended:

$1\frac{1}{2}$ quarts of water
$3\frac{1}{2}$ quarts of denatured alcohol
1 quart of acetone
1 pound of sodium sulfide (60% commercial)

Dissolve the sodium sulfide in the water before adding the alcohol and acetone. Use plenty of liquid, about two gallons to a pound of nitroglycerin, scrub with a stiff brush and sweep with dry sawdust. The sweepings should be destroyed by burning.

Disposal of nitroglycerin may also be accomplished by slowly adding the nitroglycerin to ten times its weight of a 17.5% solution of hydrated sodium sulfide, with continuous agitation. Heat is liberated but does not represent a hazard unless the agitation is interrupted.

AMMONIUM NITRATE AND AMMONIUM NITRATE/FUEL OIL (ANFO)

Ammonium nitrate was first prepared in 1859, and first used as an explosive in 1867 in what was essentially a dynamite mixture. Ammonium nitrate is so insensitive that it cannot be used alone as an explosive. It readily absorbs moisture and when moist will react with copper to form a very sensitive nitrate that is as sensitive as lead azide, a blasting cap explosive. It will corrode iron, steel, brass, and lead. It is not toxic, but since it is an oxidizing agent, it represents a fire hazard and will increase the combustion of flammable material mixed with or adjacent to it. Ammonium nitrate is used commercially as a blasting agent and in various dynamite mixtures. The fertilizer grade of ammonium nitrate is not explosive as such, and both the commercial and fertilizer grades cannot be exploded by a blasting cap; a primary boosting explosive must be used. Bombers have used ammonium nitrate as a surround to increase the explosive force of high explosives.

Ammonium nitrate/fuel oil (ANFO) mixtures are widely used in commercial blasting operations. They are sold either with the fuel oil in the mixture, or dry for mixing at the site.

TRANSPORTATION. Fire precautions only.

SOLVENT. Water.

DISPOSAL. Burning is recommended.

DYNAMITE

The most widely used commercial explosive in the United States and the most favored explosive of the bomb constructor is dynamite. In 1867, the Swedish scientist named Nobel invented dynamite, a mixture of nitroglycerin and a chemically inert absorbent earth called Kieselghur. Since this time, other absorbent materials such as wood pulp, starch, peanut hulls and plastic have been substituted for the Kieselghur. The dynamite was so insensitive that Nobel invented a blasting cap to explode it.

Dynamites are high explosives with detonating velocities of up to 24,000 feet per second. Their appearance varies from white through tan to deep brown and may be finely pulverized or quite coarse grained. Dynamites are blasting cap sensitive and most dynamites contain a nitroglycerin base. Other ingredients have been added to dynamite or substituted for nitroglycerin which has resulted in a wide range of dynamite grades. The percent strength of dynamite refers to the percentage of nitroglycerin by weight with variations of from 30 to 60 percent. The wide range of grades and strengths permits the user to select the lowest cost dynamite for the work to be performed. As an example, dynamite with less strength or shattering effect but with great heaving effect is preferred for blasting soft rock or earth. In addition to substituting other materials for the absorbent and the nitroglycerin, other ingredients have been added for specific purposes such as the addition of sodium nitrate, ammonium nitrate, and nitrated glycol which is added to prevent freezing under the lowest temperatures expected in the United States.

The various manufacturers produce their dynamites under a wide variety of trade names. No attempt will be made to identify commercial dynamites by trade name in this text, since it would serve no useful purpose. Packaging materials and dynamite wrappers are clearly marked as to their contents and specific information, if desired, may be secured direct from the particular manufacturer. Commercial dynamites are sold under a variety of packagings, the most familiar being in cartridge or stick form (Fig. 20). Diameters of the stick vary from one to two inches with the length around eight inches. The explosive is wrapped in plain manila paper that has been sprayed or dipped in paraffin. Dynamite is also packaged in larger sticks or shells of from two inches to twelve inches in diameter and up to thirty-six inches long. Again, the variety of packagings has little bearing on our

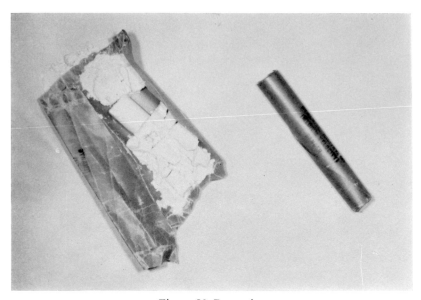

Figure 20. Dynamite.

subject as they are well marked and present no identification problem in their original packaging.

Military dynamite is in stick form, the explosive is white in color and very similar in appearance to commercial sticks. The outer wrapper is clearly marked "Dynamite" and shows its class and type. Military dynamites M1, M2 and M3, the models differing only in cartridge size, have the following explosive composition:

RDX (explosive)	75%
TNT (explosive)	15%
SAE No. 10 engine oil and Polyisobutlene	5%
Cornstarch	5%

Military dynamites are equal to 60% straight dynamite used commercially, but are much safer.

It is best to treat all dynamites as sensitive to shock, flame, spark and friction and consider them highly inflammable, although military dynamite is very insensitive.

Dynamites can be classified into four basic groups.

Straight Dynamite

This is a mixture of nitroglycerin, sodium nitrate, and an absorbent. They are named according to the percentage of nitroglycerin they contain. Sixty percent straight dynamite contains 60% nitroglycerin by weight.

Ammonia Dynamite

This is the same mixture as straight dynamite, but a percentage of the nitroglycerin and sodium nitrate has been replaced by ammonium nitrate. The addition of ammonium nitrate reduces the cost and slows the detonating rate and imparts more of a heaving effect. Forty percent ammonia dynamite indicates it is equivalent to 40% straight dynamite. It does not contain 40% nitroglycerin by weight.

Blasting Gelatin—Gelatin Dynamite

Colloiding nitrocellulose with the nitroglycerin makes this dynamite suitable for use under water.

Ammonia Gelatin Dynamite

Essentially this dynamite is gelatin dynamite with ammonium nitrate added. It combines the heaving effect of ammonia dynamite with the waterproofing properties of gelatin dynamite.

The fact that dynamites have been improved to reduce the freezing problem, safety, and exudation due to prolonged heat or age, does not mean that commercial dynamites the officer may encounter are of the improved types. There have been many instances where law officers have been called on to dispose of explosives that have been stored in old farm buildings for many years. Dynamite that has deteriorated can be recognized by its dark color and mushy feel of the stick. Exudation produces an oily brown stain on the stick and packing case. Frozen dynamite feels hard, and small extremely sensitive crystals will be seen in the mixture. If exudation or freezing is suspected, the officer should not attempt to move the dynamite but should secure the services of an explosive expert.

Dynamite has been the favored explosive of the homemade bomb constructor, since it is powerful and relatively easy to obtain for ostensibly legitimate use or by theft from storage sites. A dynamite theft is usually the tip-off as to future explosive incidents.

TRANSPORTATION. The inexperienced officer should not attempt to move or transport old exuding dynamite. It is preferable to contact military or civilian experts for advice and assistance. If no other recourse is available, move the stick or container by hand to a nearby area and burn it. The officer must definitely be prepared for a possible detonation during the burning operation. If no close area is available, then carefully transport in an automobile, a stick or container at a time, with cushioning such as a mattress will provide.

Dynamite that is not old and exuding may be transported with relative safety. Transport the dynamite in nonmetallic, covered and sealed container if it is not in its original package. Observe fire precautions in particular. Shock, flame, spark and friction are hazards associated with dynamite transport.

MILITARY EXPLOSIVES

Within the past several years, the number of instances where military explosives and munitions have figured in bombings has increased dramatically. Plastic explosive, TNT and detonating cord have been used by bombers who secured these explosives through theft from military facilities or pilfering by troops who use these items in training. See also Chapter 13 for military ammunition items.

The following explosives are peculiar to the military services, and despite the great emphasis of the military on security, these items may be encountered by police and fire service officers. They are predominately demolition types of high explosives and are most desired by bomb constructors.

Local disposal is not recommended for these explosives as a call to the nearest military installation will result in pick-up and disposal service by Explosives Disposal Units. See also Chapter 13.

Flex-X

This is the military version of Du Pont Detasheet that was previously covered in this chapter. It may be identified through prominant markings on the container and wrappings, and in some instances on the explosive itself. The charge, demolition Flex-X is olive colored.

TNT (trinitrotoluene)

First produced by the Germans in 1902, trinitrotoluene (TNT) developed into the standard high-explosive filler for military munitions of many countries. Toluene, a derivative of coke, was replaced by a synthetic toluene derived from petroleum, which gave the United States an unlimited supply of this excellent high explosive. TNT's stability, which permits melt-pour loading into munitions, stability in storage under all temperature conditions, and use in other explosive mixtures has made it the most widely used military explosive. It is light yellow in color and is used in all types of military ammunition including aircraft bombs, artillery projectiles, mines, grenades, etc. TNT is one of the main military demolition explosives. It is one of the least sensitive explosives and in the form of demolition blocks, it is virtually bullet safe. The detonating velocity is 6,900 meters per second and is not affected by moisture or sea water. When the flame of a match is applied, TNT will burn; it will not detonate unless very large quantities are burned in one pile and at one time.

Military TNT demolition blocks are produced in $\frac{1}{4}$, $\frac{1}{2}$, and 1 pound blocks. The cast TNT is encased in olive drab colored cardboard containers with metal ends. One end is threaded for insertion of a boody trap device or a blasting cap and adapter. The $\frac{1}{4}$-pound block is cylindrical in shape and the $\frac{1}{2}$ and 1-pound blocks are rectangular. All blocks are marked in yellow to indicate the explosive content and weight. See Figure 21 for the $\frac{1}{2}$-pound size demolition block.

TRANSPORTATION. This is one of the safest explosives that an officer might have to transport. Smoking and flame precautions are most important.

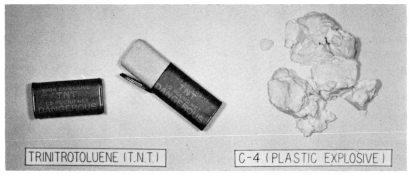

Figure 21. Military demolition explosives.

Tetratol (Chain Demolition Blocks)

Tetratol is the name given to a mixture of two explosives, Tetryl (a booster explosive) and TNT. The chain demolition blocks consist of eight tetratol blocks (11 × 2 × 2 inches) that are cast onto and connected together with detonating cord, and further packed into a green haversack. Each block has an asphalt impregnated green paper wrapper marked with the type of explosive. *Note:* Tetratol blocks are presently being removed from military service.

Transportation. This explosive is more sensitive than TNT, yet very safe to transport. Smoking and flame precautions are most important.

Composition C-3 and C-4 (Plastic Explosive)

Both Composition C-3 and Composition C-4 are popularly called plastic explosives; both consist predominately of RDX explosive in a plasticizer mixture. C-3 is an odorous, yellowish, putty-like solid and C-4 a nonodorous, white to light brown, putty-like material. Both are packaged in blocks approximately 11 $\times$ 2 $\times$ 2 inches in well marked cardboard or plastic containers.

Both are ideal military demolition explosives as they can be molded around an object and have a higher shattering effect than TNT. They are slightly more sensitive than TNT and blasting caps are used to set them off (Fig. 21).

Transportation. Same as for TNT.

Military explosives that are not considered of significant interest to police and fire service personnel, other than by name, are as follows:

1. *Composition B:* A mixture of RDX and TNT. Gradually replacing TNT as the standard high explosive filler in munitions, such as hand grenades and artillery projectiles.

2. *RDX:* This is a substitute abbreviation for cyclotrimethylenetrinitramine. Used as a base charge in some blasting caps and in explosive mixtures.

ROCKET PROPELLANT INGREDIENTS

The interest of youth in rocketry over the past years has resulted in some of these home compounded propellants being used as explosive fillers for homemade bombs. The list of various propellant mixtures is endless and would be of no practical benefit to the officer. The ingredients that are most commonly used are listed in Appendix A.

There are many commonly used substances that are explosive

under proper conditions, with gasoline being an excellent example. Given the right conditions, gasoline on a pound-for-pound basis is more powerful than TNT. No text can hope to list all possible explosive items and mixtures and still be meaningful and workable as a text. Suffice to say, it will be a rare exception for an officer to encounter an explosive that has not been covered. The particular explosive has little meaning or interest to an officer who is coping with a bomb and is primarily interested in stopping the bomb from functioning.

EXPLOSIVE TRENDS AND DEVELOPMENTS

With the increased sophistication in homemade bomb construction that has been shown by bombers and the increased use of explosives by industry, it is likely that law enforcement and fire-service personnel will encounter some perversion of industrial explosives for illegal purposes. It is further expected that both fire and police personnel will use explosives in the future to accomplish specialized objectives.

Jet-Axe

One of the first explosive devices designed for specialized use to become available is the Jet-Axe. While the Jet-Axe is specifically designed for fire department use, it is conceivable that instances might occur where law enforcement officers could apply this device to good purpose.

Through the use of controlled explosive energy (linear-shaped charge), the Jet-Axe provides the firefighter with a fast, safe method of forcible entry. When conventional techniques are impossible or when time is the factor, the Jet-Axe allows the firefighter to make an opening remotely by means of a thirty-five or fifty-foot (depending on the type of Jet-Axe used) firing line contained in the Jet-Axe. The variety of Jet-Axe models and accessories afford firefighters the capability to cut openings in concrete, cement block, or brick walls; cut openings in steel roll-up and metal clad doors; cut locks, bars and reinforcing rods. The Jet-Axe is capable of breeching 6 to 8 inch thick reinforced concrete slabs. The currently available models will cut access areas

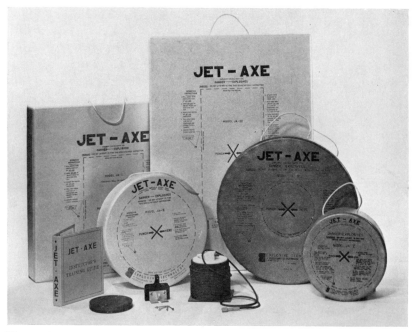

Figure 22. JET-AXE configuration and accessories. (Courtesy Explosive Technology).

from 10 inches in diameter all the way up to an area of 2 feet by 3 feet.

Inside the Jet-Axe is a linear-shaped charge called Jetcord. The Jetcord is shaped like an inverted "V" with the open side placed against the surface to be cut. Upon detonation a thin jet of material, traveling at a rate of five miles per second, becomes the cutting force. Initiation of the Jet-Axe is made by means of a firing device that contains a spring-loaded firing pin and primer similar to that found in a shotgun shell. The primer initiates a long column of explosive in a flexible firing line that in turn initiates the cutting charge. Depending on the Jet-Axe model, the amount of RDX explosive in the shaped charge varies from 2 to 6 ounces. The Jetcord and firing line, when packaged as Jet-Axe, are virtually impossible to detonate unintentionally. When thrown into a fire, the Jet-Axe burns but does not detonate. The Jet-Axe is considered bullet-safe.

Jet-Axe was designed by Explosive Technology, Inc., for use by firefighting personnel; however, it could be put to limited use by police when a surprise raid or a rapid, forcible entry must be made. While some police departments might not be interested in stocking the Jet-Axe, the fact that the local fire department has the Jet-Axe available could be of possible benefit. The need for the Jet-Axe in law enforcement is problematical but if a need is foreseen for a shaped charge application, the manufacturer should be contacted.

Astrolite Explosives

A comparatively new development in explosive technology with a high potential for employment by law enforcement and fire-service personnel is "Astrolite," a cap-fired liquid explosive. Developed by the Explosive Corporation of America, Astrolite explosives are basically liquids that can be pumped into tubes, sprayed, poured into containers, soaked into the ground, squirted into cracks, and mixed at the site from two nondetonatable components in containers. Astrolite may be used in a variety of ways that are not possible with conventional solid explosives.

Astrolite explosives are a family, that is the explosives have been adapted to a wide variety of commercial and military needs and can be tailored for virtually any application. Modifying agents can turn the explosive into gels or rubber-like solids sensitize the explosive or change a wide number of physical, chemical, and detonating properties.

Astrolite explosives can be visually identified in that they are all liquid explosives, although their consistency can vary. For example, the military version, Astrolite A-1-5, is a gray syrupy liquid whereas Astrolite "T" is a clear free-flowing liquid with a consistency of water.

Astro-Pac (Fig. 23) is the only product presently on the commercial market and holds the greatest promise for law enforcement and fire service application. Astro-Pac is prepackaged as two nondetonatable components that when mixed become a powerful, multi-purpose, liquid high explosive with a detonating velocity of 8,000 meters per second. The mixed explosive can be neutralized by diluting with at least three parts of water.

Figure 23. Astro-Pac. Prepackaged as two nondetonatable compounds. When the two components are mixed, Astro-Pac becomes a powerful, multi-purpose liquid explosive. (Courtesy Explosive Corporation of America).

Safety is unparalleled in an explosive. Both components, packaged separately, can be flown in passenger aircraft or air cargo; shipped by rail, water, or truck; transported in a passenger car; stored without an expensive explosive magazine, used simply and safely. The unmixed components are classed as corrosive and flammable and should be kept away from any source of flame, fire or sparks. They are mildly toxic. The mixed explosive is relatively insensitive to shock but precautions against flame, fire and sparks apply.

Suggested applications for law enforcement and fire service usage are as an explosive for destroying explosives and homemade bombs at a suitable destruction site and for emergency squad use.

Questions

1. Place an "X" in the column alongside those explosives that are classified as low (deflagrating) explosives.
   a. _____Dynamite
   b. _____PETN
   c. _____Smokeless Powder
   d. _____Flex-X
   e. _____Black Powder

2. Write in the probable name of the explosive opposite the description.
   a. Black with some yellow
      and white grains   _____
   b. Coarse, brown color   _____
   c. White, putty-like   _____
   d. Silver-gray flakes   _____
   e. Clear, colorless liquid   _____

3. Should you ever remove the end-cap of a pipe bomb that is suspected to contain explosive by hand? _____

4. Place an "X" in the column alongside those explosives that require a blasting cap to set them off.
   a. _____Black powder
   b. _____Dynamite
   c. _____PETN
   d. _____Smokeless Powder

5. A red color indicates the commercial version of Detasheet. What color is the military Flex-X version? _____

6. If it is absolutely necessary to transport liquid nitroglycerin, you should carefully pour the nitroglycerin onto a(n) _____ material.

7. Will a blasting cap set off commercial and fertilizer grades of ammonium nitrate? _____

8. If a rectangular container approximately 11 × 2 × 2 inches was discovered with military markings and the marking "C-

4," would it be necessary for you to dispose of this explosive?

_____

9. What is the name of the explosive in the above container?

_____

10. If you were required to transport a container of unknown explosive, which of the following precautions would you observe? Place an "X" in the appropriate space.

_____a. No smoking or flame.

_____b. Spark precautions.

_____c. Shock precautions.

_____d. Open the container and identify the explosive.

Answers to Questions

1. c, e.
2. a. Black powder.
   b. Dynamite.
   c. C-4, plastic.
   d. Smokeless powder.
   e. Nitroglycerin, or mixed Astrolite "T."
3. No.
4. b, c.
5. Olive or green.
6. Absorbent.
7. No.
8. No. (Call the military for disposal).
9. Composition C-4.
10. a, b, c.

Chapter 5

COMMERCIAL BLASTING SUPPLIES
AND ACCESSORIES

T HE FOLLOWING commercial blasting supplies and accessories used by demolition personnel are included in this book, since items such as time fuse, detonating cord and blasting caps are also used in most homemade bombs, as well as in legal commercial use. A few accessories are covered in brief, primarily for information purposes and not because they would be found as component parts of homemade bombs.

SAFETY OR TIME FUSE

Safety fuse is used to transmit a flame to a nonelectric blasting cap and in turn set off an explosive charge. When safety fuse is used by bombers in a pipe bomb, for example, that is filled with black powder, smokeless powder, or a home-compounded low explosive, a nonelectric blasting cap is not necessary to explode the bomb; the flame of the fuse alone will explode most low-explosive fillers.

Safety fuse burns at a slow uniform rate which allows the person firing the charge to retire to a place of safety before the explosion takes place. Safety fuse contains a core of black powder that is tightly wrapped with a waterproofing outer core of fabric or plastic material. The fuse outer wrapping may be any color, orange, black, green, etc., with a corrugated, semi-smooth or smooth surface, depending on the manufacturer. The burning rate can vary from 30 to 45 seconds per foot depending on altitude, moisture, and other factors that affect the burning rate (Fig. 25). Most safety fuse comes in fifty-foot lengths, two lengths to a paper-wrapped coil. Safety fuse may be transported with complete safety.

Bombers secure safety fuse through theft from commercial storage points, by ordering fuse through various fireworks outlets,

73

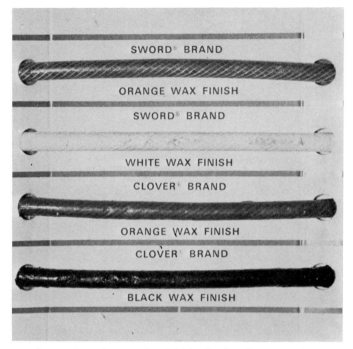

Figure 24. Various Ensign Bickford safety fuse wrappings.

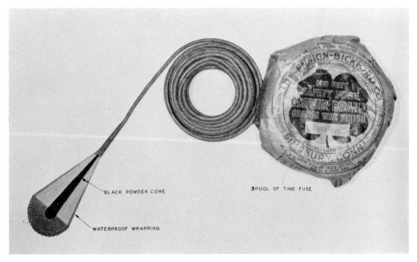

Figure 25. Safety fuse.

or by making their own fuse. Homemade fuse used by bombers is made by dipping cord in wet black or smokeless powder and allowing the cord to dry. A variation of this uses glue instead of water with the powder. Potassium permanganate, flour and sulfur mixed together and inserted into a soda straw, or potassium chlorate and sugar mixtures are also used.

Common matches are generally used by bombers to light safety fuse; however, manufactured fuse lighters are available from commercial sources. One type of fuse lighter, a pull wire type, is shown in Figure 26. It consists of a paper-wrapped tube with an open end which is slipped onto the safety fuse. Pulling the wire extending from the closed end of the lighter, ignites the

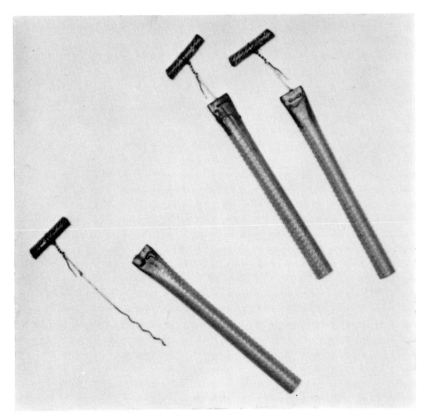

Figure 26. Fuse lighter—friction type.

friction compound which in turn ignites the black powder train in the safety fuse. Fuse lighters are used to ignite a number of explosive charges quickly and safely.

DETONATING CORD—EXPLOSIVE CORD—PRIMA CORD

Detonating cord or explosive cord, commonly called Prima Cord, consists of a high-explosive core of PETN contained in a waterproof wrapping (Fig. 27).

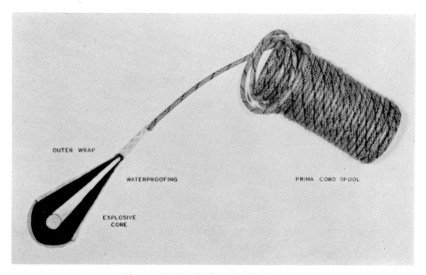

Figure 27. Explosive (Prima) cord.

Prima cord is used to transmit a detonating wave from an electric or nonelectric blasting cap through the length of the cord to directly explode an explosive charge. By means of detonating cord, the blaster can achieve a simultaneous detonation of explosive charges that are quite some distance apart and interconnected with detonating cord. Prima cord has a very high detonating velocity of 21,000 feet per second and does not require a blasting cap on the explosive charge end. Detonating cord is produced in a variety of wrappings ranging from a plain outer cover through wire and plastic reinforced wrapping, and in various colors and combinations of colors (Fig. 28). It has been

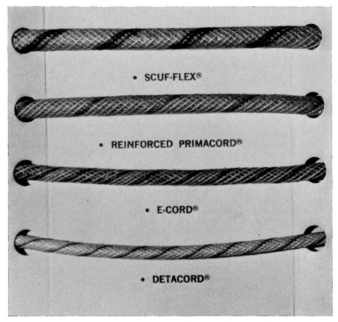

Figure 28. Various detonating cord wrappings.

used by bombers to interconnect charges set to destroy vehicles and in one attempted suicide.

Because of the many colors and wrappings associated with both time fuse and detonating cord and their similarity, both being cord and approximately $\frac{1}{4}$ inches in diameter, the only sure way for an officer to distinguish between the two is to check their cores. Safety fuse will have a black core (black powder) and detonating cord will have a white core (PETN).

Prima cord is sold in spools of 50 to 1,000 feet in length and is initiated by means of an electric or a nonelectric blasting cap.

Detonating cord is insensitive to shock and for all practical purposes is considered bullet-safe. It may be transported with safety and may be disposed of by burning or detonation.

BLASTING CAPS

When Nobel invented dynamite, he also invented blasting caps to initiate this insensitive explosive. There are two types of blasting caps in use, electric and nonelectric. They are copper or aluminum tubes, closed at one end and filled with several highly sensitive explosives that form part of the overall explosive train. They are approximately $\frac{1}{4}$ inch in diameter and their length will vary dependent upon strength and other factors (Fig. 29).

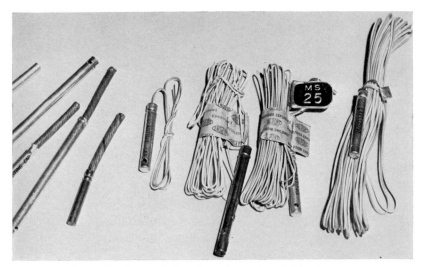

Figure 29. Assorted electric and nonelectric blasting caps.

Blasting caps contain more than one explosive. Both electric and nonelectric caps contain an ignition charge of a sensitive explosive mixture, an intermediate charge that is generally lead azide explosive, and a base charge of tetryl, PETN or RDX explosive.

Nonelectric Blasting Caps

These are small copper or aluminum tubes, open at one end to permit the insertion of a length of safety fuse (time fuse). When the length of fuse burns down, a small spit of flame out the end ignites the ignition or priming charge that is sensitive to flame, in turn setting off the intermediate and base charges in the cap. Some caps incorporate fixed delays built into the cap to permit successive detonations rather than simultaneous detonation of charges (Fig. 30).

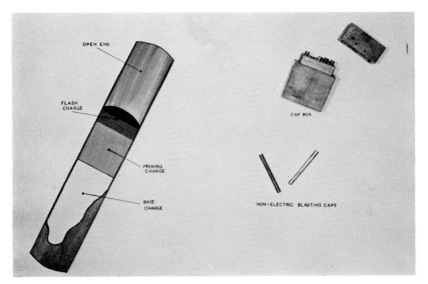

Figure 30. Nonelectric blasting cap.

Electric Blasting Caps

The electric blasting cap is used to fire or detonate many explosive charges simultaneously, or in some instances with fixed delays. Essentially electric blasting caps consist of varicolored plastic lead wires for connection to an electric power source. The ends of the wires are held together by means of a *shunt* (shorting tab or clip) to prevent an accidental firing of the cap prior to use. The shunt is removed immediately prior to connecting the lead wires to the electrical circuit. The other ends of the lead wires run through a plastic, sulfur, or rubber seal at one end of the blasting cap tube and are connected by a bridge wire imbedded in the priming explosive. When an electric current is applied to the cap, the bridge wire heats up, similar to the element in an electric toaster, and causes the priming, intermediate and base charges to explode (Fig. 31).

Electric blasting caps of various strengths are manufactured to set off explosives of various degrees of sensitivity and are numbered to indicate their strength. Other types of electric caps are produced that incorporate seconds of delay. Law enforcement

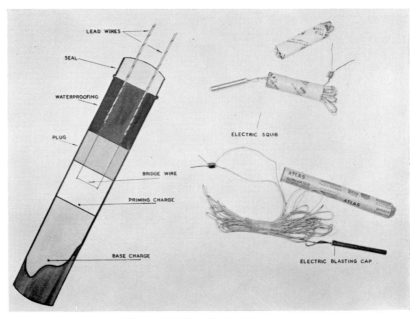

Figure 31. Electric blasting caps.

and fire-service personnel will experience little difficulty in identifying electric or nonelectric blasting caps.

The possibility of electric blasting caps being fired by induced electricity originating from mobile police-fire radio equipment is remote, but to play safe the transmitter should be shut off. If the shorting clip (shunt) is missing from the lead wires of an electric cap, twisting the bare wire ends of the lead wires together and folding the wires in an accordian fold will virtually eliminate any possibility of induced electrical energy from setting off the electric cap (Fig. 32). The high frequencies, low power and vertical antenna associated with mobile radio further preclude setting off the cap (see also Chapter 9). It is not advisable, however, to transport any blasting caps in a vehicle containing other explosives.

GENERAL TRANSPORTATION AND SAFETY PRECAUTIONS. If it becomes necessary to transport blasting caps, the following safety precautions should be observed:

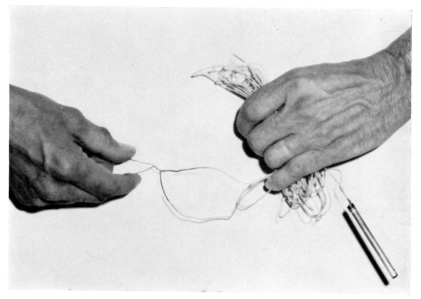

Figure 32. Protection from induced electricity.

1. Take fire precautions.

2. Carry in a covered, nonmetallic container.

3. If the caps are not in the original manufacturer's packaging, cushion the individual caps from contact with one another and from shock in particular (Fig. 33) .

4. Carry electric blasting caps with the shunt in place or the lead wires twisted together and the wires in an accordian fold.

5. Do not transport in the trunk of a vehicle that has mobile radio. The inside seat is much safer. Do not operate the transmitter.

6. Do not carry in the same container with other explosives. It is preferable to carry blasting caps in a separate vehicle.

7. Exercise common sense to protect the caps from heat or shock. *Use Your Head.*

Figure 33. Loose electric and nonelectric blasting caps should be separated and cushioned in soft cloth. Place in a nonmetallic container.

BLASTING ACCESSORIES—NONEXPLOSIVE

Cap Crimpers

To insure safety and for proper functioning, nonelectric blasting caps must be *crimped* to the safety fuse. Cap crimpers are made of a nonsparking metal, and are designed to squeeze or crimp the open end of the nonelectric cap securely to the fuse (Fig. 34).

This crimping assures a tight fit and will prevent the cap being pulled off the fuse accidentally and failing to fire the charge. Crimping also provides a good seal against moisture.

Blasting Machines (Exploders)

Several types of blasting machines are manufactured, designed to produce an electric current for firing electric blasting caps and squibs that are used to ignite black powder. Twist, push-down, and battery types are produced. A twist-type blasting machine designed to explode up to ten caps is a small impulse generator, and a twist of the handle generates the current (Fig. 34). A push type blasting machine is larger and designed to fire a greater number of electric caps. A handle geared to a generator is pushed down, generating the necessary current.

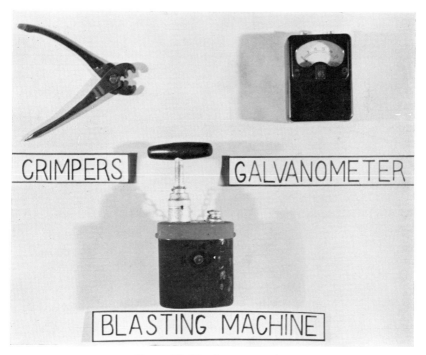

Figure 34. Blasting accessories.

Galvanometer

A galvanometer is an instrument for testing electrical continuity of a firing circuit just prior to hooking up the blasting machine to fire an explosive charge. Touching the wire ends of the blasting cap or the wire ends of the firing circuit to the terminals of the galvanometer will permit a very light current, insufficient to detonate the electric cap, to pass through the complete firing circuit. Movement of the needle indicator indicates a good complete firing circuit without a break or short (Fig. 34).

Questions

1. Safety time fuse can be positively identified by its _____ core and detonating cord by its _____ core.
2. Place an "X" in the column to indicate a correct statement about blasting caps.
   a. _____There are two basic types of blasting caps, electric and nonelectric.
   b. _____Blasting caps contain more than one explosive.
   c. _____A shunt should be connected to the lead wires in order to fire the electric blasting cap.
   d. _____Electric caps may never be transported in a police car that contains mobile radio because of the presence of induced electrical hazards.
   e. _____The most important factor when dealing with blasting caps is the exercise of common sense.
3. Cushioning blasting caps in transport is primarily designed to protect them from _____.
4. Prima cord is detonated by means of an electric or nonelectric blasting caps. Is it necessary to have a cap on the other end of the cord to detonate the explosive charge? _____
5. The detonating rate of prima cord is 21,000 feet per second. Since it is so powerful, it should never be transported in a standard police vehicle. True_____ False_____.

Answers to Questions

1. Black, white.
2. a, b, e.
3. Shock.
4. No.
5. False.

Chapter 6

EXPLOSIVE CHARGE FIRING TRAINS

In Chapter 3, we briefly discussed explosive trains and stated that since main charge explosives such as dynamite are insensitive, a powerful shock wave is required to explode them; this powerful shock is accomplished by means of a firing train. A firing train consists of a very small quantity of highly sensitive explosive, and through means of *boosting explosives,* it amplifies the shock or detonating wave until it is capable of setting off the main, insensitive, explosive charge.

In order for an officer to *render safe* or stop a homemade bomb from functioning, it is vital that he have a complete understanding of explosive charge firing trains. The object of all rendering safe procedures is to *Interrupt the Firing Train.*

The following paragraphs explain the various types of explosive charge firing trains that are employed both commercially and in homemade bombs:

Basically, homemade bomb explosive firing trains can be classified into three types:

1. Nonelectric.
2. Electric.
3. Percussion.

NONELECTRIC FIRING TRAINS

Low-Explosive Firing Trains

This is the most simple firing train that the officer will encounter and consists of a main charge of black powder, smokeless powder or a homemade low explosive, and a length of time fuse. The main powder charge is initiated by the spit of flame from the end of the fuse; a blasting cap is unnecessary (Fig. 35).

Many homemade bombs consist of a container, pipe, can, etc., filled with powder and have a length of time fuse sticking out

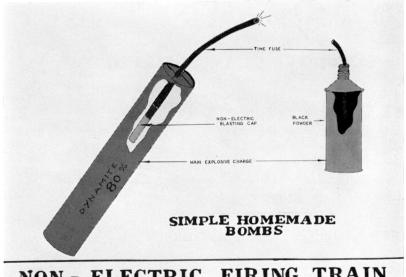

TIME FUSE

NON-ELECTRIC
BLASTING CAP

BLACK
POWDER

MAIN EXPLOSIVE CHARGE

DYNAMITE 80%

SIMPLE HOMEMADE
BOMBS

NON - ELECTRIC FIRING TRAIN

Figure 35. Nonelectric firing train.

one end. The fuse is ignited and the bomb tossed or placed at the desired location.

High-Explosive Firing Trains

In a nonelectric high-explosive charge firing train, a length of safety fuse (time fuse) is inserted in the open end of a nonelectric blasting cap and crimped. The plasting cap with fuse is inserted into the stick of high explosive and tied or taped to the explosive to prevent the cap and fuse from falling out. The safety fuse is ignited, it burns and sets off the blasting cap which detonates the explosive. The explosion of one stick of dynamite will set off any other sticks in the charge sympathetically. An example of a nonelectric dynamite charge is shown in Figure 35. The great majority of homemade bombs consist of a fuse and powder, or a nonelectric cap with fuse and dynamite.

ELECTRIC FIRING TRAIN

Low-Explosive Electric Firing Train

Blasting cap manufacturers produce an electrical cap that is similar in appearance to an electric blasting cap, but is not high explosive in design and is called a *squib*. The squib is used to initiate commercial black powder through flame rather than detonation of the cap and can be employed to set off low explosive bomb filler through flame action, similar to safety fuse.

High-Explosive Electric Firing Train

In an electric high-explosive charge firing train, an electrical impulse travels through the lead wires of an electric blasting cap causing the connecting bridge wire buried in the initiating explosive to become incandescent, firing the cap and in turn the main explosive charge.

Homemade bombs contained in packages, suitcases, etc., are for the most part electrically operated and use a battery as the source of electrical current (Fig. 36). Any electrical source can be used, such as house current direct, or through a radio, TV,

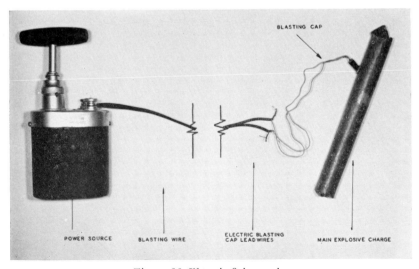

Figure 36. Electric firing train.

lamp, etc., that is connected to the house current. The electrical circuitry in an automobile is frequently employed by bombers as a current source.

Detonating cord can also be used by a bomber, although its use to date has been infrequent. In one instance it was wrapped around the waist of an individual who was attempting to commit suicide, and in another instance was used to interconnect explo- sive charges set to destroy vehicles in a parking area. Since deto- nating cord is used commercially and by the military and has been used by bombers, an example of a firing train employing Prima cord is included (Fig. 37). An electric or nonelectric blasting cap is used to set off the detonating cord which explodes at a velocity of 21,000 feet per second and detonates the explosives tied to the end of the cord.

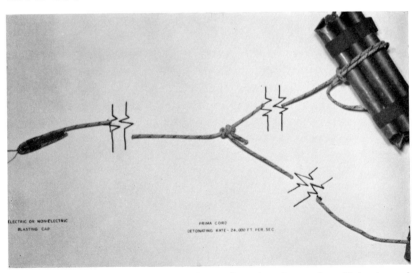

Figure 37. An example of an explosive train using detonating (Prima) cord to achieve simultaneous detonation of one or more explosive charges. An electric or nonelectric blasting cap may be used to initiate the detonating cord.

PERCUSSION FIRING TRAIN

Low-Explosive Percussion Firing Train

The functioning of a percussion firing train is very similar to the action that takes place when a weapon is fired. In a homemade

bomb employing a percussion firing train, a firing pin or a substitute for a firing pin is used to set off the primer of a round of
small arms ammunition which will explode a black powder or
smokeless powder charge.

High-Explosive Percussion Firing Train

It is possible to employ a nonelectric blasting cap, set off by
the primer, to detonate a high-explosive charge (Fig. 38).

The foregoing are examples of various firing trains. In succeeding chapters there are many more examples of these explosive charge firing trains.

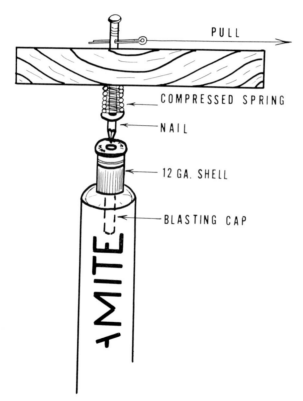

Figure 38. Percussion firing train that employs a 12 ga. shotgun shell primer,
a nonelectric blasting cap and dynamite.

Questions

1. What is the object of all "rendering safe procedures"?
   To_____ the _____ _____.
2. What two firing train components make up the nonelectric, low explosive firing train of a black powder filled pipe bomb?
   a. _____
   b. _____
3. What three firing train components make up the nonelectric, high explosive train of a dynamite filled pipe bomb?
   a. _____
   b. _____
   c. _____
4. Would an electric squib be employed to detonate Prima cord? _____
5. In a percussion firing train, can a small arms primer be used to detonate a nonelectric blasting cap?
   _____
6. What color is the core of Prima cord?
   _____

Answers to Questions

1. Interrupt the firing train
2. a. Fuse
   b. Low explosive (black powder or smokeless powder)
3. a. Fuse
   b. Nonelectric blasting cap
   c. High explosive (dynamite)
4. No
5. Yes
6. White

Chapter 7

TRIGGERING METHODS AND
FUNCTIONING OF HOMEMADE BOMBS

T HERE ARE TWO TYPES of homemade bombs which the law enforcement or fire service officer will have to cope with:

1. Straight, simple, open bombs.
2. Disguised or concealed bombs.

The straight bomb is not disguised, that is, there is no doubt that it is a bomb. Examples of straight bombs are bombs that incorporate a piece of time fuse, or time fuse and a nonelectric blasting cap in their firing train. The bombs that were shown in Figure 35 are straight bombs.

The disguised or concealed type of bomb presents the greatest threat and disposal problem to officers, as many types of homemade initiating devices and triggering methods can be incorporated in this type of bomb. An example of a disguised or concealed type of homemade bomb would be a suitcase containing a clockwork time mechanism, batteries, electric blasting cap and an explosive charge.

The armies of all nations have developed various types of booby-trap and delay-triggering devices designed to initiate an explosive charge (Fig. 39).

These triggering devices rely on disguise and concealment to accomplish their purpose, which is to kill and delay advancing enemy personnel. Manufactured triggering devices of the various nations will differ in appearance, but all will utilize one or more of the following basic functioning or triggering methods:

PULL
PRESSURE
RELEASE OF PRESSURE
TENSION
TIME DELAY (MECHANICAL-CHEMICAL)
ELECTRICAL-MISCELLANEOUS

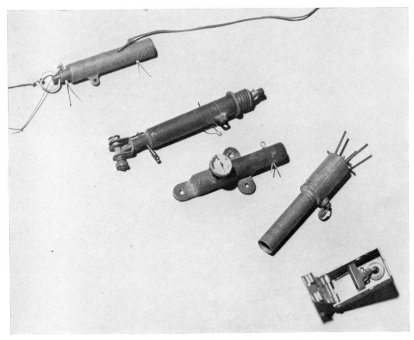

Figure 39. Assorted military booby-trap devices.

The homemade bomb, open, concealed, or disguised bomb, also utilizes triggering devices concealed inside a package, suitcase, placed under a step, etc. Since the bomber would not normally have access to manufactured military triggering devices, he must invent his own substitutes for these devices and use materials not specifically designed for triggering purposes, such as a clock, mercury switch from a house thermostat or automobile electrical system components. If ten men were each asked to construct a homemade bomb, the result would be ten bombs differing in appearance and triggering methods; however, the triggering devices would employ one of the basic functioning methods used in military booby-trap and delay devices.

In this chapter, basic triggering methods for military booby-trap explosive charges, and possible substitute triggering methods for homemade bombs will be compared and the functioning of

each described. It must be remembered that the illustrated triggering methods for homemade bombs represent but one way the
bomber can duplicate the basic functioning methods used to
trigger military booby-trap explosive charges. Many other methods
are possible, limited only by the ingenuity of the homemade-bomb
constructor. Several of the homemade bombs illustrated could
incorporate a percussion firing train in lieu of the electrical firing
train shown. Other applications of these triggering methods are
shown in succeeding chapters. For the sake of visual clarity, various safetying methods used to prevent both manufactured and
homemade triggering devices from functioning a bomb prior to
the desired time are not shown in the illustrations.

BASIC FUNCTIONING METHODS

Pull

This type of device would be used against an individual. It
requires a pull to activate the percussion firing mechanism or to
complete an electrical circuit to function an explosive charge.

A manufactured military pull type of booby-trap triggering
device is shown in Figure 40 (*1*). A pull on a wire or line will
cause a cocked firing pin to be released, striking a primer which
in turn will set off a nonelectrical blasting cap and detonate the
charge. Anything that can exert a pull can be utilized. Opening
a door, moving an object, or tripping against a taut wire will cause
this type of device to operate.

A homemade bomb constructor can duplicate this pull-type
device in many ways, limited only by his imagination. One method
is illustrated in Figure 40 (*2*). Here the bomber has used a common nail, an electric blasting cap, dynamite and an ordinary
flashlight battery. A pull on the trip wire or any object that the
wire is fastened to will pull a pin and allow the nail to move forward under spring tension, complete an electrical circuit, and
explode the bomb. It can readily be seen that the materials used
to construct a homemade bomb can be the most common objects
and are virtually impossible to trace, even if the bomb is recovered
in an intact condition.

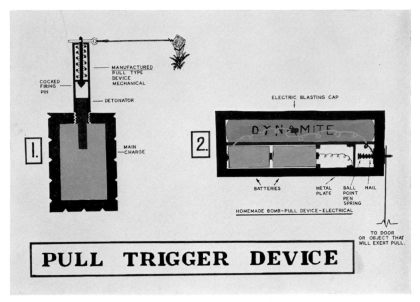

Figure 40. Pull trigger device.

Pressure

This type of device requires pressure to release a percussion firing mechanism or to complete an electrical circuit initiating an explosive charge. One type of military pressure device is illustrated in Figure 41 (*1*). Pressure on this device will release a cocked firing pin setting off the detonator and firing the main explosive charge. This device will be placed under a loose board or an object that will conceal it and at the same time is free to move down when weight is applied.

There are many ways in which a bomber can construct a pressure-activated firing mechanism and many common materials that can be used. An example of one such triggering method is illustrated in Figure 41 (*2*). The bomber in this instance has again used a common nail. Upon application of pressure, the nail would bend one metal plate against another, completing an electrical circuit, and exploding the bomb. Any piece of flexible material could be used, such as two pieces of spring, flexible wood or bamboo with metal contacts.

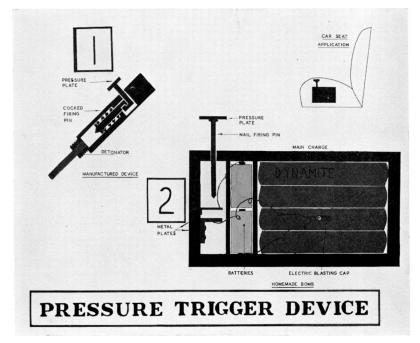

Figure 41. Pressure trigger device.

Release of Pressure

A release-of-pressure-actuated device is functioned by the removal of the object, weight, or pressure that is holding a percussion or electrical contact device from closing. An example of a manufactured military device is shown in Figure 42 (*1*). Here removal of an object will permit a pressure plate, under spring tension, to fly up allowing a spring-actuated striker to fire a detonator and explode the charge.

Duplication of a release-of-pressure device by an individual constructing a bomb could be accomplished through the use of a spring-actuated pressure plate and rod as illustrated in Figure 42 (*2*). Removal of a weight from the pressure plate will cause the pressure plate and rod to move upward and complete an electrical circuit, exploding the bomb. A bomber is not limited to the particular device illustrated; an infinite variety of materials and triggering devices may be devised and used.

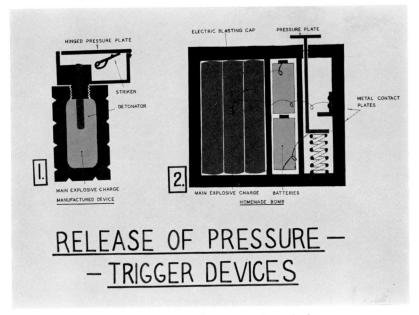

Figure 42. Release of pressure trigger device.

Tension

Tension-type devices incorporate a taut wire or cord which is physically holding back a cocked firing pin or an electrical connection contact under tension. Severing the taut wire will release the spring-actuated firing pin or an electrical contact and initiate the firing train (Fig. 43–1).

It is possible for homemade bombs to be activated using a tension type triggering device (Figure 43–2). In this instance we have a piece of bamboo held under tension by a taut wire. Cutting the wire will permit the bamboo to spring straight and complete an electrical circuit. With modification, the bamboo could act as a percussion-type device, the bamboo with metal contact acting as a firing pin. Again, any spring material may be used.

Time Delay

While time-delay can be secured by use of time fuse, it is basic; this has been covered fully in previous chapters. The more

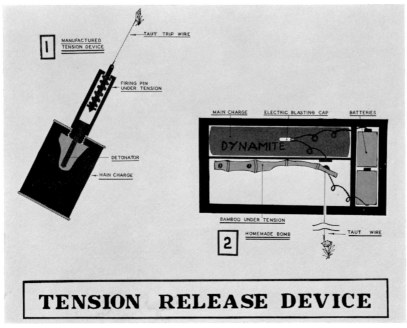

Figure 43. Tension release device.

complex time-delay triggering mechanism incorporates a mechanical- or chemical-delay mechanism. The methods used to obtain a time-delay are many, but clockwork mechanisms are used in the majority of time-delay bombs. Other ways to attain time-delay involve using a metal strip under tension that will fatigue and break after a period of time (metal fatigue), or an acid that takes time to eat through a sealant. Using metal fatigue timing is dangerous and the time is not precise; for this reason it has not been used in bombs. Chemical-delay has been used in bombs and consists of a vial of sulphuric acid with the open end stopped with a thickness of paper, plastic, or cork. To use, the vial is placed stopper down into the bomb. When the acid eats through the stopper (time-delay), it encounters a mixture of potassium chlorate and gunpowder which bursts into flame, setting off the explosive charge.

A straight clockwork time bomb is illustrated in Figure 44. The clock alarm going off at a preset time allows two metal con-

Figure 44. Time-delay.

tacts to touch, completing the circuit and detonating the bomb. The clock used would be quite silent in operation and could be rigged to release a percussion type firing mechanism in place of the electrical method shown. Wristwatches are quite frequently used as timing devices by homemade bomb constructors and are quite silent in operation; a good electronic amplifying stethoscope is needed to hear a wristwatch mechanism inside a package or pipe bomb.

Electrical-Miscellaneous

Included under Electrical-Miscellaneous triggering devices are methods of initiating an explosive charge through an electrical circuit, many of which are beyond the capabilities of the average homemade bomb constructor; for example, an explosive charge that will detonate when a radio signal of a certain frequency is received, explosive coal, an explosive cigar or pen, explosive soap, and other manufactured devices which are designed for wartime sabotage rather than for use as a homemade bomb. Manufactured devices of this sort employed by professional saboteurs are not detailed in this book, because from a practical standpoint these manufactured devices are superfluous to the existing homemade bomb problem and would serve no useful purpose.

There are certain triggering devices used by bombers that employ an outside electrical source, such as the electrical system of an automobile, or house current. An unlimited number of locations exist at which a bomb can be wired or installed in a building. Any electrical switch, plug, appliance, etc., can provide the electrical current and sometimes act as the trigger for a home-

Figure 45. Results from a bomb that was placed under the front seat of an automobile in Iowa. (*St. Louis Post Dispatch*)

made bomb. In an automobile, the horn, ignition switch, stop lights, headlights, parking lights, back-up lights, starter solenoid, and many other points in the electrical circuitry can be tapped. A bomber in Georgia employed the headlight dimmer switch in the automobile of a preacher as the trigger mechanism for an electrical firing train. In Pennsylvania, a bomb was set to detonate when the headlights of an automobile were turned on. Most frequently, homemade bombs are wired to detonate when the ignition switch is turned on. The favored position for the explosive charge is against the fire wall or under the front seat.

An explosive bomb connected to the distributor of an automobile is shown in Figure 46. Turning on the ignition switch to start the automobile will detonate the bomb. The ignition switch acts as the trigger and the automobile battery as the source of electrical power. The homemade bomb employing dynamite and an electrical blasting cap is prepared prior to installation so that

Figure 46. Automobile bomb—Electrical firing train.

the actual installation time is a matter of seconds; it takes less than half a minute for a professional to raise the hood, install the bomb, close the hood and depart from the scene.

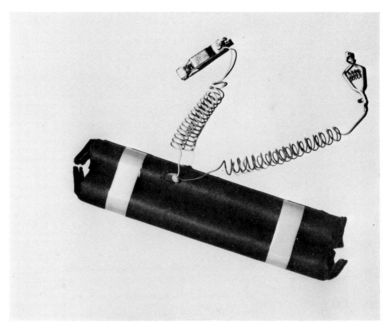

Figure 47. Alligator clips, an electric blasting cap and dynamite constitute this prewired automobile bomb. Installation takes only seconds.

Two other methods of using an electrical contact as the trigger are illustrated in Figure 48. Turning the doorknob will cause a steel ball inside the tube to roll down and contact two needle points inside the tube and complete an electrical circuit. A mercury switch from a washing machine or a house thermostat could also have been used as illustrated. Turning the doorknob will cause liquid mercury to be squeezed and to contact the two wire ends, completing an electrical circuit. Other more common mercury switches are constructed so that when the glass container is tipped, the mercury will flow to one end of the glass container and contact two wires in one end of the container, completing the circuit.

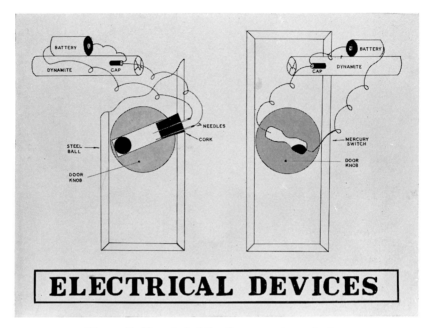

Figure 48. Electrical—Miscellaneous trigger devices.

Figure 50 shows another triggering method that employs the action of a doorknob to explode a bomb. In this instance the lead wires of an electric blasting cap are used as the electrical contacts. Turning the doorknob in either direction will cause the blasting cap lead wires to touch and complete the electrical circuit. Bombs of this sort can be prepared at another site and installed in a matter of seconds.

The miniaturization of components has resulted in the construction of homemade bombs that are the size of a package of cigarettes or smaller (Fig. 51). Transistors, photographic and hearing aid batteries, mercury switches, and small wristwatches that are coupled with small amounts of high explosive have been used in bombs and can cause serious injury or death. Bimetal strips and thermostat springs that make contact when a change in temperature occurs can be used to trigger a bomb; however, the triggers are somewhat hazardous for the bomber and it is unlikely

Figure 49. Mercury switches in a house thermostat, easily secured from this source by a homemade bomb constructor.

they would ever be used. A collapsing field type of bomb that will explode when a wire is cut is not preferred by bomb constructors as there are easier ways to booby-trap a bomb. Bombers desire a bomb that is simple to construct and to assemble as there is much less risk and less chance of a malfunction or dud.

A movie titled "Doomsday Flight," written by Rod Serling, concerned the flight of a passenger plane with a barometric (pressure) bomb hidden aboard. Supposedly the bomb would detonate when the plane descended to five thousand feet altitude. The plane landed safely at Denver, Colorado, altitude five thousand two hundred feet, without an explosion. Since the television presentation, extortionists have used this plot several times. In

Figure 50. Electrical—Miscellaneous trigger device.

August, 1970, an airline paid $25,000 dollars to an extortionist who claimed a bomb was aboard the Alaska to Seattle flight. No bomb was found on the plane. In May of 1971, Quantis, Australian Airlines, paid $560,000 dollars to a gang who claimed a barometric bomb was aboard a Boeing 707 jetliner in flight. As proof of the bomb the gang reported a similar bomb was in an airport locker. Police rushed to the locker and found a barometric bomb that was not electrically connected, but which if connected would explode the bomb at twenty thousand feet altitude on descent. The barometric trigger was an aircraft altimeter and the explosive glegnite (dynamite). After the payoff to the extortionists, several similar threats were received but no bomb was found aboard any plane. Several days after the Australian incident, National Airlines in Miami, Florida, received a similar threat. Police were also

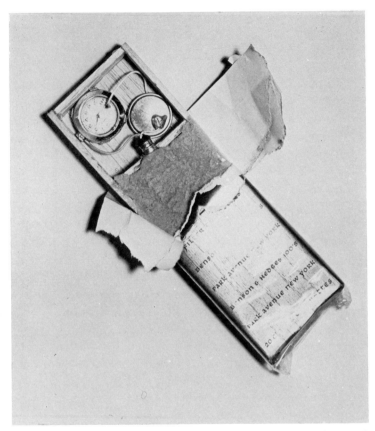

Figure 51. Cigarette package bomb employing a wristwatch timing device designed to arm the bomb after being placed by the bomber. A wristwatch, battery, electric cap and dynamite complete this bomb.

told that a bomb similar to the one in the plane could be found in an airport locker. A bomb was located in a locker, the components were a clock, wire and batteries, but it was so crudely assembled that it could not trigger and explode.

The simple uncomplicated bomb is still the most effective tool of the bomber who has no desire to risk his safety or the effectiveness of the bomb by making a complicated device that may very well malfunction. Sound reasoning and good common sense on the part of the disposal officer will enable him to cope with any explosive incident with minimum risk to himself and maximum protection to the public.

In many instances, in trying to fit a homemade bomb triggering-functioning method into one of the seven categories (pull, pressure, etc,), the author and the officer are placed in the position of trying to answer "Which came first, the chicken or the egg?" As an example, the twist of a doorknob can set off a bomb, and categorizing the triggering method as electrical-miscellaneous is not quite true since the action was a twist. The seven classifications listed in this chapter represent the best practical compromise at classification, or categorizing. If the officer understands the triggering method and the firing train of the homemade bomb, he is in a position to safely stop the action. For instructional purposes, however, this classification was deemed the best method of enabling an officer to understand the triggering method and functioning of the more complex homemade bombs and still allow for some variations that may be encountered. While it is very desirable that an officer fully understand the triggering method and functioning of a homemade bomb, instances have occurred where the officer could not determine the triggering method, but through his knowledge of firing trains alone, he was able to safely interrupt the explosive train and render the bomb safe. By the same token, the opposite is also true, that is, the trigger can be interrupted.

Fortunately most homemade bombs are simple in construction and functioning and do not reflect a great deal of knowledge or desire on the part of the bomber to turn out a complicated bomb at much greater risk to himself. Many bombs present more of a safety hazard to the bomber during construction than they do to the disposal officer. The majority of homemade-bomb constructors are not well educated in the safe assembly of the more complex bombs, and the rendering safe of most homemade bombs is not to be especially feared. Several bombs have incorporated more than one triggering method, and in several instances, more than one bomb have been placed. The officer should never assume that because one trigger is identified or one bomb located, he can relax. Bomb searches must be thorough.

This chapter has dealt primarily with the basic functioning and triggering methods employed by bombers. Succeeding chapters will present many more examples and variations of the basic triggering and functioning methods.

Questions

1. Write the "most probable" triggering method in the space provided opposite the functioning description.

   a. A bomb that functions when a headlight dimmer switch is activated. _____

   b. A bomb that explodes when a desk drawer is opened.

   _____

   c. An explosion occurs when a package is opened.

   _____

   d. A bomb that functions thirty minutes after a bomb threat is received at a local industry. _____

   e. A disguised package bomb explodes when jerked remotely.

   _____

   f. An explosion occurs when a TV set is turned on.

   _____

   g. A taut wire is sheared and a bomb explodes.

   _____

   h. An explosion occurs in a suit coat pocket among a rack of suits in a men's clothing store. _____

   i. A bomb detonates when an automobile is shifted into reverse. _____

2. An officer, when confronted with a bomb that he must physically disarm, should attempt to identify both the explosive train and the triggering and functioning methods. With this in mind, what is the object of all rendering-safe procedures?

Answers to Questions

1. a. Pressure
   b. Pull
   c. Release of pressure
   d. Time

    e. Electrical-miscellaneous (vibration)
    f. Electrical-miscellaneous (twist)
    g. Tension
    h. Time
    i. Electrical-miscellaneous
2. Interrupt the explosive train.

Chapter 8

UNEXPLODED HOMEMADE BOMBS

Most articles and publications dealing with law enforcement activities either ignore the explosive and homemade-bomb problem, or simply state the hazard and recommend that an explosive expert be called. This is no help, since most communities do not have an explosive expert trained and qualified to cope with a homemade bomb. Since bombings are infrequent in most communities, the community cannot justify the funds for special bomb-handling equipment. A state police crime laboratory may have an individual who is qualified, and if time permits, may be called on for advice and assistance in bomb disposal or in the investigation of a homemade-bomb incident.

If a police agency is suddenly confronted with a call, "A bomb is going to explode at the high school in thirty minutes," what can be done? The absence of a prepared plan developed through thought and coordination with other interested agencies, and which outlines the procedure to be followed in evacuating the school and conducting a search, and the procedure to follow if a bomb is located, etc., places the unprepared city and police agency in an unenviable position. A major disaster is possibly in the making, followed by recriminations and acrimony. A rash of bombings and bomb threats will follow many labor, racial and militant meetings, most of which are false but which must be investigated and acted upon promptly. The police department of a large city can be completely disrupted when confronted with continuous bomb threats while at the same time having to deal with the primary cause of the trouble which might be labor, racial or anti-establishment inspired.

THE BOMB THREAT PROBLEM IS NOT RESTRICTED TO OUR LARGER CITIES. EVERY CITY REGARDLESS OF SIZE IS NOW CONFRONTED WITH THIS PROBLEM.

BOMB PLAN

The author strongly recommends that all law enforcement agencies prepare a plan that outlines the procedures to be followed should an explosive or homemade-bomb incident occur. The contents of the plan should be made a permanent part of the police training program. Preparing a draft plan and circulating the plan for coordination and approval among interested sections of the police department, Civil Defense unit, school officials, fire department, and responsible city officials will result in a safe, efficient, practical, and workable plan. The plan should include, but need not be limited to, the following: actions concerning schools, hospitals, specific public buildings, bus stations, airports, railroad stations, etc.; notification, evacuation procedures, conduct of search, traffic control, disposition of an intact bomb, evidence, agencies and individuals responsible for operations and control, etc. The officer responsible for performing any rendering-safe procedure on a bomb should not be held to a detailed rendering-safe procedure. A detailed procedure is virtually impossible to outline because of the multiplicity of possible bombs and triggering devices that may be encountered in a variety of locations, and the disposal officer must have freedom of choice in deciding what to do in the particular circumstance. The disposal officer who is responsible for performing the rendering-safe procedure is the one whose life is on the line.

Since incendiary devices may be encountered, fire department personnel can provide valuable assistance and support in preparing a plan of action and the local fire chief should be consulted. Most city and state laws governing the normal movement, handling, and storage of explosives are the responsibility of city and state fire officials.

Advice, assistance, and some live lecture-demonstration training on explosives can be secured by a letter of request to the nearest Army Area Headquarters. All Army areas have Explosive Disposal Detachments that are available for assistance in the explosive area.

The following represents a skeleton outline of factors to consider in the development of a bomb plan that is unique to a particular building, industry, city, etc. It is intended to guide and stimulate the thoughts of an officer who is responsible for the preparation of a bomb plan. Statements in a bomb plan should be detailed in most areas; list the names and phone numbers of individuals to be contacted, yet keep the plan as simple as possible, practical and workable. Try to organize the plan in sections that can be distributed to specific interested agencies rather than having to reproduce and pass on the entire plan.

CITY OF _____

Police Department
Explosive and Homemade-Bomb Plan

SECTION

1. *Responsible Agencies*

   Outline here the responsibilities of your agency and others such as the fire department, county, etc. List any mutual assistance agreements between city and county, etc.

2. *Consultants and Assistance*

   List private civilian agencies such as explosive companies, out-of-house crime laboratory service, military explosive disposal assistance, rescue units, Civil Defense units, etc., that can be called on for advice and assistance, and to what extent.

3. *Public Information Policy*

   List official spokesmen and any restrictions on information given to local news media. (Following some incidents, local news media have published detailed artist drawings on bombs, showing construction and functioning, which further compounds the problem).

4. *Bomb Squad Organization, Equipment and Procedures*

   Include an organizational chart with names, responsibilities, equipment, and the initial procedure to follow when a call is received that requires action by the squad. (The term "squad" is used here for want of a better word.) It is an actual fact that the majority of communities do not have the funds or the number of incidents to justify assignment of this duty to an officer on a full-time basis.

5. *Bomb Threat Procedure*
   a. *General*

   This section should contain general procedures for distribution to schools, public facilities, industry, etc. List recommendations for individuals and facilities receiving a bomb threat, to include recommended actions and steps that any private security force can take.

   b. *Detailed*

   A list of the detailed procedures for your agency to take, such as notification of officials or groups concerned. Any notification of fire, rescue, medical, utility, Civil Defense, city engineer, city attorney, etc., should appear here.

6. *Search Procedure*
   a. *General*

   Give a recommended general procedure for all types of facilities in your area: what they can do to help themselves; what assistance you require of them. This is a general procedure, as a facility will have to fit it to their particular situation.

   b. *Detailed*

   Outline detailed procedures to include search steps, by priority, for community facilities that you are responsible for. Any special floor plans with special search procedures might be included here. Give less detailed step-by-step procedures for an officer to follow when required to conduct a search of an unfamiliar building. Consider using inhouse building personnel to conduct the search.

7. *Unexploded Bomb (UXB) Procedure*

   List general guidance for coping with an unexploded bomb, if found, and specific guidance for officers concerning a bomb that is located in a very sensitive or hazardous location such as a hospital, communication center, oil refinery, power plant, etc. List those locations or special circumstances where every attempt must be made to keep a bomb from exploding, regardless of risk to an officer's life. These special situations should be quite rare.

   Give general guidance for handling an open bomb, disguised bomb, suspicious package, etc. and general guidance for handling and rendering safe a known or suspected bomb.

Note: This should be a rarity, as in virtually every instance a bomb can be tumbled remotely and removed from a building remotely. A building can be repaired, but the life of an officer cannot be replaced.

8. *Transportation, Storage, Disposal*

List the transportation procedures for unexploded bombs, the storage-destruction site that explosives and bombs would be carried to, special precautions such as escort and routes.

Note: While explosives are never taken into a court room for presentation as evidence, the city attorney should be contacted in regard to any required preservation of explosive evidence. See also Chapter 10, on explosive evidence.

9. *Exploded Bomb (XB) Procedure*

List the plan of action to take if a bomb explodes, or has exploded, to include the gathering of evidence.

10. *Other Explosive Incidents*

Give procedures for other types of explosive incidents such as downed aircraft (military), rail and truck accidents involving explosives, etc.

11. *Reports*

List those agencies that will furnish after-action reports, to whom and when. List information such as who received the call, actions taken, who was notified, etc. If a bomb was found, list in a report the details desired, such as the description, markings, type, functioning, explosive and amount, safing procedure if required, disposition, etc. If the bomb had exploded, describe in detail any evidence that was recovered.

Note: The following paragraphs concerning threats, evacuation, search, etc., will assist in the development of detailed procedures for inclusion in the bomb plan.

BOMB THREATS

By virtue of their very numbers, bomb threats account for more actual disruption of activities than do bombs, and represent a major economic loss to the nation. There has been little guidance available and agencies have had to formulate their own decisions as to what action to take—decisions that are for the most part based on common-sense reasoning. Some communities do not evacuate schools when a bomb threat is received; most communities do. The common-sense practical approach is fortunately the right one to take. Certain guidelines can be set forth in a textbook of this sort; however, the individual agency must inject their own particular situations into the guidelines to come up with a truly workable solution; the one that is right for their community. Avoid publicity, this only encourages additional bomb threats. The following guidelines will assist in the development of the procedure to take when a bomb threat is received:

1. The switchboard operator or person receiving the call should attempt to secure as much information as possible from the caller, information such as what time the bomb will explode and the location, if possible; note the tone of voice, sex, and any background sounds. The operator may even ask the name of the caller on the off chance of response to the question.

   Note: If numerous bomb threats are received, an inexpensive telephone pickup and tape recorder can be used to monitor calls.

2. Notification of designated authorities should be accomplished immediately after the call is received.

   Note: Some agencies that are notified may not respond to the call but are placed on stand-by in case the bomb explodes.

3. The responsible official should direct the evacuation procedure. This may be accomplished through use of existing fire alarm systems that are not tied directly into a fire station, or separate warning systems such as horns or public address systems may be used.

   Note: The determination to evacuate or not is a management decision.

   Personnel working in the building should be instructed that, *if time permits,* they should open doors and windows (to reduce blast damage), shut off electrical equipment, and check their immediate work area for a nonstandard condition (bomb), prior to evacuation of the area. If possible, employees should be used for all bomb searches, as they are more familiar with the facility, and more likely to recognize an out-of-place object.

   Evacuation distances should be further than for normal fire evacuation: 150 to 300 yards from a building situated in a large open area. If in a downtown area with closely surrounding buildings, evacuating around a corner where other buildings will provide protection from blast and fragmentation will suffice.

4. Employees, security personnel, competent volunteers, or the designated responsible agency should perform the search with consideration given to the following:
   a. Search outer building walls and window ledges at ground floor level, nearby trash cans, sheds and vehicles.
   b. Restrooms should be searched early. Since they are not always occupied, they are a favored location for placement of a bomb.
   c. Check hallways and stairwells.
   d. Search janitorial closets and supply rooms.
   e. Remaining areas that are normally occupied at all times during working hours.
   Note: It is recommended that personnel performing a search have some means of communication such as walkie-talkies and that the search be performed by people who work in the building.

5. Insure complete evacuation of the building, including all search personnel, a minimum of five minutes before any given time for the bomb to explode; restrict entry into the building until a minimum of five minutes after any stated time. If a time has not been given, evacuate the building and wait at least one hour.
   Note: This is a local policy decision. Many communities require the police to continue the search through any given time for the bomb to go off. The author does not recommend this, as an officer's life is more valuable than most properties and not to be risked unnecessarily, or taken lightly.

6. If a bomb is found, then trained individuals who are designated to deal with the bomb should be notified. The fact that one bomb has been found should not deter completion of the search, as more than one bomb may have been placed by the bomber.

Many private security forces should give serious consideration to expanding their security net to a point beyond the front and rear doors of a building. Visual surveillance of the outer walls, window ledges, streets near the building, and parking lots should be given increased attention. Many bombs have been placed on window ledges and tossed through windows; in one instance a large bomb was contained in an automobile parked in the street in front of a building.

Because of threats and bombings directed against police facilities, consideration should be given to screening all lower windows of stations and providing a lighted and enclosed parking lot for private and official police vehicles. Visitor movement should be restricted, and if necessary, curtailed entirely. In extreme instances, outside outer walls bordering sensitive inner areas should be reinforced. Inner blast walls may be constructed to divert blast away from such sensitive divisions as communications and records.

EVACUATION

Evacuation of Schools

The decision as to the necessity of evacuating a school if a bomb threat or call is received is difficult, to say the least. Youth are prone to make false reports of this sort and quite literally will raise havoc with the orderly function of the school, police and fire agencies. The individuals responsible for the safety of the children are subject to some adverse comment no matter how they decide to deal with a rash of false reports of this sort. A decision as to the course of action requires coordination between city officials, the school board and police. Telephone companies have had some success using special equipment in tracing threat calls.

Some communities have had success by treating every bomb threat as bona fide, and having the children make up the lost time on Saturdays or evenings. Extension of the school day or having Saturday morning classes has proved to be an effective deterrent to false reports.

Evacuation distances for schools are dependent on many factors; the type of explosive, the amount of explosive, type of building construction, and the area surrounding the school all have a bearing on the evacuation distance. Since most of these factors are not known in advance and the officer does not carry a card with evacuation distances in his pocket, the practical officer must apply rule-of-thumb distances. In general where the school is located on a large open plot of ground and where shielding from blast does not exist, it is recommended that the children evacuate to a distance of a city block from the school (150 to 300 yards). This should provide more than enough protection from blast and flying debris caused by the explosion of most homemade bombs. The distance can be reduced if the school is located in an area where the school building is surrounded by other buildings. The surrounding buildings would act as a shield to protect the children from blast and debris, should the bomb explode. In this instance and if time and conditions permit, citizens in these nearby buildings should also be warned and evacuated, or instructed to open doors and windows and to remain in the portion of their building farthest from the direction the blast will come from.

Evacuation of Other Areas

An outline drawing of a small shopping area with a bomb located in one of the stores is depicted in Figure 52. The decision as to the extent of evacuation is based on the effects of an explosion that were covered in Chapter 3. Such factors as blast travel and debris (in this instance, glass fragments), should the bomb

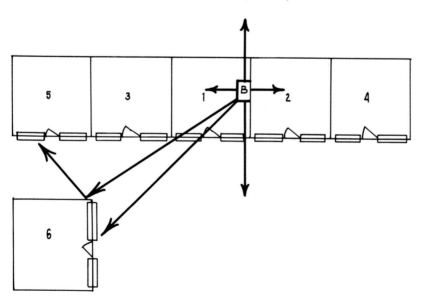

Figure 52. Arrows depict blast travel should the bomb in the store explode.

explode, are the primary effects to consider. As can be seen by the arrows in Figure 52, blast would radiate outward in all directions; however, blast seeks the point of least resistance such as the window areas, and at a distance is deflected by solid objects such as walls. I would recommend that stores 1, 2, and 3 be evacuated for a bomb of up to two sticks of dynamite. If the bomb consisted of more than two sticks, the stores numbered 4 and 5 should also be evacuated. If the amount of explosive is unknown, then play safe and evacuate all stores numbered 1 through 6. The wall between stores number 1 and 2 would probably be holed and the wall between 1 and 3 would probably suffer major damage. Brick and cinderblock walls are very susceptible to blast damage, and dividing walls in shopping areas are notoriously thin. The area to the open front and to the rear of the store should be cleared to a distance of 150 to 300 yards. Stores number 5 and 6 should be evacuated or personnel instructed to remain in the rear areas for protection against flying glass. Note how blast may bounce off the wall of store 6 and affect the glass of store 5.

Looking at this text situation in a practical sense, the first officers at the scene would have their hands full with evacuating and dealing with the problems of the affected store, let alone having to clear a crowded shopping area and considering blast bouncing off walls a distance away. However, the officer should not throw up his hands, but do the best that he can under the circumstances.

In any bomb or evacuation plan the originator must look at his plan from a practical point of view and while planning for the best must still blend practical realities into the plan. Obviously the size of the department—number of personnel available—affects the plan in a practical sense. The ultimate determining factor in the success of any plan is the trained officer who is accustomed to dealing with emergencies on a day-to-day basis and can be trusted to exercise sound judgement.

SEARCH PROCEDURES

The following search procedures are examples to build upon in the development of a department procedure and should be tailored to the departments' unique situations:

Schools

In the school layout example depicted in Figure 53, the officers conducting the search will be hampered by a multitude of closed and locked student lockers, any one of which could contain a homemade bomb. In general the search should include the following:

1. Outer ground floor walls and window ledges.
2. Latrines, restrooms or lounges.
3. Trash baskets.
4. Stairways and stairwells.
5. Storerooms, boiler room.
6. Open lockers.
7. Auditorium, gymnasium.
8. Library.
9. Unoccupied classrooms.
10. Office and remaining areas.

Figure 53. School layout example.

In any search procedure, check those areas that are not occupied full-time, such as a latrine. Obviously the bomber prefers to place his bomb with a minimum chance of his being observed and to provide for concealment of the bomb. Rooms that are normally occupied full-time would be searched last. It is recommended that school personnel assist in any search.

Public and Commercial Buildings

No text can outline an exact step-by-step procedure, as every building is different in layout and function. For public buildings and buildings that are not familiar to the officer, the procedure listed at the start of this chapter under "Bomb Threats" should be used to build upon: to devise a plan that is detailed and workable for municipal and public buildings and which at least provides a general search procedure for the officer to follow when required to search an unfamiliar building.

Hospitals

In developing a plan to cope with bomb threats, provide for limited evacuation, and provide a detailed step-by-step procedure for a local hospital search, various factors that are unique to a hospital only must be taken into consideration. Hospitals are particularly vulnerable to bomb threats, and total evacuation and work stoppage cannot be accomplished when a threat is received. Preparation of a plan for evacuation and search is influenced by many entrance and exit points, a large number of daily deliveries of supplies, certain hazards pertaining to hospital equipment and supplies, intensive care patients and restricted areas, etc. If the hospital has reason to suspect they may be bombed or the administration decides that the number of threats requires some protective action, then normal security must be strengthened to include consideration of the following:

1. Strict control and check of incoming supplies.
2. Restricting entrance-exit points of visitors and employees. Include signing in and out and package surveillance.
3. Pinpoint areas where hazardous equipment and supplies are located. Tighten security at these points when deemed necessary.

4. In coordination with hospital personnel, assign search priorities by functional and/or patient priority.
5. Enroll selected hospital personnel to participate in the search of restricted or hazardous areas. Since many patients cannot be evacuated, the search must be rapid and complete.
6. If funds are available, purchase fluoroscopic equipment and mats that can be used to dampen the possible explosion of a suspected bomb.
7. Extend the security perimeter to include the area outside the hospital building and the parking lot. Install outside security lights at sensitive points.
8. Plan for the use of existing hospital communication equipment during any emergency.

The foregoing are but points to consider when devising a plan for coping with hospital threats and employing search procedures. Coordination with hospital authorities who are cognizant of their particular hazards and problems must be accomplished. Hospital personnel *must* be available to advise and assist in the search.

Aircraft

Because of the variety of aircraft models and their varying construction and layout, it is best to enroll selected airport employees and airline personnel who are familiar with the layout of their particular planes and facilities into any search procedure. They would be more likely to recognize a nonstandard condition than any officer called to the scene. Airport security personnel in coordination with the management should formulate their own bomb plans and procedures to follow.

Homemade bombs for use against aircraft can be made as small as a cigarette package, or consist of a small amount of dynamite with a time mechanism as shown in Figure 54.

A small bomb of this sort can be inserted into a very small opening so all exterior openings in an aircraft must be searched such as the engine nacelles, wheel wells, and any break between stabilizers and the fuselage. Other points to search are exterior and interior baggage compartments, heads, galley, seats, and crew areas.

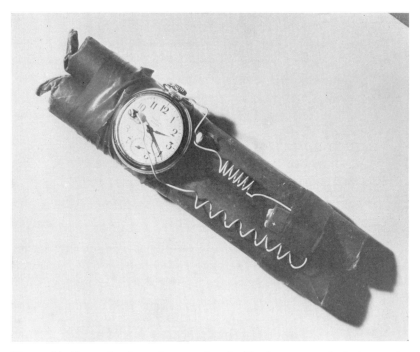

Figure 54. Dynamite, batteries, nonelectric blasting cap and clock are the components of this small bomb which would be relatively easy to conceal in many small spaces of an aircraft. A bomb of this sort can be concealed in a suitcase or package and is virtually impossible to detect except with a fluoroscope.

Consideration should be given to the establishment of a suspect area for aircraft and construction of a bomb pit at that location. A pit may be constructed that is as elaborate as a reinforced concrete hole at least four feet square, or as simple as an excavated hole in the ground. Consider the construction of concrete blast walls on the surface to deflect blast away from facilities if a bomb should explode and behind which a suspect aircraft and baggage may be placed. If a fluoroscope is not available, baggage may be held in the suspect area for one hour or total flight time to destination. Passengers may be requested to open their baggage for search.

Automobiles

Any point in the electrical circuitry of an automobile may be used to trigger a bomb electrically; therefore any automobile search must be detailed and complete. A complete search must include the areas under the hood, seats, dash, frame and fenders. The areas most favored by bombers have been under the hood and front seat. Check the suspension areas, steering, fuel tank, and drive shaft under the automobile.

Officers who wish to reduce the bomber's opportunity to connect a bomb to their automobile should always lock their automobile, install a locking gasoline cap, lock the car in a garage at night, install a hood lock and perhaps a burglar alarm. While the foregoing will not stop a determined bomber, it will help to reduce the number of points at which a bomb can be attached and simplify the officer's search.

Many agencies are primarily concerned with training their officers only to identify a bomb, relying on an outside agency to perform the rendering safe of any bomb that is found. I consider this to be a mistake and strongly recommend that all officers, even in those departments that have bomb squads, receive at least basic instruction in bombs, to include immediate actions to take if an active open (undisguised) bomb is discovered. (A simple open bomb, such as dynamite and burning time fuse, that the officer should know about in order to make an intelligent decision for his protection and the public's, could through lack of training result in a major disaster.) In one major city a bomb was discovered and the police waited four hours for a disposal unit to arrive and deal with the bomb. An open (not disguised) time bomb that is discovered in a sensitive location such as an oil refinery or a hospital, is still active and working, and a delay can be catastrophic. A bomb located in a hospital will likely require immediate action; time is of the essence and neither the hospital nor the responsible agency can wait for hours. Hospital personnel and security personnel at other sensitive locations should be trained to cope with a bomb, if necessary, and to recognize a bomb that can be left undisturbed for the arrival of disposal personnel.

A stockpile of bomb mats on a wheeled cart for quick movement would be invaluable at these sensitive locations.

Looking at a bomb search in a practical sense, the officers who are conducting the search are to some extent putting on a show for officials and the public. Open bombs (not disguised) would probably be located during any search; however, a disguised bomb is quite another matter. It is not reasonable to assume that every package or possible disguised bomb container can be identified and checked during the search of a large, perhaps unfamiliar building. The officer must do the best that he can under the circumstances considering that a disguised bomb, as compact as the cigarette pack bomb that was shown in Figure 51, will be virtually impossible to detect during a search. The disguised bomb and the attendant difficulty of detecting the bomb during a search are two of the reasons that officers conducting a search should also evacuate the building during any announced time for the bomb to explode. The officer should never risk his life unnecessarily and must always balance the risk to his life against the expected property damage and/or the lives of others, should the bomb explode. A hospital search would probably continue despite the threat to the lives of officers.

PROTECTIVE MEASURES

Protection of the public is the officer's first duty and is accomplished through warning, evacuation, blocking and rerouting traffic, protective works, informing other interested agencies, search and disposal. The news media should be requested to cooperate, since a flash bulb being fired at the wrong time, or interference with an officer performing a rendering safe procedure could have dire consequences. The very tone of a news article can cause an increase in the number of bomb threats. Following preliminary measures, a search is made if necessary. If a bomb is discovered, protective measures to reduce possible damage to a facility and provide protection to the public and the officer who is to perform the rendering safe procedure is considered.

The officer who understands the effects of an explosion (fragmentation, blast, incendiary, and vacuum covered in Chapter 3) can do much to protect himself, the public and his equipment from the damaging effects of a possible explosion. The proper technique is to copy the actions of the soldier when he expects to be, or is, subjected to enemy fire. The soldier will dig a foxhole, take shelter behind a tree, rock, or building; slide underneath a vehicle, or lay flat on the ground; construct a barricade, etc. Fragmentation, blast and flying debris are the main effects against which to take protective measures. In certain instances officers could use their own vehicle as a shield or for cover, and officers within an expected-danger area should make every effort to protect themselves while performing their duty. Knowing that fragmentation and blast travel in a straight line from the point of detonation indicates that protection may be secured by taking a position where an object will be between the explosion and the person or equipment to be protected. Note the following news account of a fire and accumulated gas explosion in Atlanta, Georgia: "Police Sergeant . . . said that a parked fire truck, standing between the source of the blast and spectators, probably saved many people from injury and death." Vacuum does not present much of a hazard, since very large quantities of explosives must be involved, and the police officer may disregard this effect. If a very large blast were to be expected, keeping the mouth open would help prevent injury to eardrums and lungs by permitting more rapid equalization of pressure between the inside and outside of the body. When lying flat on the surface of the earth, raise the chest off the ground slightly to prevent knockout from transmitted earth shock.

In general, the explosion of a quantity of explosive will have less effect than one is led to believe. The delusion that massive destruction will be caused by the explosion of small quantities of explosives has been fostered by television programs that show a small vial of liquid explosive, supposedly nitroglycerin, and indicate that a large building or an entire city block would be destroyed if the vial were to explode. A person can be within the area of explosive damage and suffer very minor injuries, if any, since the human body is much more resilient than window glass and other brittle materials. When an explosion occurs on the surface of the earth, or underground, there is a tendency for the explosive effects to raise upward. This is due to the fact that a part of the explosive force is directed downward and as the earth becomes denser, it turns the explosive force back in an upward direction. A person lying on the ground, even though quite near the explosion, may escape the effects entirely.

If the facilities and competent personnel are available, it would be excellent training for both police and fire service personnel to witness the explosion of a single stick of dynamite, and also larger charges of five and ten sticks respectively. (See Appendix B, Evacuation Distances.) These charges should be exploded in the open and at a safe distance. Officers would be able to see and feel the blast, and immediately after each explosion proceed to the explosion site to observe and smell the surface of the earth at the point of detonation.

It is a natural tendency for a person to seek cover when an explosion is expected, and this natural tendency will work to the advantage of the officer. Police and fire service personnel have a duty to perform; however, they owe it to themselves and to their community to exercise as much care as possible while doing so. Firefighters are a very real problem as they just cannot standby and watch a fire involving explosives without attempting to fight the fire. Some have perished as a result.

Aside from the protective measures that an officer can take to protect himself, he must also consider means to protect the general public and reduce damage to a facility, should the bomb explode. To this end the bomb mats and equipment listed in the next section of this chapter are of great value. However, it is a recognized fact that the very great majority of departments do not possess any special equipment, and in a practical sense the officer is again faced with having to make a common sense decision to accomplish any protective measures. A few of the factors that the officer with knowledge of the effects of an explosion may consider and selectively apply to provide protection are as follows:

1. The bomb could possibly be removed remotely to a less hazardous location using a length of line and a slow pull.

2. Hazardous or sensitive materials could possibly be removed from the vicinity of the bomb.

3. Mattresses, or even furniture and other materials at the site could be used to buffer or direct the blast of a low-explosive or small high-explosive bomb in a safer direction. *Note:* Never place any buffer or barricade directly against an object to be protected. Always leave one or more feet of air gap to prevent the buffer or barricade from transmitting the explosive force directly to the item being protected.

4. If time permits, open all doors and windows to vent the blast. Window glass can also be taped to help reduce breakage and flying debris.

5. Attempt to estimate the direction that the blast would take and to prevent personnel from entering these areas. Remember that blast can bounce or ricochet.

The foregoing are recommendations, simply factors to consider, since each bomb and its location will require a judgment-type decision on the part of the officer. The time factor and some types of bombs will prevent an officer from taking any preventative measures in many instances.

The trained officer is indispensable to the welfare of a community, and as a consequence has a duty to safeguard himself commensurate with the performance requirements of that duty. An officer who possesses the knowledge of the effects of an explosion and who applies common-sense reasoning, can be instrumental in saving lives and reducing property damage if an explosion should occur.

PROTECTIVE EQUIPMENT

Bomb squads of several of our larger cities have equipment specially designed for the handling and transportation of explosives and homemade bombs. Design and purchase of equipment for this purpose is quite beyond the means of most local governments, nor can they justify the purchase or use of this equipment based on the number of bomb incidents with which they may have to contend. Law enforcement agencies are faced with the problem of infrequent explosive incidents, yet they need the equipment in order to provide for the maximum protection of life and property when a bomb incident does occur. If the purchase of special equipment is not possible, then the next best solution to the problem must be found. Common commercial materials and equipment that can be obtained on short notice and adapted to provide protection during the handling and transportation of explosives offers the only solution.

Protection for the individual law enforcement officer performing the rendering-safe procedure is virtually nonexistent. An armored flack vest, helmet, gloves, etc., would offer some protection from the explosion of a small bomb, but for a larger bomb are mostly of psychological value.

Placing or carrying a bomb in a container of water or oil, the object being to stop a clockwork mechanism from operating, is not recommended. It must be assumed that the contained explosive is waterproof or is in a waterproof container. Water is too volatile and will not guarantee the stopping of a clockwork mechanism. If a wristwatch time mechanism is used, the probability is that it is waterproof anyway. A thicker liquid such as oil must be used to stop a non-waterproof alarm clock and then jarring in transportation will probably cause the clock to operate sporadically. If the bomb is in a container, water or oil will probably not enter easily and holes or vents would have to be made in the container. If holes are to be cut into an active bomb container, then a complete rendering-safe procedure might just as well be undertaken. The following section covers equipment that is presently available or can be adapted or constructed for use in bomb handling.

Protective Armor

Body armor offers protection against the fragmentation of a bomb container in particular and partial protection from the blast effects of a small bomb. It is most suitable for any carrying operation involving a small bomb and in conjunction with a portable hand carrier. It is a matter of officer's choice for other operations. I do not recommend wearing body armor or any cumbersome protective equipment for any delicate rendering-safe procedure, as dexterity, vision and coordination are affected, thereby increasing the risk to the officer.

Colt Industries of Hartford, Connecticut, offers a lightweight body armor made of laminated ballistic fiber glass that will defeat a .45 caliber, hard ball at a distance of ten feet. This lightweight armor is offered for use with the Colt-Tabor bomb-handling system covered in subsequent paragraphs. Also offered is a helmet of lightweight fiber glass with ear, temple and face protection.

The Federal Laboratories of Saltsburg, Pennsylvania, also offer a lightweight armor used by many bomb squads.

For the department that does not possess body armor and cannot justify the purchase of this equipment, a motorcycle helmet that covers the ears would offer some protection from fragmentation and blast effects of a small bomb. Padded, fireproof or fire resistant clothing will also offer some measure of protection.

Portable Hand Bomb Carriers

The most popular portable bomb carrier is made of a woven wire mesh. The bomb is enclosed in the wire mesh and is carried suspended from a pole by two officers. It is suitable for carrying small bombs, reducing fragmentation and partially muffling blast. Officers carrying the bomb must wear full protective body armor for maximum protection.

X-ray Fluoroscopes

Portable x-ray fluoroscopes are available that are satisfactory for use by officers in checking the contents of suspicious packages and/or containers. The operation of fluoroscopic devices is not particularly complex but does require an individual who is trained in explosives and homemade bombs to recognize any concealed explosive train. Available fluoroscopic devices are fairly portable and are particularly valuable when large numbers of suspect bomb containers must be checked (Fig. 55).

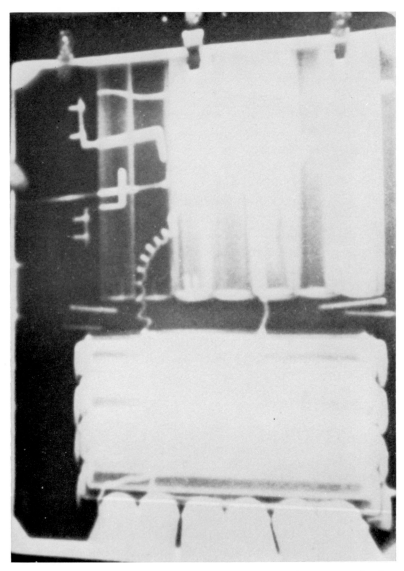

Figure 55. Fluoroscope of suspected container. Dynamite, cap, and trigger are visible.

Electronic Amplifiers

Electronic amplifiers or stethoscopes are used to check a suspicious package or container for the presence of a mechanical time mechanism, such as a clock or watch. A wristwatch buried in a package cannot be heard except through the use of a device to amplify sound. These amplifiers rule out the possibility of a clockwork mechanism but do not eliminate the possibility that the suspicious container is triggered by some other device such as release-of-pressure (Fig. 56).

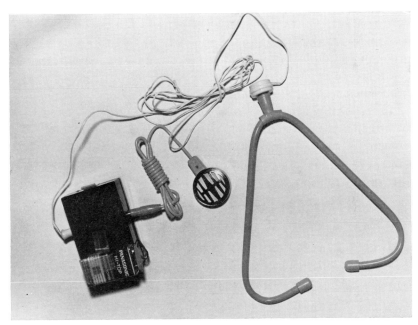

Figure 56. Electronic amplifying device. Stethoscope is designed to eliminate all outside sounds.

Blasting Mats

Blasting mats are heavy mats woven of rope or steel wire that are designed to muffle and contain blast and fragments should a bomb explode. They may be spread directly over a bomb or a light explosive charge; if heavier charges are involved, then railroad ties or logs are put down first and the mats spread over the top. Because of the weight involved, steel mats are not too satis-factory for police use.

For most bomb applications, plain gunny-sacks partially filled with sand would be the most valuable matting available. They are cheap, portable, and lend themselves to a variety of stackings and configurations and may also be used as a barricade to direct blast away from a threatened object.

Colt-Tabor Bomb-Handling System

A development in bomb-handling equipment is the introduc-tion by Colt Industries of the Colt-Tabor bomb-handling system. The system was specifically designed to cope with the principal problem facing departments that are unable to maintain regular bomb squad units, that is, the initial handling, removal and transportation of a homemade bomb to a safe area for disposal.

The hazards associated with the all too frequent practice of an officer picking up a suspected or actual explosive bomb and carrying it to another location, and/or the wearing of cumber-some armor, are greatly reduced by the use of the Colt-Tabor system. The system is built around a portable ballistic fiberglass basket and will reduce the need for close physical handling of the bomb. The basket is 24 inches high, 26 inches wide and weighs 65 pounds. Plastic rope loops are located around the outer top and bottom areas of the basket. Inside the basket is a nylon net that is suspended from the rim and that hangs to a point midway in the basket. The shape of the basket enables it to be easily carried, placed in a car trunk, passed through doors or windows, and lifted or moved by a two-man team. The design and strength of the basket enables it to withstand a sizable explosion by venting the explosive force upward while containing horizontal frag-mentation. Testing indicated the basket will contain and vent the effects of most black powder pipe bombs and a number of sticks of dynamite. While the explosion of over eight sticks of 40% commercial dynamite, unconfined, or a military high explosive will probably shatter the basket, it will still reduce the horizontal effects of an explosion. Considering that the great majority of homemade bombs involve relatively few sticks of dynamite, three to five, or a low explosive such as black powder, the basket should be effective in handling the majority of bombs encountered by departments.

The basket is part of a system that includes related equipment for use by a two-man team. The related equipment includes two pull ropes, a net and drawstring, jointed ten-foot poles, a special clamp-pulley device, two shields, two sets of front and rear light-weight fiberglass body armor, and two helmets with face shields. Figure 57 through 62 portray the use of the system and equipment.

Figure 57. (1) Clear area of all unauthorized personnel. Place bomb basket near suspected bomb. Attach cords and bridle to basket at this time.

Bomb Transport Trucks

There are two types of bomb-handling trucks in use by a very few metropolitan law enforcement agencies: the woven steel mesh

Figure 58. (2) Place net over bomb from behind cover or shield.

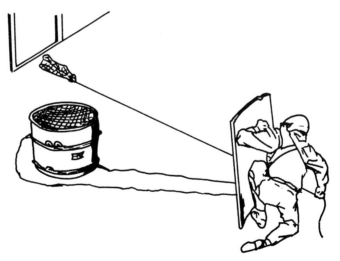

Figure 59. (3) Pull drawstring on net from protective cover, jerk and tumble the bomb to determine if the bomb is boobytrapped. Do not touch bomb with hands. Pull bomb to asket. *Author's Note:* Jerk and tumble from a greater distance than shown in the illustration. Use a long length of cord.

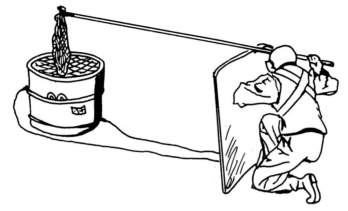

Figure 60. (4) From behind a shield, lift bomb into basket. Use notch on the shield as a fulcrum point.

(basket weave) type in use by the New York bomb squad and the "tub" type used by most other departments (Fig. 63). While a bomb transport truck that could contain all the forces of an explosion would be most desirable, neither of the two types in use will provide this complete protection. It is doubtful that a truck can be designed to do so for other than a small bomb. Both types of trucks will provide major protection to the public during transport of a bomb, with both types employing a controlled

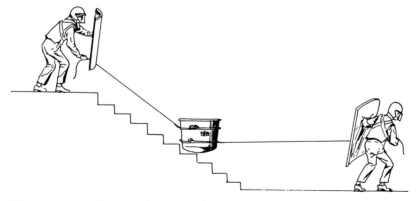

Figure 61. (5) The curved bottom of the basket makes it possible to pull it like a sled, negotiate stairs, and handle it from a greater distance.

Figure 62. (6) Poles may be placed through the loops for shoulder carry if absolutely necessary. Floor level movement of the bomb by pull and restraining cords is preferred.

venting action to direct and dissipate the blast effects of an explosion.

The truck depicted in Figure 63 has an angled (45°) deflection plate of $\frac{1}{2}$ inch steel at the forward part of the truck bed to protect the driver. The tub itself is 48 inches high, 42 inches in diameter, and is made from $\frac{3}{4}$-inch cold rolled steel with a concave bottom from one inch boiler head steel. The drum is surrounded by sand and sandbags. This truck has been tested and withstood the effects of 30 sticks of 40% ammonia gelatin dynamite. Further information may be obtained from the Ontario Attorney General's Office, Toronto, Ontario, Canada.

Equipment Expedients

Most departments cannot justify the cost of special bomb-handling equipment, or if they do have the funds, the equipment that they need is not available for purchase. Most of the equipment presently available was designed for other purposes than for

Figure 63. "Tub" type truck in use by the metropolitan Toronto Police Department. Note the tub, boom, and equipment storage compartments. (Courtesy D. M. Lucas, Ontario, Canada)

bomb handling, but has been adapted or applied to bomb usage also. For the most part, trucks have been designed and constructed by large metropolitan departments that have been able to justify the truck cost by virtue of the large number of incidents they have to cope with. Potential sales have not justified the cost of research and development, so departments have been forced to design and test their own.

As a stimulant to thought, as a spur to the local design and construction of equipment for bomb handling, and most of all for public and officer safety, the following represents a practical exercise problem with the step-by-step reasoning and development of a solution to the problem. The wordage is purposely designed to provide a practical insight into the reasoning process that the officer must go through when coping with a homemade-bomb handling problem. It should always be remembered that if the very best equipment is not available, or if the very best rendering-safe procedure under ideal conditions cannot be performed, the officer should do the next best thing possible under the circumstances.

Practical Exercise Problem

Devise a simple, minimum cost, remote handling aid that will reduce jarring of a homemade bomb to a minimum during remote removal, and hold to a minimum the length of time that an officer must spend in close proximity to the bomb.

Practical Exercise Solution

Because an officer should not expose himself to a hazard unnecessarily, the problem of removing a bomb from a building is a very real one, and an aid that can be used to remove the bomb remotely can greatly reduce the time that the officer is exposed to possible bomb action. While the Colt-Tabor system may be highly desirable, a department that does not have the number of incidents or funds for this system must employ the next best technique. Sadly enough, in too many instances the officer picks up the bomb and carries it away. A better technique would be to suspend the bomb on a fishing pole for carrying, as every foot of air gap between the bomb and the officer will reduce his personal hazard. However, full remote handling calls for the officer to use his ingenuity.

If a bomb is found in a building and the officer decides to remove it remotely, he must expose himself to the bomb's action in order to secure a length of line to the bomb either by hand, or through use of a pole and hook. He can then pull the bomb from its location from a safe distance. There are several options that the officer has at this initial point. If an explosion at the bomb's location can be tolerated, he should jerk the bomb with the line in an attempt to deliberately explode the bomb. If the line is jerked and the bomb does not explode, it indicates the bomb is probably not sensitive to jarring, but does not rule out the possibility of a time bomb if a container is involved. If the bomb is in a location where an explosion cannot be tolerated, or if after jerking the bomb it did not explode, the officer can take a chance and carry the bomb from the area, or drag the bomb from its location using a length of cord. For maximum safety, however, he would remotely load the bomb into a cushioned handling container for remote pull from the location and loading into a bomb transport vehicle, or remote removal to a pit dug in the ground area at the building site. Since in this instance there is no handling device of this sort available, the officer must use his own ingenuity and fabricate the device himself. The remote handling aid depicted in Figure 64 is a workable aid that was constructed and tested by the author. It is simple, inexpensive and represents a next best substitute for a commercially manufactured piece of equipment.

Note that provision for holding a door open during remote removal operations has been provided. A skid to slide the bomb

Figure 64. Remove handling aid consisting of a net bomb holder, plastic clothes basket and a length of remote line. Note door stops for holding doors open if the bomb must be pulled from a room. The harness is designed to prevent hangup of the aid on an object. The pull line will slip on the harness and cause the aid to skid and turn.

into the aid has also been provided. While the aid will not contain a blast, it will cushion the bomb and provide for an air gap between the bomb and floor and between the bomb and the disposal officer.

For the sake of the exercise, let's assume that the bomb is located in a washroom. The disposal officer, at his option, may open a window and toss the bomb outside or carry the bomb to the outside of the building by hand.

Note: Neither of these options are recommended unless the bomb is in a vital location and the circumstances are such as to require immediate removal, regardless of risk to the officer's life. Throwing the bomb outside the window means accepting the risk that the bomb will explode on contact with the ground. If the bomb detonates on contact, it may injure others unless the ground floor of the building and area have been cleared.

The disposal officer can secure a length of line to the bomb and give the line a series of jerks in an attempt to deliberately explode the bomb, if an explosion can be tolerated, and then continue to pull the bomb from the building. If time permits, open as many doors and windows as possible to reduce blast damage should the bomb explode. If an explosion cannot be tolerated at the bomb location, the disposal officer can inert the bomb, carry it off by hand, or tie a length of line to the bomb for slow, careful remote removal. Place a length of prepared board between the bomb and the window ledge and run the remote pull line out of the window to a safe distance. From natural or artificial cover, slowly pull the bomb up the board and allow it to drop to the ground. If the bomb does not explode on impact with the surface outside of the building, then the officer again at his option may carry the bomb to the transport vehicle (not recommended). This may still be an active bomb, however, and the officer is taking a chance. A better choice would be to continue to pull the bomb remotely to the rear of a placed transport vehicle and up a prepared skid into the vehicle.

The disposal officer may decide to place the bomb which is located in the washroom by hand into the remote-handling aid, or secure a length of line to the bomb, place the remote-handling aid and skid and pull the bomb remotely up the prepared skid into the cushioned aid (Fig. 65), or place the bomb into the aid using a fishing pole. The handling aid would then be pulled remotely from the building. The officer would be exposed to a possible explosion when securing the line and positioning the aid, but this is better than hand-carrying the bomb with increased exposure time. The disposal officer must carefully run the remote line and place door stops if necessary. This step is very important and should not be hurried, as a hangup of the remote-handling aid would necessitate the officer's returning to free the aid. With the bomb in the aid, the cord secured to the lower front of the aid would be pulled slowly from a safe distance, moving the bomb from its location. If stairs are encountered, a second line is attached to the lower rear of the aid. The lowering would require a second officer and coordinated action to lower the aid and the bomb down the stairs. The front harness of the aid and the curve of the skid are designed to prevent hangup of the aid when

Figure 65. If the bomb is on a ledge, it may be pulled off into the cushioned aid. If the bomb is on the floor, it may be pulled up a skid into the aid.

rounding a corner. A pre-prepared wood skid with side rails will assist in properly directing the aid when it is pulled remotely up into a properly placed in-line vehicle.

Note: All prepared bomb skids and handling aids should be constructed of wood, cardboard, masonite, soft celotex, plastic, or a material that will not add materially to fragmentation should the bomb explode. A metal container that would fragment is not satisfactory for this purpose.

From the foregoing exercise it can be seen that prearranged skids and pre-planning on the part of the officer can substantially reduce his exposure time to possible injury and still enable him to cope with the bomb. Since the bomb encountered could be an active disguised time bomb, the officer should consider pulling the bomb to a pit that has been dug in the ground outside and letting the bomb sit in this pit for one to twelve hours, then re-motely load the bomb into the transport vehicle. The area would have to be guarded to keep the unwary away during this period of time.

Although the foregoing was quite wordy, the objective of the exercise was to present the many alternate routes (options) the officer may take in disposing of a bomb where a handling problem exists. There were many routes the officer could take which would accomplish the purpose, but the route that is safest for the officer and the general public should be taken. The exercise also exempli-fies the fact that the only person who is competent to make a de-cision concerning the disposal of a homemade bomb is the officer at the scene. Prerecognition of problems and performing the best possible procedure for the time and place is the key to the safe and successful handling of unexploded homemade bombs.

A field expedient type of bomb truck may consist of a dump truck with a foot or more of sand in the bed and several rows of sandbags around the extremities of all four sides. In all instances, try to leave an air gap between the explosive, or bomb, and the bed and sides of the truck. If the bomb should explode in transit, the primary force of the explosion would be directed upward.

The cost of a basket weave or tub type bomb truck is too high for the very great majority of departments, who must do the next best thing: design and construct their own substitute truck with materials that are available to them. The city engineering department can render valuable assistance in the design and construction of a bomb carrier that could be set in the bed of a truck or trailer. While a good solid steel drum may be preferable, many communities do not have steel plate readily available. Substitute materials such as wood chips, celotex, sawdust, sand, etc. can be used to cushion, absorb, and direct the force of any explosion upward, yet not add to the fragmentation should the bomb explode. While damage to the carrier will occur, the benefits of even partially directing an explosion upward will compensate for the efforts in construction. A dump truck with heavy steel sides is preferred from the standpoint of directing the blast and affording some protection to the driver. Cutting off the rear portion of a salvage dump truck and converting it into a bomb trailer is even more satisfactory as far as protection to the driver is concerned. A wood skid with wood strips on the sides to direct the bomb, similar in construction to coal chutes, is very desirable for remote pull of a bomb up into the truck. The line should be left attached for remote removal of the bomb from the truck at the disposal site.

The disposal officer, in conjunction with the city engineering department, may produce a container for the bed of a specifically designated city truck and made from materials that are readily available. The design of expedient bomb-handling equipment is essentially a common-sense proposition, and the time to construct the equipment is prior to the occurrence of a bomb incident.

The United Nations Security and Safety Section has coped with the problem of rapid response to any bomb or threat within their building complex in New York. Their gear is mounted on a rubber-tired, wheeled cart that can be quickly moved to any floor or building. Included in the equipment is a fluoroscope and a woven wire mesh hand-type of bomb carrier.

Because of the many bombings and bomb threats in Canada, the Center for Forensic Services in Toronto has experimented quite extensively with bomb equipment. One device that was tested and approved was developed by the Montreal Police Department: a portable shield with a wood base and a V-shaped wood front to which spaced armor is attached. The armor consists of two $\frac{1}{8}$-inch thicknesses of aluminum alloy separated by a $\frac{1}{8}$-inch air gap. The armor has a window made of two layers of $\frac{1}{8}$-inch lucite separated by an air gap. Holes exist in the front of the sloping armor for the insertion and use from behind the shield of poles designed to tie a rope around a bomb, or the use of several manipulative devices for gripping, lifting, cutting and probing a suspected bomb. The shield has proven to be effective against the blast of at least twelve sticks of 40% dynamite that was exploded six feet in front of the shield. The Center for Forensic Services decided that while armor suits offer considerable protection, they seriously limit vision and mobility. A physical barrier with manipulative action offered the best solution.

DEACTIVATION (RENDERING-SAFE) EQUIPMENT

Bomb Kits

A rendering-safe procedure can be as simple an operation as the removal of a piece of time fuse, or time fuse and nonelectric blasting cap from an explosive and carrying the bomb away, or a time-consuming procedure involved with rendering safe a disguised, trigger-actuated, homemade bomb. The object of the rendering-safe procedure is to interrupt the explosive train and to do so will require a kit of common tools being readily available to the disposal officer. As a minimum, it is recommended that the small hand kit with contents as shown in Figure 66 be assembled. The following items are recommended for inclusion in any bomb kit:

Equipment	*Use*
1. Packet of single edge razor blades.	For gaining access through paper and fiber containers.
2. Small jack knife.	
3. Small pointed scissors.	
4. Hand metal cutter.	For gaining access into light metal containers.
5. Beer can opener.	
6. Small wire cutters.	
7. Claw hammer.	For gaining access into wood containers.
8. Pliers.	
9. Screwdrivers or wood chisels.	

10. Several rolls of 1 inch or larger adhesive tape.

For securing a line to a container and remote pull of a suspected bomb.

11. At least 500 feet of strong, light flexible line, fish hooks, snaps, and jointed pole.

12. Common paper clips.

For triggering device interruption.

13. Clamp wrench (vise grips).

14. Pieces of rubber inner tube.

15. Wood tongue depressors.

16. Cotton batting.

To cushion blasting caps for handling and transport.

17. Roll of electricians plastic or rubber tape.

For taping electrical leads etc.

18. Penlight flashlight and spare batteries.

For viewing interior of a container.

19. Small mirror.

20. Magnifying glass.

21. Container to hold equipment.

Figure 66. Small bomb kit made up of commercially available items. Plenty of good strong light cord should be included to jerk or pull a bomb remotely to a less hazardous location.

Miscellaneous Tools and Techniques

There are no tools specifically designed for the great majority of rendering-safe procedures, but common tools may be used. Scissors, tape, cutters, remote line, etc. are all easily obtained from commercial stores. A more elaborate bomb kit might include tools that are available from Army surplus, hardware stores, etc., such as pulleys, wood stakes, rope, pipe wrenches, picks, and shovels can be invaluable for digging a bomb pit if necessary. Figure 67 illustrates the use of a 12 gauge shotgun with a deer slug cartridge employed to gain access to a suspected pipe bomb container remotely. This operation must be performed at a suitable range location, as an explosion must be anticipated and planned for. While the services have used cartridge de-armers for a number of years and they are perfectly suitable for many of their procedures, when applied to a disguised homemade-bomb container this

Figure 67. A 12 ga. shotgun may be employed to gain access into a suspected bomb container remotely.

technique becomes less satisfactory. There is no guarantee that the bomb will not explode, that the bomb will be disarmed, and the indiscriminate shattering or edge opening of a package could result in a most hazardous condition inside the package. The slightest jar, or even a movement of the torn package due to wind, could cause the bomb to explode. Nevertheless it is a technique, but it is recommended that it be employed with the utmost discretion by a disposal officer.

Some departments have devised modified ice tongs for the remote pull-apart, on a range, of a suspected bomb container. These devices are not used on every bomb, but are special tools for highly selective use, if deemed necessary by the disposal officer.

Electrically nonconductive glass knives for gaining access into a package are part of the components of several bomb squad kits in use by metropolitan departments; however, there are other nonconductive materials, such as Delrin, that are much easier to make and keep sharp. There are many non conductive materials, wood, rubber, plastic, formica, etc., that are suitable for bomb squad usage.

Common aluminum tent poles may be used to hook onto some bombs from a distance and for remote pull to another area (Fig. 68) .

For gaining access into a steel bomb container, a strong acid may be used to eat through the metal. To prevent acid from entering a container and perhaps reacting with the explosive, do not spray or drip the acid onto the top of the container but direct the acid onto the lower side or edge.

The batteries in a homemade bomb may be immobilized through the use of dry ice, CO_2 and alcohol, and other freezing materials. It must be remembered that once frozen, the batteries must be kept frozen during transport to the disposal area.

While the use of acid and freezing is mentioned, it would be a very rare circumstance where either of these methods would be employed. Obvious disadvantages exist; the difficulty of using and controlling the corrosive acid, the time element, and not being positive that a battery is frozen, are some of the shortcomings of these techniques. Other equipment to use the acid and to hold

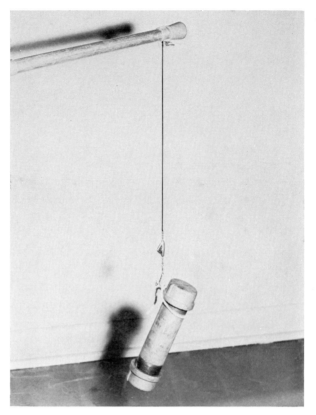

Figure 68. Use tent poles to hook onto and remove a bomb remotely. Fishing snaps can be used to aid in securing a line to the bomb for remote pull.

the freezing material would have to be devised and employed. The use of these two techniques is not recommended by the author.

Plaster of paris and similar mixtures may be employed as an interrupter. They may be specifically used to interrupt a trigger mechanism when other forms of interruption are not desirable or possible. There are certain plastic, quick-hardening foam mixtures in aerosol type sprays that give promise as a quick means of interrupting trigger mechanisms (Fig. 69).

Law Enforcement Assistance Administration funds have been allotted for the research and development of tools and equipment

Figure 69. Spray foam expands to twenty times original volume and hardens quickly.

to handle and render-safe homemade bombs. It is expected that special tools for remote spin-off of pipe bomb caps, for opening of disguised bombs and improved fluoroscopic and transport equipment will be devised. There is no doubt that remote handling equipment can be improved upon.

Virtually all homemade bombs may be rendered safe using only the most common types of tools that can be readily assembled by any department at reasonable cost. With the addition of some small tools, many emergency-rescue trucks could be employed for bomb squad usage.

RENDERING-SAFE PROCEDURES (RSP'S)

The particular rendering-safe procedure for coping with any unexploded bomb is determined at the site by the officer charged with disposal of the bomb. Any procedure may be used including the deliberate disposal of the bomb by demolition at the site. The bomb disposal officer assigned to deal with the bomb will go through the following basic procedure:

1. Survey
2. Initial RSP decision
3. Protective measures
4. Gaining access if necessary
5. Apply RSP if necessary
6. Transportation and final disposal

Survey

When the disposal officer arrives at the scene, he initially surveys the existing situation to determine the best RSP for the particular circumstances. His initial survey is concerned with the following:

1. The type of bomb (open—disguised).
2. Known or estimated amount of explosive.
3. Location of the bomb in relation to the threat to life and property should the bomb explode.

All of the foregoing have a direct bearing on the decision as to the initial rendering-safe procedure that the officer will employ.

Initial RSP Decision

With the survey completed, the officer uses this knowledge to make an initial RSP decision that will include one of the following options:

Conditions	*Initial RSP Decision—Options*
1. Explosion of the bomb can be tolerated.	*Option 1.* Take protective measures and deliberately explode the bomb in place.
	Option 2. Jerk the bomb remotely in an attempt to explode the bomb. If an explosion does not occur, remove the bomb remotely.

2. Explosion of the bomb can be tolerated, but is not desired.

Option 1. Carefully, slowly, remove the bomb remotely to a safe or less damaging location.

3. Explosion of the bomb cannot be tolerated.

Option 1. Use cushioned remote handling aid. Use steady, slow pull.
Option 2. Carry to another location using a jointed pole and hook.
Option 3. Carefully remove the bomb by hand carrying.
Option 4. Attempt to RSP in situ prior to any movement.

4. Explosion of the bomb cannot be tolerated. *There is not time for slow remote removal or RSP in situ.*

Option 1. Carefully remove the bomb by hand to a less damaging location and apply 1 or 2 above.

The decision to move any bomb by hand, or to perform a rendering-safe procedure *in situ* that involves cutting into a container should be considered as a last resort and reserved for a bomb in a location where the threat to life and property is so extreme that risk to the life of the disposal officer is judged necessary. It must constantly be remembered that property can be replaced, but the life of an officer cannot be.

Protective Measures

The application of protective measures such as the employment of blasting mats and placement of material to direct a possible blast, opening of doors and windows, and perhaps removal of a threatened object are all part of the decision-making process the disposal officer must apply to any incident that he encounters. In some instances where time is of the essence, the officer will not be able to apply any protective measures but will immediately apply a rendering-safe procedure.

Gaining Access

Initially the disposal officer can categorize any homemade bomb encountered as:

1. *Disguised or concealed:* This may be a known or suspected bomb but in each case the firing train is concealed, as in a package or suitcase.
2. *Open or straight bomb:* There is no doubt that this is a bomb. Examples are a stick or dynamite or a section of pipe with a fuse protruding. The firing train is generally exposed to the officer's view.

If the bomb is open, there is no need for the disposal officer to gain access to the firing train; however, a disguised or concealed bomb may in a rare circumstance require gaining access into the container to determine the firing train and to decide as to how best to interrupt the train. This gaining access would be a last resort when no safer method can be used because of unique circumstances. If this unlikely instance occurs, the disposal officer would use any equipment that is available to him that was covered previously in this chapter.

The possession of a fluoroscope would be invaluable at this point since a determination could be made as to whether the suspected bomb is in fact a bomb; further, the location and position of the explosive and trigger, type of trigger, and layout of the firing train within the container could be determined. It is obvious that positive identification of a bomb and interior workings would permit the disposal officer to decide on the safest disposal method and, if required, the safest point for entry into the container.

It is a fact that most departments do not possess a fluoroscope; for this reason, the author recommends the slow careful remote removal of all disguised-contained bombs through the use of a remote-handling aid, or lacking an aid, the steady slow removal with a length of cord.

The following are the authors recommendations if the unique situation occurs and the disposal officer decides that entry must be made into a suspected bomb container, regardless of personal risk, and no other possible alternative exists.

SUITCASE ACCESS. Entry into a canvas or leather suitcase is quite simple, and cutting into a corner edge is easily accomplished using a sharp knife or razor blade. Make as small an initial opening as possible. If the opening exposes explosives, the officer should stop and make a hole of entry in another location. Removing the explosive without identifying the triggering method might allow a mechanism such as a release-of-pressure device to settle and function the bomb. The object of gaining access is to determine the firing train and then to decide the best method of interrupting the firing train, to permit safe removal and transport to a disposal area.

While gaining access into a canvas or leather suitcase is relatively easy, a metal or high-impact plastic suitcase is quite another matter. An acid or plastic solvent could be used, but what a mess and acid-solvent hazard for the officer who must peer through the resultant hole to determine the inner contents and workings. For this type of suitcase container, the author recommends careful remote removal only. Using a drill or cutting tool on metal suitcases will most assuredly jar the suitcase anyway. A drill or cutting tool being used on heavy metal will create friction and possible sparking that could be most hazardous. The risk of an explosion is not acceptable in this instance.

HEAVY METAL CONTAINER ACCESS. Do not cut into a heavy metal container, as the risk of an explosion is considered unacceptable. Use careful remote removal.

LIGHT METAL CAN CONTAINER ACCESS. If the suspected bomb is incased in a light metal can container, or if upon cutting into a package, a light metal container is encountered, make sure the container is secure and will not accidentally open during operations. A cut may be made on the top edge using a beer can opener. Oil the metal surface of the container prior to making the cut (Fig. 70). When opening a container, if a powder explosive starts to flow from the cut, tape the cut immediately and make a cut at another location. If the explosive powder is allowed to flow from the container, the settling of a release-of-pressure device might activate the bomb. If black powder is exposed then wet the powder.

WOOD CONTAINER ACCESS EXAMPLE. Wood presents much less of an access hazard than metal containers since wood is a nonsparking material. A small hole to permit viewing may be made

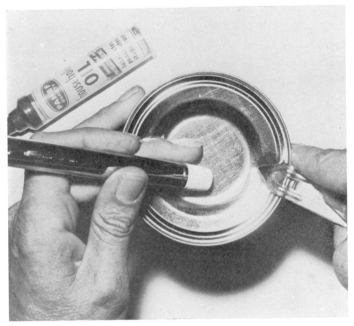

Figure 70. Cutting into a light metal container. Use oil to reduce the metal-to-metal contact.

in a corner edge of the box using a sharp knife. In lieu of using a knife, an edge of the container may be pried up just far enough to permit a slight view through a crack. This *slight* raising is to prevent possible functioning of a release-of-pressure or pull device (Fig. 71).

PAPER WRAPPED CARDBOARD PACKAGE ACCESS EXAMPLE. Prior to commencing any access procedure, make sure that the package bindings are secure. Using a small knife, razor blade, small scissors, etc., carefully make a layer-by-layer series of cuts into the wrapping material. Hold the cutting tool parallel, or as flat as possible with the wrapping material surface. Cut and enlarge the area of each layer of paper, in turn. Cut as small a hole as necessary for vision into the cardboard container (Fig. 72).

Caution: When cutting into a package, if a layer of foil is encountered, *Stop.* The bomb may employ two layers of foil

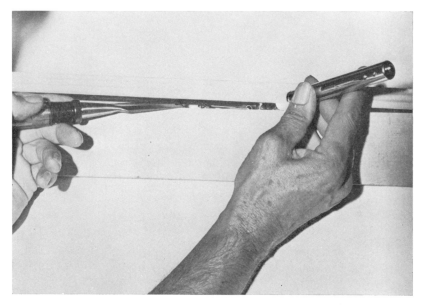

Figure 71. Gaining access into a wood container may be accomplished by shaving a hole using a sharp knife, or by slightly raising the lid using a screwdriver or wood chisel as shown.

separated by a nonconductive insulating sheet. An electrical current source within the package is applying continuous current to each layer of foil, but the circuit is not complete due to the nonconductive sheet. A cut into the package will carry part of the outer foil sheet through the insulator sheet and into contact with the inner foil sheet, completing the circuit and firing the bomb. If this type of bomb is encountered, the outer foil sheet must be carefully cut, pulled back and taped to prevent accidental contact and then, in turn, smaller openings made in the insulating and inner foil sheets before continuing further with the rendering-safe procedure (Fig. 73).

Note: This foil-lined type of bomb has only appeared in one homemade bomb and it failed to function. The foil-lined bomb is very difficult and extremely hazardous for a bomber to construct.

In a practical sense, an undue amount of attention is given to

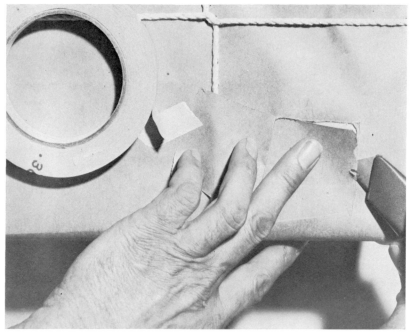

Figure 72. Make a layer-by-layer flat cut into the wrappings and in turn into the cardboard inner container. Note that the package is secured by bindings.

the rendering-safe procedure of a disguised bomb *in situ* by various publications, television programs, and disposal personnel, the reasons being that this is perhaps the most hazardous RSP to perform, and by far the most dramatic to portray and discuss. Yet, this RSP *in situ* of an active disguised bomb is a rarity. The disposal officer must consider every possible option other than an RSP *in situ,* which is a last resort, a method employed when there is a failure to come up with anything better.

As an example, follow the author's reasoning if he was to be confronted with a disguised, supposedly active bomb located in a washroom of the Capitol in Washington, D.C. It is daytime and there are officials and tourists present. Considering the heritage associated with the Capitol building, is the potential damage worth the life of an officer? While this is a personal decision the officer must make, looking at the incident dispassionately and

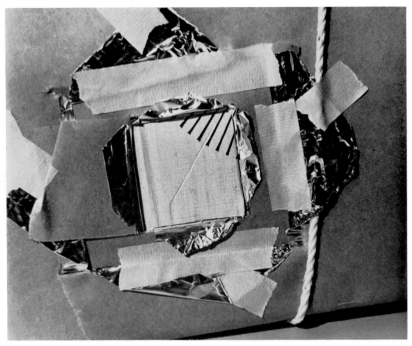

Figure 73. The two electrically charged foil sheets must not come into contact with each other during the access procedure. Each layer must be carefully cut and taped before proceeding further with the RSP.

with common sense, I am sure the reader will agree with the author in saying *no*. It would be far better to concentrate on protection to lives by evacuation of the floor and the areas above and below the washroom, and to preventing persons from entering the danger area accidentally. The author would wait one hour at least, before attempting removal of a disguised bomb by remote means. If the incident occurred at night, the same RSP would be applied.

First priority would be given to protecting the lives of officials and tourists, second to the life of the officer, and third to any damage that might be incurred to the Capitol. The damage that the Capitol actually sustained in the 1971 bombing is negligible when compared to the loss of a single life. The RSP is remote removal of the bomb.

Apply RSP

If the officer decides to perform a detailed rendering-safe procedure *in situ,* then the detailed procedures covered in succeeding paragraphs will apply.

Transportation and Final Disposal

Suggested transport vehicles and expedients have been covered previously in this chapter under equipment. As a practical note, it must be recognized that the very great majority of bombs encountered to date have been transported in conventional commercial vehicles, as only a few departments have other than conventional patrol vehicles at their disposal. Transport in a patrol vehicle is discouraged by the author. It is recommended that departments give immediate thought to the utilization of other types of city vehicles such as a dump truck, perhaps with a foot or more of sand in the bed.

Final disposal by burning or detonation is covered in the next chapter. It is recommended that the district attorney be consulted when formulating any final disposal policy on homemade bombs, as evidence requirements must be considered if any prosecution is contemplated.

The following general and detailed rendering-safe procedures are applied *after* access to the initiating-triggering device has been accomplished and the firing train is understood by the disposal officer. They do not specifically make allowances for the odd-ball type of bomb, such as one that may incorporate a collapsing field circuit, or mercury switches. It is assumed that the officer will identify the firing train and then apply his own innate intelligence and knowledge to the RSP. Certainly if the conditions and time permit, all bombs should be jarred and handled remotely with minimum exposure to the disposal officer. The RSP's represent the worst possible situation, that is minimal tools and equipment, and a very compelling necessity for the disposal officer to physically work on the bomb to interrupt the firing train.

The rendering-safe procedure varies according to the type of bomb and the initiating-triggering source. One detailed RSP cannot be outlined that will apply to every conceivable type of homemade bomb, although the methods and the object behind all RSP's are based on *interrupting the firing train.* Because of the impossibility of outlining an RSP that will apply to every conceivable type of homemade bomb, the following procedures are divided into two main subsections:

1. General Rendering-Safe Procedures by *Initiating* Source.
2. Detailed Rendering-Safe Procedures for *Triggering Method* (Device).

An additional subsection is devoted to a detailed example of a step-by-step rendering-safe procedure.

GENERAL RENDERING-SAFE PROCEDURE BY INITIATING SOURCE

Initiating sources are divided into three basic sources as follows:

1. Flame (time fuse) —heat
2. Percussion (firing pin-blow)
3. Electric (electric blasting cap—electric source)

Note: Detailed RSP's for the various triggering devices that may be encountered are outlined in the next subsection.

Flame (Time Fuse)—Heat

Bombs using flame as the initiating source, for all practical purposes can be called straight or open bombs. An open bomb can be recognized on sight as being a bomb. This type of bomb will incorporate a time fuse, or time fuse and nonelectric blasting cap, to initiate the explosive. The explosive may consist of one or more sticks of dynamite or a container, such as a section of pipe, containing black powder, smokeless powder, dynamite, etc., as the main explosive filler.

If a flame-initiated bomb is found with the fuse burning, a decision must be made by the disposal officer as to whether to seek cover and let the bomb explode, throw himself on the bomb, pick the bomb up and throw it to a less critical spot, or to attempt to break the active firing train. The location of the bomb has a direct bearing on the decision to be made. For example, if the bomb is located in a crowded facility, then every effort should be made to protect the lives of citizens.

Note: It is not inconceivable that an officer might consider throwing himself on the bomb or using his own body to protect fellow officers or the general public. Officers have given their own lives for the same purposes in connection with incidents in the past.

If the decision is to interrupt the firing train of this active bomb, then accomplish the following *quickly:*

1. Pull the fuse and nonelectric blasting cap out of the explosive if possible, and bend the fuse and cap away from the explosive charge (Fig. 74). Seek cover; put distance between yourself and the explosive charge; wait for the nonelectric cap to explode with small chance of the main explosive charge detonating.

Figure 74. Removing blasting cap from explosive to interrupt the explosive train.

2. If the blasting cap cannot be pulled out of the explosive because of the construction of the bomb, then consider throwing the bomb to a less hazardous location, or cut the fuse as close to the bomb body or cap as possible, and seek cover.

Note: When looking at a burning piece of time fuse, it is virtually impossible to tell where in the fuse the powder train is burning. For this reason, pulling the fuse and blasting cap from the explosive and retiring to safe cover is recommended.

3. Once the fuse has been pulled and the blasting cap has gone off or the time fuse has been cut successfully, the firing train has been interrupted and the bomb may be considered safe. It will not go off of its own accord. Remove the bomb and transport it to a safe disposal area for temporary retention as evidence followed by final destruction.

A fuse may burn out and fail to fire the nonelectric blasting cap and charge if the bomber cut the fuse crooked, or did not seat the fuse into the blasting cap properly. A wet fuse or a fuse with a broken powder train inside the fuse, because of the fuse having been kinked, may also cause a misfire (dud) . Perhaps the bomber was interrupted and never ignited the fuse in the first place. For all practical purposes the bomb is safe. A rendering-safe procedure should not be necessary.

Caution: In 1970, a bomb specifically constructed to kill police officers was used in California. The bomb consisted of a piece of pipe capped at each end, with a piece of *burned* time fuse protruding from one end cap. The disposal officer observing this pipe bomb notes the burned fuse and decides that the fuse has gone out and the bomb is a dud. Upon picking up the bomb, it explodes (Fig. 75) .

The burned fuse is a fake and is not connected to the firing train. The pipe bomb firing train consists of an explosive filler, electric blasting cap, battery power source, wristwatch to arm the bomb after it has been placed, and a mercury switch to trigger the bomb when it is disturbed.

Note: The purpose of the wristwatch is for the bomber's safety. The bomb cannot explode during movement by the bomber until

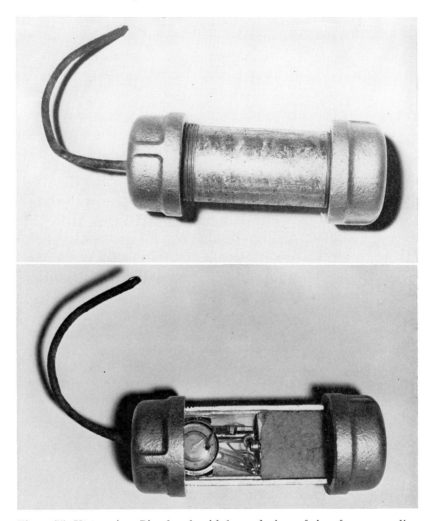

Figure 75. *Upper view:* Pipe bomb with burned piece of time fuse protruding from one end cap. *Lower view:* Interior view of anti-police boobytrap pipe bomb. Note the antidisturbance mercury switch.

the wristwatch has closed an open break in the electrical circuit sometime after the bomber has placed the bomb.

The bomb has two switches, or breaks, in the electrical circuit. The clock arms the bomb by closing one open section of the circuit which allows current to flow to the open mercury switch. When disturbed, the mercury switch will close, completing the circuit and firing the bomb.

Apply protective measures, then carefully secure a cord loosely around the bomb body and jerk the bomb from a safe distance (Fig. 76). This will either cause the bomb to detonate, or if the bomb does not explode, it will indicate the fuse probably was lit, burned out, and the bomb is a true dud. *This procedure is recommended for all open bombs.*

Figure 76. Carefully secure a cord to the bomb body and jerk the bomb from a safe distance. Note that the cord is initially loose on the body. Attempting to secure it tightly to the body might accidently disturb and function the bomb.

A hidden mercury switch could be inserted into a stick of dynamite. If in doubt, the disposal officer should always play it safe by jerking the bomb remotely.

Typical pipe bombs are shown in Figure 77. A straight pipe bomb is more effective if a file is used to cut grooves in the side of the pipe body, or BB's, nails, etc., are added for increased fragmentation.

Figure 78 shows the components of a very small black powder bomb, one of several constructed and used by a schoolboy. This bomb was filled with homemade black powder and used the container that had held the potassium nitrate (saltpeter) as purchased

Figure 77. Typical pipe bombs.

Figure 78. Black powder bomb.

from a drug outlet. A piece of cord dipped in a chemical and dried was used as a fuse. The effect of the bomb was concussion.

Percussion—Electrical

The recommended rendering-safe procedure for homemade bombs using percussion or electrical initiation is combined, since both types of homemade bombs can appear as straight bombs (one that can easily be recognized as a bomb) or disguised bombs (one that requires penetration of a container to identify it as a bomb). The general RSP's are the same for percussion and electrical initiation.

The percussion type of initiated homemade bomb uses one of the triggering devices (pull, pressure, etc.) to release a firing pin and detonate a primer which fires the explosive charge.

An electrically initiated homemade bomb utilizes an electrical power source such as a dry battery, a trigger device, and an electric blasting cap to detonate the main explosive charge.

Since a disguised bomb, such as a package bomb, may contain either a percussion initiating device or electrical initiation and a triggering mechanism, access to the interior of the package or disguise must be accomplished. Apply the recommended detailed RSP when the initiating source (percussion or electrical) and triggering method is located and identified.

Prior to attempting to gain access or applying any of the recommended RSP's to a disguised homemade bomb, thought should always be given to remote removal, sandbagging, and destruction of the bomb in place. The resultant damage, should the bomb explode, may be minor when balanced against the life of an officer.

It is very important that the disposal officer identify the firing train, as there is a slight possibility that a bomb that incorporates a collapsing field electrical circuit or other unusual triggering device might be used. The collapsing field circuit has current applied at all times to one circuit which is holding a switch open. If a wire is cut, the circuit collapses, the switch springs closed and a second electrical circuit is activated, firing an electric blasting cap and the main explosive charge. It is always advisable to remove the blasting cap from the explosive first. When cutting a wire, cut as close to the blasting cap as possible. The possibility of encountering a collapsing field circuit is remote. There are easier and better ways to trap a disposal officer through employment of some metal detectors, commercial security alarms, etc., that will trigger a bomb if anyone is in the near vicinity; infrared beams, photoelectric cells, mercury switches, sensors or proximity switches, etc., can be used. It is possible to construct a bomb where there is little possibility of rendering the bomb safe. Fortunately these more complicated and exotic triggers are for the most part speculative on the part of knowledgeable disposal personnel, rather than being employed by bombers. Most bombers realize that the simpler bomb is easier to construct, that there is less hazard to them and less chance of a dud.

The bomb disposal officer does run a risk and from time-to-time must accept the risk as an occupational hazard. Driving to and from an incident, in many instances, is more of a hazard than the hazards associated with the homemade bomb.

The following is a step-by-step general rendering-safe procedure for either percussion or electrically initiated homemade bombs and is based on bombs that have been used, rather than the one in thousands that might be more complex. Bear in mind that identifying the firing train, using knowledge gained from this text, and making a decision based on personal observation at the scene is the only valid RSP the disposal officer can apply.

1. Use fluoroscope or electronic amplifier to determine if the bomb is actuated by clockwork time mechanism. If it is a clockwork-actuated bomb, then a decision as to whether to go ahead with the RSP or to wait out the explosion must be made. (See Note No. 1.) If a fluoroscope or amplifying equipment is not available, start with No. 2, below.

2. If the trigger and explosive is in a container, that is, not out in the open, then access to the inside of the container must be gained and the triggering method and initiating source identified. *Important:* Two triggering methods may be used in combination.

3. a. If after gaining access the initiating method is determined to be percussion, then apply the recommended detailed RSP to the triggering device. (See next subsection on detailed RSP's for triggering devices.)

b. If the initiating method is determined to be electrical (electric blasting cap and battery), remove the blasting cap from the explosive, if possible, and cut the blasting cap lead wires as close to the cap as possible and remove the cap. Tape the wire ends if the cap cannot be removed to prevent accidental contact and detonation.

4. Both types of initiated bombs are for all practical purposes safe and can now be transported to a disposal site.

Note No. 1. If the decision is made to evacuate and let the bomb explode, a further decision is necessary—that is, how long to wait? If the bomber has given a detonation time, wait *at least* five minutes beyond the given time; if no time was given, wait one hour. Maximum safety would be attained with a twelve-hour waiting time. After the waiting period has elapsed, carefully attach a long cord to the bomb and jerk it several times. If the bomb does not explode, then continue with the RSP.

Figure 79 illustrates a percussion-initiated homemade bomb. An electrically initiated disguised homemade bomb, an explosive book, is illustrated in Figure 80. When the book cover is opened, an insulating tab is pulled, permitting a wire and metal plate to

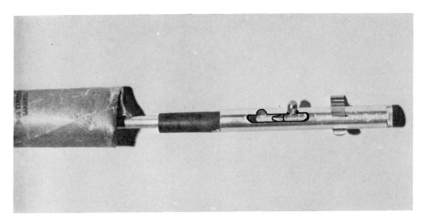

Figure 79. Percussion initiated homemade bomb consisting of a tear gas gun trigger, 410 ga. shotgun shell primer, nonelectric cap and dynamite.

Figure 80. Explosive book.

touch. This completes an electrical circuit and fires the blasting cap and charge.

Additional examples of percussion and electrically initiated devices are shown in succeeding paragraphs.

DETAILED RENDERING-SAFE PROCEDURES
BY TRIGGERING METHOD

In Chapter 7, triggering devices, are listed according to their functioning method as follows:

1. Pull
2. Pressure
3. Release-of-pressure
4. Tension release
5. Time-delay
6. Electrical—Miscellaneous

The recommended rendering-safe procedure for homemade bombs, incorporating each of these triggering methods in turn, is detailed in the following paragraphs.

Pull

This device requires a pull to actuate the mechanism to release a percussion firing pin or to close an electrical circuit and explode the charge. Pull triggers usually consist of a wire or cord that is fastened at one end to an object, such as a lid, or door, and at the other end to the device itself (Fig. 81). The following RSP is recommended:

1. Observe carefully and determine the triggering method and initiating source (percussion, electrical).

2. If possible, secure the door or lid etc., so that the pull device cannot function accidentally during the rendering-safe procedure.

3 a. If the device is percussion-initiated, determine from the operating method if a wedge, tape, wire, plaster of paris or similar materials can be used to prevent the firing pin or striker from making contact with the primer. If this cannot

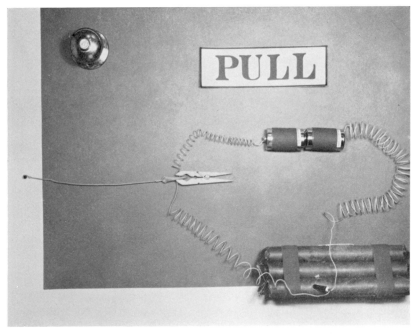

Figure 81. Application of a homemade *pull* type trigger device to a door.

be accomplished, attempt to break the firing train through removal of primer and/or explosive.

    b. If the device is used to complete an electrical circuit, the safest and easiest method of rendering safe is to pull the blasting cap, if possible, and to cut the electric blasting cap lead wires.

    4. Remove safed bomb to the disposal site.

Pressure

This device requires pressure to release a percussion firing mechanism or complete an electrical circuit to fire a charge (Fig. 82). An unsuspecting individual, stepping, sitting, pressing, etc. on an object concealing a pressure device will cause it to function the bomb. The recommended RSP is as follows:

    1. Observe carefully and determine the triggering method and initiating source (percussion, electrical).

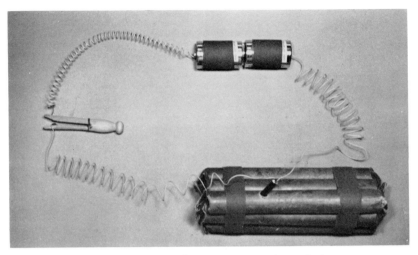

Figure 82. Homemade *pressure* type trigger device.

2. a. If the device operates electrically, pull the blasting cap from the explosive, if possible, and cut a blasting cap lead wire.

b. If the device operates by percussion, or if a lead wire cannot be cut, block or wedge the underside of the pressure plate or plunger, and tape in place. Insert wedge between striker and cap. If possible, break the firing train elsewhere in addition to interrupting the trigger.

3. Remove safed bomb to the disposal site.

Release-of-Pressure

Removal of a weight or pressure on this release-of-pressure device will cause it to function a percussion primer, or close an electrical circuit (Fig. 83). This release-of-pressure triggering device works very well in a disguised or contained type of bomb and should be a suspected trigger for all disguised bombs. Release-of-pressure is one of the triggering devices favored by bombers. The recommended RSP is as follows:

Caution: This is an Extremely Dangerous Device

1. Observe carefully and determine the triggering method and initiating source (percussion, electrical).

Figure 83. Homemade *release-of-pressure* triggering device.

2. a. If this device is determined to operate electrically, pull the blasting cap if possible, and cut the blasting cap lead wires.

b. If the bomb is determined to be percussion-initiated and in a container, securely fasten the lid using tape or cord, and remove the bomb as is, to a disposal area.

c. If the release-of-pressure device is open and not in a container, then attempt to secure the weight on the device so that it cannot be accidentally removed and permit the device to function the bomb, or attempt to secure the pressure plate or arm of the device so that it cannot function when the weight is removed; place a wedge or cushion under the striker. Attempt to break the firing train through removal of the cap or explosive. *Caution:* Removal of the explosive may permit the release-of-pressure device to move down and explode the bomb if the pressure plate or striker has not been secured. If the release-of-pressure device cannot be secured, that is, the striker cannot be wedged, pressure plate taped down, or explosive removed, then consider the possibility that the weight, release-of-pressure device and charge can be secured together and moved, as is, to a disposal area. It may be possible to get plaster of paris, plastic quick-hardening foam, or a similar material up into the device and let it harden, thus interrupting the firing train.

3. Remove safed bomb to the disposal site.

Tension

Tension devices utilize a taut wire or cord that is under tension preventing a cocked firing pin from moving forward or an electrical contact from closing and completing a circuit. Cutting the taut wire or cord releases the tension (Fig. 84). The recommended RSP is as follows:

1. Observe and determine the triggering method and initiating source (percussion, electrical).

2. a. If the device is electrically initiated, pull the blasting cap if possible, and cut the blasting cap lead wires.

b. If an electric wire cannot be reached and cut, or the device is percussion initiated, attempt to insert a wedge between the striker and primer or electrical contact, and break the firing train.

3. Cut tension wire if necessary.

4. Remove safed bomb to the disposal site.

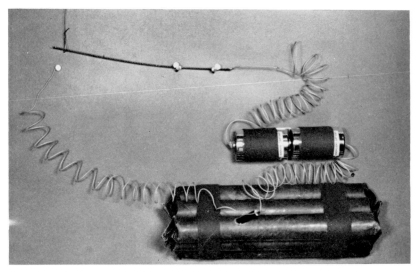

Figure 84. Homemade *tension* triggering device.

Time Delay

There are many ways of securing time delay in a homemade bomb. The methods most commonly used employ mechanical clockwork mechanisms, or a chemical delay (a chemical eating through, or softening a material) (Fig. 85). These time triggering devices may or may not release, or trigger another device in

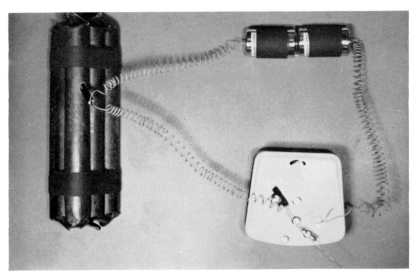

Figure 85. Homemade *time delay* triggering device.

turn. These are active bombs; that is they are working while the individual disposal officer is performing an RSP and are very hazardous as a result. Whenever a bomber telephones a bomb threat, a time bomb is to be suspected. Evacuation and protection of life should be the primary consideration. If a decision is made to attempt an RSP on a time bomb, the following RSP is suggested:

1. Attempt to make positive identification of the triggering method and initiating source.

2. a. If the bomb is actuated by a mechanical time mechanism and is electrically initiated, pull the blasting cap if possible, and cut the blasting cap lead wires.

b. If the device is actuated by a mechanical time mechanism and utilizes percussion initiation, consider one or more of the following in any order as determined by the disposal officer:

    (1) Wedge or secure trigger mechanism.
    (2) Disconnect any mechanical linkage.
    (3) Break the firing train.

c. If the device is actuated by a chemical delay, attempt to remove the acid vial. If this cannot be accomplished, then the officer should consider wetting the bomb and/or moving the bomb remotely to a less hazardous location and burning, or letting the bomb function.

3. Remove safed bomb to a disposal site.

Electrical-Miscellaneous

Electrical-miscellaneous devices include such triggering methods as connecting a bomb to an electrical circuit in an automobile, house, etc. Any one of innumerable electrical triggers and sources may be used. These bombs while hidden are generally not in a container, as such. Once discovered, the mechanism can generally be seen and must be rendered safe. The recommended RSP is as follows:

1. Observe and determine the triggering method and initiating source.

2. Pull the blasting cap, if possible, and cut, unplug, or remove the connection from the electrical source; or cut the blasting cap lead wires.

3. Remove safed bomb to a disposal site.

Miscellaneous devices include items such as explosive letters, pens, cigars and pencils, designed more as sabotage devices and for wartime usage rather than as homemade bombs. Rather than being homemade, these devices are manufactured and most will require a pull or twist to function. If the object is known to be explosive and is small, and if functioning cannot be determined, sandbagging and disposal in place is recommended. If this cannot be accomplished or is deemed inadvisable, then it can probably be carried away safely after jarring remotely, and if due care is taken not to pull, twist, etc., any portion of the disguise.

If at any time military manufactured devices from any country are encountered, look for one or more small holes running through the side of the device. Safety pins were formerly in these holes. Insertion of a strong wire such as a straightened paper clip or nail, will in effect replace this safety pin and prevent functioning because of its position between the cocked firing pin and the primer (Fig. 86). The presence of a hole in the side of a package or pipe bomb might indicate that the bomber has removed a wire or cord that was his safety, to prevent the bomb from accidentally functioning during handling. Trying to reinsert any safety in a homemade bomb is *not recommended* unless the officer is positive it will safe the bomb.

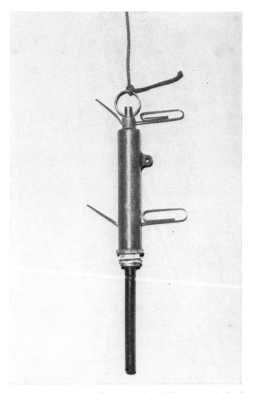

Figure 86. Note safeties in this military pull device.

The foregoing recommended RSP's are recommendations only and do not represent the only possible rendering-safe procedures. Just as no two bomb constructors will construct identical bombs even though they use the same triggering method and initiating source, a disposal officer may differ in the RSP that he uses from that of another officer. Certainly each officer can perform an RSP in a safe manner and accomplish the same ends despite this difference. The officer performing the RSP *must* have freedom of choice and be the sole authority as to the procedure that he employs. A most important step in any rendering-safe procedure is to *use your head.*

RENDERING-SAFE PROCEDURE EXAMPLES

Example No. 1

An explosion has occurred in a federal building and a security guard has been killed. From evidence, fragments, and the condition of the body, it was determined that the guard had picked up a pipe bomb which had exploded in his hands. A short time later a call was received from another federal building that a suspected pipe bomb had been located in an employee lounge during a routine security check.

Upon arrival at the lounge, the disposal officer noted that the suspected pipe bomb consisted of a two-inch diameter pipe approximately six inches long, capped at each end. There was no protruding fuse; however, a small hole was observed in the side of the bomb near one end cap (Fig. 87).

The disposal officer decided that if this was a bomb, the hole might have contained a safety that the bomber had pulled after setting the bomb and that since no fuse was visible, either disturbance or unscrewing the end cap would cause the bomb to explode. The triggering method was *most probably* release of pressure, but could also be time. The bomb could incorporate an anti-disturbance switch of some sort with any of these triggering methods. A short length of wire was found on the floor of the lounge.

To play it safe, the disposal officer carefully secured a length

Figure 87. Suspected pipe bomb. Note the small hole in the side of the pipe near one end-cap, and the small wire apparently used by the bomber to arm the bomb.

of line around the bomb body and jerked the line remotely from a safe distance. The bomb did not explode.

Note: At this point the disposal officer has many options. He could sandbag the small bomb, or use a blasting mat and blow the bomb in place, or continue to pull the bomb remotely from the building and blow it up outside of the building. He might transport the bomb, preferably in a dump truck, from the outside area to a disposal site. He may assume that the bomb is not sensitive to shock, pick it up and carry it away by hand. Picking the bomb up without jarring and carrying it off has been quite common in the past. This is not recommended if there is any other alternative open to the disposal officer.

The disposal officer in this instance decided after jarring that the bomb did not have an anti-disturbance switch, and it was probably safe to move by hand; however, he decided to reinsert the piece of wire into the hole in the side of the bomb and tape it in place. Nothing happened on reinsertion of the wire, and the officer picked the bomb up and carried it to a patrol car for transport to a police firing range. The bomb was transported without incident.

At the firing range, the disposal officer decided that instead of destroying the bomb using one of the methods described in the next chapter, he would attempt to open the bomb remotely for intelligence purposes. The equipment he would use consisted of two pipe wrenches, several lengths of stout cord (window sash cord in this instance), a roll of good adhesive tape, pulleys, wood stakes and a knife. He rigged the equipment and bomb for remote removal of the end cap as shown in Figure 88. The officer first tried to spin off the end-cap closest to the hole in the pipe body using tape and sash cord wound around the cap. The cap was too tight and would not loosen. Next, he used a second pipe wrench

Figure 88. Tape and cord wound around end cap in an attempt to unscrew the end-cap.

to partially loosen the end-cap. The bomb did not explode. Using the tape and cord still wound around the end cap, the officer spun the cap off the end of the bomb. In Figure 89, we note that the trigger is a military release-of-pressure device; that the wire the officer has reinserted into the hole in the side of the bomb did not enter the trigger holes and safe the device, and that the bomb is now in a very dangerous condition. The triggering device is hung by the wire, but could loosen at any moment and the bomb would explode. Since the bomb is on a firing range, the officer decided to explode it remotely with rifle fire.

Figure 89. Pipe bomb with end-cap off. Trigger is in a very sensitive condition.

Note: Normally, rifle fire is not recommended for remotely exploding a bomb. There is no assurance the explosive is not bullet safe, that the officer will not be within missile distance of exploding bomb fragments, that high velocity rifle bullets will not present a hazard to people some distance away, and that the bomb will explode and not be left in a highly dangerous condition.

Author's Comments: There are many *if's* and *but's* about this practical example that were purposely placed in the example to make a point, or to disturb the reader. The officer-reader should now go back and read the example again, fitting his own unique equipment situation and his knowledge into the example. Perhaps the officer, if confronted with this problem, would not have a remote line available to jar the bomb; would he wait one or twelve hours on the assumption that there might be a clockwork mechanism in the bomb? Would the reader pick up the bomb after jarring, as the officer did in the example, or would he pull it remotely from the building? At the destruction range would the bomb have to be preserved for a time as evidence, or could it be destroyed by burning or demolition? Can the reader think of a safer method to open the bomb, employing equipment that is available to him? Should an officer even attempt to open the bomb with makeshift tools? Did the disposal officer in the example make mistakes in a safety sense? Would using a shotgun to pop off the end cap have been a better technique?

The value of this particular example to the officer studying this text is in answering the foregoing questions in the light of his own unique circumstances. Bear in mind that the disposal officer in the example may have had a compelling reason for many of the actions he took, one that the reader may rate as unsafe. The reader's actions in like circumstances would be influenced by local conditions and policy decisions. The RSP in the example was successful even though most readers will find they can rate several of the actions as unsafe and/or unnecessary.

A large percentage of the homemade bombs actually encountered have been handled by officers with little experience or equipment and, too often, the favored RSP has been to pick the bomb up and carry it away. One of the objectives of this text is to present information and options for the disposal officers consideration to eliminate this most hazardous pick-up-and-carry-away RSP and substitute safer steps. At the least, a department should be able to purchase several five-hundred-foot rolls of good strong cord, fishing hooks and snaps for jarring a suspected bomb and removing it from a building. Do not forget, if it is planned to remove a bomb from a building remotely with cord, some rubber door stops should be included in the disposal kit.

Because of the more enlightened outlook by officials who have come to realize that in most instances the loss of an experienced officer can be more costly to the community than the cost of repairing a bomb-damaged facility, there should be very few instances where a disposal officer would ever have to gain access into a suspected disguised package bomb *in situ.* In the preparation of a Standard Operating Procedure (SOP), the known areas where an explosion cannot be tolerated, and where the disposal officer must do all that he can to prevent an explosion regardless of risk to his life should be listed. Examples of areas that might be listed as critical in an SOP are certain hospital areas; perhaps a costly computer, fixed and programmed with material that would be virtually irreplaceable; areas that would lend themselves to a major disaster should a bomb explode as specific locations within gas-oil storage sites and refineries, explosive and chemical plants and storage, power plants including atomic, etc. Each responsible agency must survey and list any priority areas within its jurisdiction. The prime criterion should not be money loss, but the effect on life and vital services. It is strongly recommended that the individual preparing a critical list coordinate with other local agencies such as the fire department, who may already have this critical listing. Too often a department or individual is inclined to a narrow view and tends to ignore other agencies rather than take advantage of the expertise of others. To this end, Civil Defense, fire-service personnel, the city engineer and private security personnel at some locations should be consulted.

Example No. 2

For the sake of the following practical example, the author assumed that the unlikely has occurred and a disposal officer is confronted with the problem of gaining access into a suspicious package *in situ;* an explosion cannot be tolerated and evacuation has been accomplished. Guards have been posted to prevent personnel from accidentally entering the danger area, and the disposal officer possesses only the most common tools.

The disposal officer surveyed the immediate site for any equipment or material that could be used to baffle, buttress, or direct the possible forces of an explosion away from the most vital points of the critical area and found nothing at hand that was suitable for this purpose; however, doors and windows were opened. A quick description of the package was taken and all personnel except the disposal officer left the danger area.

The bindings of the suspected bomb package were visually checked for tightness, as having a package spring open that may contain a release-of-pressure device during an RSP could be disasterous.

A razor blade was used to cut a small flap in the outer paper wrapping of the package. A colored inner wrapping was uncovered and a portion of this was torn away exposing a metal can-container (Fig. 90). The original cut in the wrapping was enlarged without cutting the outer binding of the package, as the metal container lid must be held down to prevent possible function of a trigger device.

A cut was made in the upper side of the metal container with a beer can opener (Fig. 91). Dynamite was exposed. The cut along the upper side of the container was enlarged until a portion

Figure 90. Initial opening of a suspicious package.

Figure 91. Opening metal container of package bomb.

of the trigger device was exposed. Using a flashlight, the trigger device was seen and found to be a common mousetrap (release-of-pressure) device with electrical initiation (Fig. 92).

A rubber pad was placed on one electrical contact to prevent detonation should the device be accidentally released. A section of the electric wire running to one of the contacts was cut and the cut ends taped to prevent accidental contact.

The open part of the bomb was taped and the bomb was removed by hand and transported, as it was, to the disposal site for destruction.

Note: If a cut is made into a container and powder flows out of the cut, tape it up immediately and try a cut in another location. Powder flowing out of the cut might allow a release-of-pressure device to settle and detonate the bomb.

The foregoing example is imaginary, but the importance of a

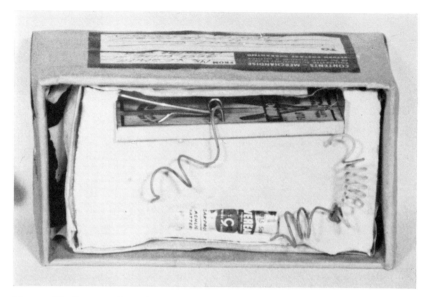

Figure 92. Cross-section of opened package bomb. Device is release-of-pressure with an electric blasting cap.

department having an SOP for dealing with homemade bombs is indicated. Coordination with other agencies is vital.

In this instance the blasting cap was not pulled from the explosive, as it could not be seen. By the same token, there could have been a second triggering device, perhaps incorporating a mercury switch in the circuitry. Jarring the bomb precludes this possibility. The disposal officer should take his time and attempt insofar as possible to determine if a second trigger is present. He also must expect to run some risk in a situation such as the one in the example.

Again, the reader of this text should fit his knowledge, circumstances, and imagination into the example, questioning each step in the procedure to attain maximum benefit from the example.

Questions

1. What are two actions that should be taken by a person receiving a bomb threat?

   a. _____

   b. _____

2. If time permits, what are two actions that personnel in a building can take prior to evacuation?

   a. _____

   b. _____

3. A good rule-of-thumb for determining evacuation distance in an open area is _____

4. Except for very compelling reasons, insure complete evacuation of a building, including search personnel, a minimum of _____ minutes prior to any given explosion time.

5. If a bomb is located during a search, should the search be terminated? _____. Reason: _____

6. Opening doors and windows will reduce _____ effect damages should a bomb explode.

7. One of the most favored areas for placing a bomb inside a building is in a _____ and should be one of the first areas searched.

8. When placing a buffer or barricade, at least a _____ foot air gap should exist between the buffer and bomb, or buffer and object to be protected.

9. An explosion occurs and there is a vehicle between you and the explosion. What primary effects of an explosion are you protected from?

   a. _____   b. _____

10. It is preferable to cut holes in a container of a suspected time bomb and transport the suspected bomb immersed in an oil-filled drum. True _____ False _____

11. Fragments of an exploding pipe bomb are a hazard to a greater distance than blast. True _____ False _____

12. Perhaps the most basic indispensable item in any bomb kit is a five-hundred-foot roll of good strong cord for remote pull. True _____ False _____

13. Homemade bombs may be classified two ways as open or straight bombs. True _____ False _____

14. The disposal officer should only attempt to gain access into a suspected package bomb in situ if an explosion cannot be tolerated and time is of the essence. True _____ False _____

15. If a hole is cut into a container and explosive is observed, remove the explosive and work backwards along the firing train from main change to blasting cap and trigger. True _____ False _____

16. Examples of nonsparking materials are plastic, rubber, wood, steel and glass. True _____ False _____

17. When gaining access into a paper-wrapped suspected package bomb, the cut should be made at a right angle (90°) with the side of the bomb. True _____ False _____

18. When ever possible, it is always advisable to first pull the blasting cap from the explosive before proceeding with an RSP or transport. True _____ False _____

19. The object of all rendering-safe procedures is to _____ the _____ _____.

20. Homemade bombs may be basically classified by initiating source as _____, percussion, or electrical.

21. If an explosion can be tolerated, the disposal officer should always consider remote jarring of the suspected or known bomb. True _____ False _____

22. It is virtually impossible to tell where the burning action is taking place in a burning piece of time fuse. True _____ False _____

23. When securing a line onto a bomb for remote jarring, always initially secure the line tightly to the bomb body to prevent slippage. True _____ False _____

24. A pipe bomb containing dynamite, nonelectric blasting cap, and fuse is an example of a _____ initiated bomb.

25. A bomb incorporating a release-of-pressure device and an electric blasting cap is classed as an _____ initiated homemade bomb.

26. A bomb incorporating a release-of-pressure device and a 12 ga. shotgun shell is a typical _____ initiated homemade bomb.

27. The disposal officer at the scene is the only individual qualified to determine the RSP for the particular bomb incident. True _____ False _____

28. Prior to performing an RSP, it is always desirable to secure a package, lid, etc., to prevent accidental opening and functioning of a bomb. True _____ False _____

29. Before a disposal officer can determine a safe detailed RSP, he must make every effort to identify the initiating source and triggering method (firing train) . True _____ False _____

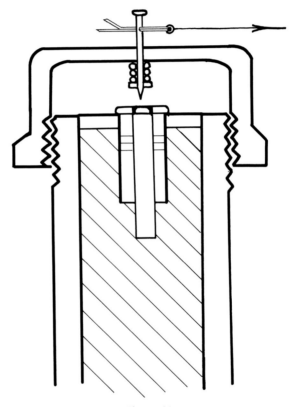

Figure 93.

30. In Figure 93, what is the initiating source and type of triggering method?
    Initiating source _____
    Triggering method _____

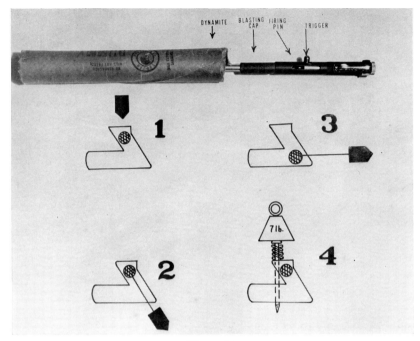

Figure 94.

31. Figure 94 depicts a "Penguin" tear gas gun incorporated as a trigger for a homemade bomb. In the illustration of the trigger, identify the triggering method for No's 1, 2, 3, and 4.

    1. _____ 3. _____
    2. _____ 4. _____

Answers to Questions

1. a. Attempt to secure as much information as possible from the caller.
   b. Notify the responsible individuals.
2. a. Open doors and windows. Disconnect electrical equipment.
   b. Check the immediate area for a nonstandard condition (bomb).
3. One city block (150-300 yards)
4. Five minutes

5. No. There may be a second bomb.
6. Blast
7. Restrooms
8. One
9. a. Blast
   b. Fragmentation
10. False
11. True
12. True
13. False
14. True
15. False
16. False
17. False
18. True
19. Interrupt the explosive train
20. Flame—heat
21. True
22. True
23. False
24. Flame
25. Electrically
26. Percussion
27. True
28. True
29. True
30. Percussion. Pull.
31. 1. Pressure
    2. Pull
    3. Tension
    4. Release-of-pressure

Chapter 9

DESTRUCTION OF EXPLOSIVES
AND HOMEMADE BOMBS

I T IS NOT THE INTENT, nor is it within the scope of this chapter, to produce a disposal officer who is competent to destroy explosives and homemade bombs, but rather to familiarize officers with the general requirements and procedures involved in the destruction of explosives. There can be no substitute for training conducted by an expert instructor, which includes actual handling and hookup of live explosive charges under competent supervision.

The Institute Makers of Explosives in their *Safety Library Publication No. 21,* states:

> Expert assistance is positively recommended in destroying explosives. The Institute Makers of Explosives have agreed to supply assistance in destroying commercial explosives to fire departments, law enforcement agencies, inspection and regulatory agencies, as well as to users of explosives. If the manufacturer is known, seek his assistance. If the manufacturer is unknown, a member company of the Institute Makers of Explosives will supply the assistance required.

Note: This assistance does not include bombs or military munitions which must be disposed of by the appropriate police or military agency.

Note: A list of member companies of the Institute Makers of Explosives appears in Appendix C.

For those departments that do not have the capability to destroy homemade bombs, inquiries might be made to the state police, state fire marshal, and to the nearest military facility as to support that they can provide.

It is recommended that states, perhaps through the Law Enforcement Assistance Administration (LEAA), give consideration to providing destruction assistance and/or training to those communities that do not possess range facilities or the expertise to cope with the destruction of homemade bombs and explosives.

The Destruction Site

The preferred method of destruction for most explosives and homemade bombs and bomb components is by *burning;* however, there is always the chance of an explosion. A known or suspected homemade bomb that has a blasting cap in conjunction with the explosive charge or an explosive that is confined as in a pipe bomb, is almost certain to explode during the burning operation; however, the explosion will probably be less violent than that produced by proper firing train functioning.

Departments without destruction support have preferred burning bombs due to the lack of qualified personnel who can destroy the bomb through demolition. It is important that the destruction site be located at a distance that will preclude the possibility of damage or injury to persons, should an explosion occur.

Most homemade bombs consist of less than five pounds of explosives. As an assist to an officer in estimating the amount of explosive in a homemade bomb, a standard stick of dynamite ($1\frac{1}{4}$ inches in diameter x 8 inches long) will weigh one-half pound. The American Table of Distances, prepared by the Institute Makers of Explosives, specifies the amount of explosives in pounds that may be *stored* safely at various distances from inhabited buildings. The table for barricaded and unbarricaded distances is given below. Note that the barricaded distance is one-half of the unbarricaded distance.

Explosives (Pounds)	Inhabited Building Distance—Unbarricaded	Inhabited Building Distance—Barricaded
2-5	140	70
5-10	180	90
10-20	220	110
20-30	250	125
30-40	280	140
40-50	300	150
50-75	340	170
75-100	380	190

The above minimum distances will protect persons against

blast but not from fragmentation (missiles) which is effective out to a greater distance than blast. At these minimum distances, personnel should be behind or under suitable cover. The distances do not preclude minor damage to buildings. If practical, disposal operations should be carried out at greater distances than specified.

The *missile safe* distances for persons in the open from bare charges placed on or in the ground are shown in the chart below.

Explosives (Pounds)	Safe Missile Distance (Feet)	Explosives (Pounds)	Safe Missile Distance (Feet)
1-27	900	65	1,200
30	930	70	1,230
34	969	80	1,299
38	1,008	90	1,344
40	1,020	100	1,392
44	1,050	200	1,754
48	1,080	300	2,008
50	1,104	400	2,210
55	1,141	500	2,381
60	1,170		

In a practical sense, the one to twenty-seven pound distance should suffice for virtually all homemade bombs, considering that from two to fifty-four sticks of dynamite would be involved. ($\frac{1}{2}$ pound per stick). If a pit approximately four feet square, or a four-sided earth barricade of approximately the same dimensions is used, the distance is more than enough. With a pit or barricade, the blast would be directed upwards and most of the fragmentation would be caught by the earth.

The destruction site should be free of dry grass and flammable material within a radius of 200 feet. During any destruction operation the fire department should stand by to combat any fires that may develop from the burning operation or from hot flying fragments of metal. The site should be wet down at the close of any burning operation.

The number of individuals in the disposal area should be kept to a minimum, but in any case there should never be less than two men present for safety reasons.

If the explosive bomb components are separated, only one

type of explosive should be burned at a time; the main explosive charge, Prima cord, priming-boosting charges, and blasting caps should be destroyed separately.

Smoking, matches and lighters should not be permitted closer than one hundred feet of a burning or blast area, or within fifty feet of a building containing explosives. Explosives should be protected from excessive heat, sparks, or impact.

It is recommened that any vehicle used to transport a bomb to a demolition site be plainly marked, that an escort be provided, and that a route be selected that will present a minimum hazard to facilities and to the public.

WEATHER CONDITIONS FOR DISPOSAL OPERATIONS

Clear to partly cloudy days with fleecy white clouds, or cloudy days with rapidly changing winds are the most favorable conditions for conducting blasting operations. Conversely, the most unfavorable days occur when the air is relatively still. Smoke fanning out horizontally with little swirling or vertical motion might indicate a temperature inversion that causes an increase in noise level and may bring complaints from persons living some distance away. A call to the local weather bureau prior to any destruction operation is suggested. No destruction operations should be carried out if local thundershowers and lightning are anticipated.

METHODS OF DESTRUCTION

The destruction of explosives can be accomplished through chemical neutralization, burning, demolition, or dumping at sea. Dumping at sea is not covered in this text because it is not feasible for most communities, clearances are necessary, expertise is required to insure that explosives will sink and not wash back ashore, for ecological reasons, and because the cost of dumping at sea can be quite high.

The burying of explosives or dumping into waste sites, wells, marshes, shallow water, and inland waterways is prohibited except for small amounts of black powder which may be dumped in a stream or body of water, if not prohibited by local law.

Destruction by Neutralization

BLACK POWDER. In all instances where black powder is exposed in a bomb, the disposal officer should wet the powder immediately to reduce the possible ignition of this very sensitive explosive by static spark or flame. Wet black powder may be destroyed by burning in a good hot fire, but leaching with water is recommended. The water dissolves the oxidizing salts (potassium or sodium nitrate) and should be disposed of separately from the residue.

Black powder may be placed in a hole in porous ground and leached out with large quantities of water. The residue may then be covered with earth.

NITROGLYCERIN. Chemical neutralization of nitroglycerin *in situ* is recommended and should be supervised by a chemist, as direct contact between the explosive and the chemical agent is necessary.

If nitroglycerin is encountered, the liquid should be sopped up with an absorbent material, such as a sponge, cotton, dry sawdust, etc. The remaining residue may be neutralized using the following solution:

> 1 pound of sodium sulfide (60% commercial) in 1½ quarts of water. Add 3½ quarts of denatured alcohol and 1 quart of acetone.
>
> *Warning:* Never add the solution to the standing liquid or unabsorbed nitroglycerin. Use the solution freely until the oily stain of the nitroglycerin is decomposed.

The solution should be mixed just prior to use, as the strength of the mixed solution weakens in storage. Users should wear rubber gloves. The absorbent material should be destroyed by burning.

Destruction by Burning

The preferred method of destroying explosives and most homemade bombs is by burning, but the possibility of an explosion must always be taken into consideration, particularly if a contained homemade bomb with firing train components intact is to be destroyed.

It is recommened that local fire service personnel be consulted prior to any burning or destruction operation for expert advice or assistance. In instances where the explosive can be identified, refer to the appropriate manufacturer.

FLAME RETARDANT CLOTHING. Flame resistant coveralls or outer clothing may be desired wear for disposal officers who perform burning operations or even for normal disposal duty wear. Clothing may be made fire retardant if immersed in a 15% aqueous solution of diammonium phosphate or ammonium sulfamate, or a solution of 2 pounds of ammonium sulfate, 4 pounds of ammonium chloride and 3 gallons of water. A stronger solution may be used without effect on the wearing life of the clothing.

BURNING OPERATIONS. A bed or train of readily combustible material such as excelsior, paper, kindling etc., should be laid down and a small pilot fire or an ignition train of suitable length arranged on the *downwind* side to allow the person lighting the fire ample time to retire to a safe place. In certain instances it may be desirable to pour a little kerosene or diesel fuel over the combustible material.

Warning: Never use gasoline or a highly volatile fuel for any burning operation. Pound-for-pound, gasoline has nearly sixty-four times the destructive effect of dynamite.

HOMEMADE BOMBS. Bombs including package and pipe with their firing train complete or partially disassembled may be destroyed by placing the bomb on a pile of combustibles large enough for a sustained burning time and letting the bomb burn. There is almost certain to be an explosion and for this reason a pit or an above-ground earthen barricade should be used to direct any blast upward and reduce fragmentation. Unless an explosion is known to have occurred, do not approach the burning area until the fire has gone out and the ground has been allowed to cool. It is advisable to have firefighting equipment readily available.

DYNAMITE. Dynamite which has exuded and shown obvious signs of deterioration, such as excessive softness, discoloration, or exudation, should not be touched, except by a representative of the explosive manufacturer, a military explosive disposal unit, or an agency designated to handle such explosives.

Loose dynamite recovered from a bomb incident may be safely destroyed by burning, provided some basic safety precautions are observed. It is advisable to limit the amount of explosive burned at any one time to a safe missile distance listed in the beginning of this chapter.

Dynamite should never be burned in its shipping container or in deep piles. Wooden shipping containers should be opened using wooden wedges and mallets. The cartridges should be slit open and spread in a row on a bed of combustible material. Separate the dynamite sticks from one another on the bed. If the dynamite is wet, use kerosene or diesel fuel on the bed. Use an ignition train on the downwind end, ignite the train, and retire to a place of safety until burning action has stopped.

PRIMERS AND BOOSTERS. Commercial primers and boosters should be removed from any packaging, spread on a bed of combustibles in a single layer, and burned observing the same procedure and precautions as for dynamite. Check before burning to insure that no detonators that would cause an explosion are present.

WATER SLURRYS. Slurry or water gel explosive and blasting agents may be destroyed by burning. Use a generous supply of combustibles, as some of these agents are difficult to ignite. Use techniques and safety precautions as for dynamite.

DETONATING CORD (PRIMA CORD). Detonating cord should not be burned on the spool. String the cord out in parallel lines, one-half inch or more apart, on a combustible bed and burn.

ANFO (AMMONIUM NITRATE/FUEL OIL). ANFO mixtures require considerable fuel to provide sufficient heat to effect decomposition during burning. Precautions as for burning dynamite apply.

BLASTING CAPS. The preferred method of disposing of detonators and blasting caps, with or without delays, is by detonation; however if only a few blasting caps are involved, place them on a bed of combustibles, approximately one foot apart, and burn as for dynamite.

OTHER EXPLOSIVES. Small quantities of smokeless powder may be spread in a long, narrow train, not over one inch wide by one inch deep, and ignited from downwind using a long ignition train. All propellant explosives burn very fast and hot, so the longer the ignition train and the thinner the train of powder, the more safety for the disposal officer. Maximum precautions against spark, heat and flame should be taken.

Other loose explosives such as TNT, C-4, etc., may be burned with procedures and precautions as for dynamite. Unless an emergency exists, report all military explosives to the nearest military facility for disposition by military explosive disposal units.

Safety fuse may be burned without special precautions. If the safety fuse is on a spool, it is advisable to unwind it to aid the burning action. Safety fuse is a flame hazard only; it will not explode.

Destruction by Detonation

There are two methods used to fire demolition charges—nonelectric and electric. The priming method for each is different and both systems will be covered. There are advantages and disadvantages to each method. Nonelectric firing is less complex, is not affected by storms or induced electricity, requires less equipment, but has a big disadvantage in that once the fuse is lit the disposal officer has no control over the explosion. While electric firing is more complex and requires more equipment, control over the exact time of the explosion is in the hands of the disposal officer. This is a big advantage if there is a possibility of persons accidentally entering the danger area, or of a low-flying plane accidentally flying over the site. In addition, an electric misfire is less hazardous than a nonelectric misfire. The particular method that is selected by a department depends on whether control over the explosion is necessary, on the area and equipment that is available, and on disposal expertise within the department.

NONELECTRIC PRIMING. A nonelectric primed charge consists of a length of safety fuse, a nonelectric blasting cap, and the main explosive charge. Assembly and use of the nonelectric charge with dynamite as the main explosive is as follows:

1. Being careful not to kink the fuse, cut off and throw away a six-inch length from the free end of the roll of time fuse. The black powder core of the time fuse may have absorbed moisture and the chance of a misfire is greatly reduced. The cut should be made square across the fuse with a clean sharp knife, or by using the cutting portion of the cap-crimpers to insure good contact of the fuse core with the cap explosive. If the burning time of the fuse is not known, cut off a three-foot section of fuse and time the burning rate. Then cut a section of fuse, *never less than three feet,* that is long enough to allow the person igniting the fuse to retire to a safe distance.

2. Check the open end of the nonelectric cap for grit or the presence of foreign matter. Gently insert the open end of the nonelectric cap onto the end of the vertically held time fuse until the cap charge firmly contacts the end of the time fuse. Do not twist or apply undue pressure. The cap should then be crimped (squeezed) to the fuse at a point $\frac{1}{8}$ to $\frac{1}{4}$ inch from the open end of the cap. Standard cap crimpers are recommended for use, rather than using teeth, knife blade, pliers, etc.

3. Dynamite may be capped at either end or in the side. Use a pointed wood dowel, a wood pencil, or the pointed leg of the crimpers to punch a hole in the dynamite for insertion of the crimped blasting cap and fuse. Use cord or tape to tie the cap and fuse securely to the dynamite (Fig. 95).

4. Place the capped charge in direct contact with the explosive or bomb to be destroyed. As a rule of thumb, it is recommended that three sticks of dynamite be used to destroy all homemade bombs, particularly for a package or suitcase bomb where the exact location of the explosive within the container is unknown. Tape the sticks together and place them on *top* of the bomb. Placing the bomb and charge in a pit is recommended to direct the explosion upward and to reduce the scattering of fragments that may be be desired for evidence or intelligence purposes (Fig. 96).

5. A signal to fire the charge, "Fire in the hole," should be given by the disposal officer after he has assured himself

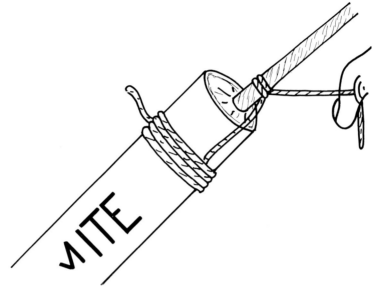

Figure 95. Use cord or tape to secure the fuse to the dynamite cartridge. This is to prevent the cap from being accidently pulled from the dynamite.

that all persons are in a safe place. There are several methods of using matches to ignite safety fuse. One method is to split the end of the fuse to expose the black powder core. A match head is placed on the exposed train and the match is lit by striking it with the box or using another match (Fig. 97).

There is a possibility that the explosive within a bomb container will not detonate sympathetically because of an air gap and may be scattered by the explosion of the charge. After the charge has detonated, search the area carefully. If a scattered explosive is found, then there is a good possibility that there is also a blasting cap nearby.

A nonelectric misfire presents a very hazardous situation. *For this reason it is recommended that all charges be double primed;* that is, two caps and fuses should be prepared as a safety factor. This is particularly important when an officer performs demolition or destruction infrequently. If a misfire occurs, *wait at least*

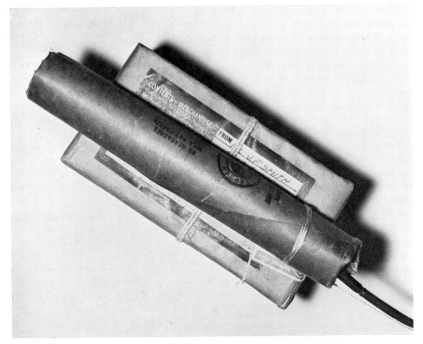

Figure 96. Place the charge on the top of the bomb. If a sandbag is placed on top of the explosive charge, it will further assist to drive the explosive force downward and increase the explosive effect on the bomb.

30 minutes after the time programmed for the explosion. Place a new primed charge without disturbing the old misfired charge and ignite.

ELECTRIC PRIMING. A complete electric priming charge consists of a power source, a firing wire of proper length, an electric blasting cap, and the main explosive charge. Necessary blasting accessories include the power source (generally a hand generator), the firing line of double strand wire, and a galvanometer for checking circuit continuity.

SPECIAL PRECAUTIONS, RADIO FREQUENCY (RF) ENERGY. Electric blasting caps under certain rare conditions may pick up enough induced electrical energy from radio transmitters to fire the cap. Electromagnetic fields of electrical energy are created in

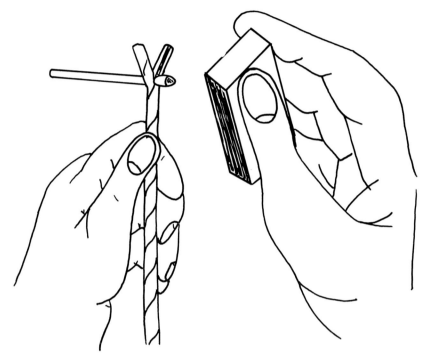

Figure 97. Slit the end of the safety fuse and insert a match head. Light by using another match or striking with the box.

the air surrounding the antennas of RF transmitters, as AM or FM radio, television and radar.

While the possibility of an explosion of an electric blasting cap from induced electricity is *very remote,* it is advisable for officers to be aware of this possibility and of the precautions to take to prevent a premature explosion.

All RF *receivers* are harmless and there is no danger from RF transmitters to nonelectric blasting caps, Prima cord, and dynamite.

If electric blasting caps are near a strong RF transmitter, the lead wires and/or any circuit wires involved, shunted or not shunted (twisted or open ends), will act as an antenna similar to the antenna on a television or radio set. This induced RF electrical current may be enough to cause the bridge wire in the electric blasting cap to heat up and fire the cap.

Commercial AM transmitters (0.555 to 1.605 MHz) are rated potentially the most hazardous because their high power and low frequency result in little loss of RF energy in the cap lead wires. FM and TV are less likely to produce a hazardous condition, as the high frequency currents are rapidly weakened or dissipated in cap or lead wires. Mobile radios, including walkie-talkies, must be rated as potential electrical hazards even though their power is low. While the possibility of mobile police-fire transmitters or walkie-talkies setting off an explosion prematurely is remote, it is recommended that when electric blasting caps are carried in a patrol car, the transmitter be turned off and that walkie-talkies not be used closer than five feet to an electric cap.

Electric blasting caps in their original packaging do not represent a problem during normal storage or transportation; however, when removed from their carton with the lead wires stretched out, the potential hazard exists. Twisting the bare wire ends of the lead wires together and folding the lead wires into an accordian fold will virtually eliminate any possibility of induced electricity from setting off the cap. See Appendix D for publications available on RF energy that contain tables for AM, HF, VHF-TV and FM, and UHF-TV transmitters; these are available from the Institute Makers of Explosives.

ASSEMBLY AND USE OF THE ELECTRIC PRIMED CHARGE. If electric firing is the chosen method of the disposal officer, then the following steps in the assembly and use of an electric primed charge should be closely followed. The disposal officer should never compromise safety in favor of speed or expediency:

1. Make sure that the power source is secured and cannot be accidentally connected during priming operations. A hot line has accounted for many deaths among disposal personnel.

2. Test the galvanometer, if used, by placing a metal contact across the two poles. A wide deflection of the needle indicates the galvanometer battery and circuitry are operative (Fig. 98).

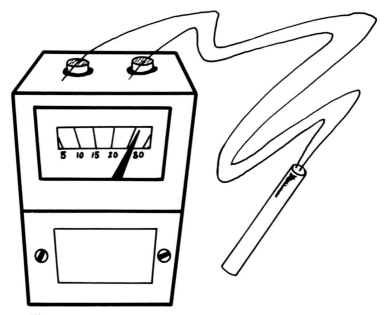

Figure 98. Testing blasting cap continuity with a galvanometer.

Warning: Galvanometers use a special mercury chloride battery. Use of any other battery in the galvanometer during a cap test will cause an explosion.

3. Lay out two strand firing line from the safe firing point to the location of the charge. Use the galvanometer to test the firing line for continuity or short circuits by separating the bare wires at both ends of the firing line. There should be no needle deflection registered on the galvanometer when the wires are touched to the two poles. Then twist the bare wires on one end of the firing line together and touch the open wires at the other end to the galvanometer poles. A meter reading indicates continuity; there is no break in the firing line.

4. Ground your body by touching the bare wire ends of the firing line to eliminate static electricity, then remove the shunt from the electric blasting cap lead wires, point the cap away from the body and touch the open ends to the

terminals of the galvanometer. A reading indicates a satisfactory blasting cap. Immediately after the test, twist the bare ends of the cap lead wires together and keep the wires short-circuited (twisted together) until ready to connect to the firing circuit.

5. Carefully uncoil the lead wires of the blasting cap. Do not hold the explosive end of the cap in the hand. Lay out the lead wires by hand without waving the cap wires in the air, or throwing the wires to straighten them out. Run the lead wires close together and parallel to each other without loops in the wire.

6. Punch a hole in the end or side of the dynamite stick and insert the cap. Use two half hitches to secure the lead wires to the dynamite to prevent the cap from being pulled out accidentally (Fig. 99).

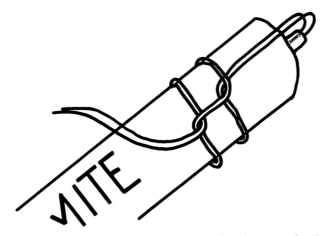

Figure 99. Use two half-hitches to secure the electric cap to the charge.

7. Evacuate all unnecessary personnel from the area. Unshort the blasting cap lead wires and connect the open ends to the bare wire ends of the firing wire. *Caution:* The bare wire connections to each firing line wire must be tight, clean, and separated from the other line to prevent a short and misfire (Fig. 100).

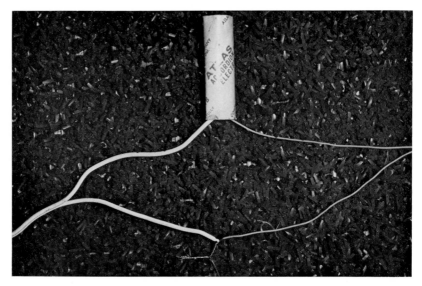

Figure 100. Make sure that wire connections are separated and carefully insulate the connections to prevent a short circuit and misfire. The packing tube of the blasting cap is used as an insulator in this instance.

8. Place the capped charge in direct contact with the explosive or bomb to be destroyed. Use at least three sticks for a package or suitcase bomb where the exact location of the explosive is unknown. Place the charge directly on top of the bomb.

9. Go to the firing point; untwist the firing line wire ends and again check the line for electrical continuity. A reading indicates there is continuity.

10. Fasten the two ends of the firing line securely to the terminals of the power source, and after assuring that all personnel are in a safe place, give a signal, "Fire in the hole," and fire the charge.

For safety reasons, *only one officer should be responsible for connecting the blasting cap to the explosive and firing the charge.* He must be certain at all times that the power source is under his complete control.

With a contained bomb there is a possibility that the explosive in the bomb will not detonate sympathetically. After the charge has detonated, search the area for scattered bomb explosives and cap.

If a misfire occurs, attempt to fire the charge several times, then disconnect the power source. *It is recommended that all charges be double primed to reduce the possibility of a misfire.* Secure the power source and check all electrical circuitry for a short or loose connection. If the circuit checks out, then prepare a new primed charge, place alongside the old charge, and try again. Repeated failure indicates there is a short between the firing wires or that the power source is weak.

Do's AND Don'ts. The following are some of the more pertinent *do's* and *don'ts* applicable to the destruction of explosives and homemade bombs. A complete listing may be secured from the Institute Makers of Explosives:

Don't store or transport detonators in the same box, container, magazine, or vehicle with other explosives.

Don't use any explosive unless you are completely familiar with the explosive and the correct and safe procedure for its use.

Don't use sparking metal tools to open any container of explosives.

Don't carry explosives in the pockets of clothing or elsewhere on your person.

Don't tamper with or remove or investigate the contents of a detonator, or try to pull the wires or detonating cord out of any cap.

Don't insert anything but safety fuse in the open end of a nonelectric blasting cap.

Don't allow smoking or unnecessary persons in the destruction site area.

Do make up primer charges using approved methods. Insure that the cap is secure and completely encased in the explosive.

Don't force a cap into the explosive.

Do test all electric caps and circuitry for continuity using only an approved galvanometer.

Do insure that all wire ends of the firing line and caps are bright and clean and securely connected.

Do keep the bare wire connections insulated from contact with one another and from the ground during electrical firing.

Don't use or uncoil wires of an electric blasting cap in the vicinity of an RF transmitter, or during dust, snow, or electrical storms.

Don't use short lengths of safety fuse. (3-foot minimum length). Know the burning speed.

Do handle fuse carefully to prevent kinks and possible misfire.

Do cut off an end of the roll of safety fuse and throw it away to insure a dry fuse. Cut square across the fuse.

Don't crimp blasting caps with other than an approved cap crimper.

Don't fire a blast without being sure personnel have cleared the area and without giving warning.

Do wait thirty minutes if a nonelectric misfire occurs.

Do keep electric blasting cap lead wires short circuited shunted, until ready to fire.

Do make sure that the electrical power source is sufficient to fire the cap.

The author has observed demolition personnel, and has himself used an automobile battery as a power source, crimped a nonelectric cap with other than approved crimpers, and failed to use a galvanometer in some instances. There is a very definite risk when other than approved tools and methods are used. Any departure from safety must be for the most compelling and emergency reasons only. The officer must be on his guard against the axiom that "Familiarity Breeds Contempt."

To some extent there has been a duplication of steps in describing the use of the two firing systems, nonelectric and electric. This is intentional on the part of the author, as this is a text and redundancy is a teaching technique. It will further assist the officer who wishes to prepare an SOP for the destruction of explosives and bombs, and who may wish to duplicate the sequence of steps for each firing system.

NOTE: A list of safety pamphlets including those covering the destruction of explosives and available from the Institute Makers of Explosives, is contained in Appendix D. The *Blasters*

Handbook published by the Sales Development Section, E. I. Du Pont de Nemours & Co., Inc., is available for six dollars. For departments that contemplate performing destruction operations, this is a most excellent detailed book.

Questions

1. The preferred method of destroying explosives and most homemade bombs is by _____.
2. When conducting a burning operation, the officer must always be prepared for a(n) _____.
3. A homemade bomb in which the explosive is confined, or has the blasting cap as a component part of the bomb, is almost certain to _____ during a burning operation.
4. Most homemade bombs consist of less than five pounds of explosives. True _____ False _____.
5. The weight of a standard stick of dynamite ($1\frac{1}{4}$ inches diameter x 8 inches long) is _____ pounds.
6. Inhabited building distances, listed in the American Table of Distances, will not protect the officer from flying _____.
7. Smoking or flame-producing matches or lighters should not be permitted around explosives, or in the blast area. True _____ False _____.
8. Using a pit or barricade at the destruction site will direct the _____ and catch most flying _____.
9. The number of persons in the disposal area should be held to a minimum, but in no case should there be less than _____ officers present.
10. The three methods of destruction are chemical *neutralization*, _____ and _____.
11. Destruction operations using electric caps may be carried out if a thunderstorm is anticipated. True _____ False _____.
12. The only explosive that may be neutralized by dumping in a stream or body of water, if not prohibited by local law is _____.

13. If the officer can identify the commercial explosive, he should refer to the _____, or if military, to an _____ _____ unit.

14. Ignition of a train or bed of combustibles for a burning operation should always be from the _____ end of the train.

15. It is advisable to limit the amount of explosives to be burned at any one time to the _____ distance.

16. When burning dynamite, the cartridges should be _____ prior to placing on a bed of combustibles.

17. Explosive components such as blasting caps, prima cord, and dynamite should never be destroyed together by burning. True _____ False _____.

18. If exposed black powder is encountered when opening a contained homemade bomb, the powder should be _____ prior to transport.

19. Chemical neutralization of nitroglycerin should always be supervised by a trained _____.

20. If wet explosives are to be burned, gasoline should be poured over the explosive to insure burning. True _____ False _____.

21. After a burning operation, the officer is uncertain that the explosives have been destroyed. He should not approach the site until the burning has stopped and the ground cooled. True _____ False _____.

22. It is best to always use a good bed of combustibles when burning dynamite, ANFO, or a homemade bomb. True _____ False _____.

23. When opening a box of dynamite, or any explosive, a metal chisel and wooden mallet may be used. True _____ False _____.

24. It is advisable to burn detonating cord on its spool. True _____ False _____.

25. Safety fuse may be burned without special precautions. True _____ False _____.

26. The disposal officer should destroy military C-4 by burning. True _____ False _____.

27. An advantage of using an electric blasting hookup for de-

struction is that the explosion time is under the complete control of the officer. True _____ False _____.

28. A complete basic nonelectric charge consists of a _____ _____, _____ and _____ _____.

29. A six-inch length of safety fuse should be cut off and discarded, a _____ foot length should then be cut and timed.

30. When cutting safety fuse, the cut should be made _____ _____ across the fuse.

31. The disposal officer should never use less than a _____ _____ foot section of safety fuse for a nonelectric charge.

32. A nonelectric cap should be crimped approximately one-third of its length from the open end of the cap. True _____ False _____.

33. Dynamite may be capped at either end or on the side. True _____ False _____.

34. The cap lead wires may be used to secure a nonelectric cap to dynamite. True _____ False _____.

35. If a nonelectric misfire occurs, the disposal officer should wait _____ minutes before approaching the charge.

36. To reduce the possibility of a misfire, the charge should be carefully assembled and preferably _____ primed.

37. After a misfire, the old cap and fuse should be removed and a new priming charge inserted. True _____ False _____.

38. Induced electricity presents little hazard if the bare wire ends are twisted together and the wires are in an accordian fold. True _____ False _____.

39. The basic components of an electric primed charge are dynamite, electric cap, firing wire, and safety fuse. True _____ False _____.

40. Electric blasting cap lead wires should run parallel and be without loops. True _____ False _____.

41. Before removing the shunt from electric cap lead wires, the

officer should ground himself by touching the bare wire ends of the blasting cap. True _____ False _____.

42. It is advisable to check continuity of the firing wire, blasting cap, and last, the complete hookup at the firing point. True _____ False _____.

43. A one and one-half volt penlight battery may be used in a galvanometer. True _____ False _____.

44. With two officers at the destruction site, one officer should be in charge of the power source and the other should make the hookup. True _____ False _____.

45. Prior to checking an electrical misfire, the firing line should be disconnected from the _____.

Answers to Questions

1. Burning
2. Detonation-explosion
3. Detonate-explode
4. True
5. One-half
6. Missiles-fragments
7. True
8. Blast, Missiles
9. Two
10. Burning, demolition
11. False
12. Black Powder
13. Manufacturer, Explosive Disposal
14. Downwind
15. Missile
16. Slit-open
17. True
18. Wet
19. Chemist
20. False
21. True
22. True
23. False

24. False
25. True
26. False (report to military)
27. True
28. Fuse, nonelectric cap, dynamite (main charge)
29. Three
30. Square
31. Three
32. False ($\frac{1}{8}$ inch to $\frac{1}{4}$ inch)
33. True
34. False
35. Thirty
36. Double
37. False
38. True
39. False
40. True
41. False (firing wire)
42. True
43. False
44. False
45. Power source

Chapter 10

EVIDENCE OF EXPLODED BOMBS (XB's)

A KNOWLEDGE of the effects of an explosion is of value to a disposal officer who may be called on to investigate a blast scene to determine if the explosion was caused by an explosive or bomb, or was the result of the accidental explosion of a common flammable substance, such as gas, chemicals, dust, etc.

Earlier in this text we learned that a chemical explosion involved the sudden violent transformation of an unstable explosive into stable byproducts (gasses) which expand at considerable speed. We further learned that explosives were classified as primary-initiating, low, or high explosives depending on the speed of decomposition or detonation; that temperatures (heat) of an explosion were 3000-4000°C, with pressures around 700 tons per square inch; that the production of gasses and heat produced certain effects that concerned the disposal officer, primarily fragmentation-debris, blast, and incendiary effects. The disposal officer at the scene of an explosion of undetermined cause must look for clear signs of chemical explosive effects or the absence of such signs to determine the true cause of the explosion.

DETERMINING THE CAUSE OF AN EXPLOSION

Determining the cause of an explosion might at first thought seem to be a hopeless undertaking. Doesn't the explosion destroy the evidence? *The answer is* NO. A liberal application of common-sense reasoning tenacity and in some instances painstaking labor, will in virtually every instance provide immediate answers to the investigator; that is, did an accident occur that involved a common explosive substance, or was this a planned bomb explosion that will require further investigation?

Important: Have the police photographer take numerous photographs of the scene of the explosion as soon as possible. These photographs are necessary for the preservation of the scene as it existed at the moment, for future study, investigation, possible prosecution, and police training. Following an explosion, the property owner and/or well-meaning individuals may destroy many clues that are necessary to the conduct of a full investigation and study.

In determining whether an explosion was accidental or involved an explosive bomb, the disposal officer-investigator has many signs that will point the way to a proper decision. The most important signs are mentioned below.

Explosion Site-Crater

Look for any crater on a floor area, or a definite spot where to the eye it appears that an explosion occurred. A cement floor will be chipped or there will be a hole in a more fragile surface. There should be signs of carbon blackening from the combustion of the explosive. If the bomb was contained, there should be marks on the surface of the floor (striation marks) radiating out from the point where the explosion took place. A peculiar acrid smell of explosive combustion may still be present.

Fragmentation

Look for evidence of scabbing (chipping) of walls, ceiling and floor surfaces from flying fragments of the bomb container and components. Fragments of the container, if a container was used, will be found in any rubble or imbedded in plaster walls, etc. Do not confuse marks left by flying debris due to the blast.

Blast

Here we can differentiate between a gas explosion that has a relatively slow burning rate and the high detonating rate of most chemical explosives. The slower burning gas will exert a push, rather than a punch as a detonating explosive will do. An unbroken light bulb, a large section of wall that has toppled with mortar intact, a window frame pushed out from the wall surface with some or all of the glass intact, are all indications that a slow burning or pushing occurred, rather than a rapid detonation that would shatter brittle substances such as glass, cast iron or mortar.

A small black-powder bomb may not do much shattering, but other signs such as an observable explosion site should be evident.

Incendiary

Look for carbon blackening and the peculiar smell of burned explosives in the area where the blast was centered. Material that is blackened from the explosion should be sent to the criminalistics laboratory. Fires and explosions are chemical and physical affairs and lend themselves ideally to examination in a laboratory. Since blast radiates outward in all directions from the point of detonation, the direction that debris has been thrown and the possible presence of a crater, or scarred concrete area, will enable the investigator to determine the location of the explosion. It is much harder to trace the point of origin in a gas explosion. This difficulty, absence of a clear detonation point, is a further clue to the type of explosion.

EVIDENCE

Normally, evidence must be preserved for introduction in connection with the prosecution of a case; however, it is obvious that explosives and homemade bombs cannot be taken into a courtroom for introduction as evidence. In compelling circumstances and dependent upon the wishes of the prosecutor, explosives and bombs may be retained at a safe and secure storage site that complies with state laws governing explosive storage. It is recommended that in most instances all explosives and bombs be destroyed. Photographs, testimony of the disposal officer and other evidence should suffice for prosecution purposes.

The evidence referred to in this chapter, however, is evidence that will be found after an explosion has taken place, evidence that would identify the type of bomb, initiating source, the triggering-functioning method and main explosive used. Surprising as it may seem, after every bomb explosion enough evidence remains to establish one or more of these indicators. In some instances, debris, fire and water may preclude any detailed search. Every effort should be made to secure evidence after an explosion and to make an analysis which coupled with expert testimony is necessary for proper intelligence and prosecution purposes.

To demonstrate and show that evidence does exist after the explosion of a straight or disguised bomb, the author has constructed and detonated several types of bombs and photographed the residue or evidence that remains to identify the type of homemade bomb exploded, the initiating source, and the triggering-functioning method. The following is representative of a cross section of exploded homemade bombs and evidence that a disposal officer may expect to encounter.

Straight Bomb

This straight bomb consists of a stick of dynamite, a nonelectric blasting cap and a length of time fuse (Fig. 101). The photographs show the straight bomb and the evidence remaining after the explosion. As can be seen in Figure 102, pieces of burned safety fuse remain. A streamlined object such as safety fuse withstands the forces of an explosion very well. Dirt or material blackened by the explosion should also be gathered and retained for laboratory analysis by criminalistics personnel.

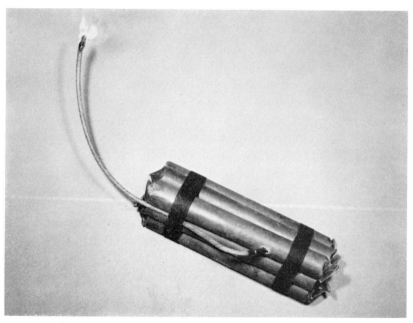

Figure 101. A straight bomb consisting of dynamite, nonelectric cap and fuse.

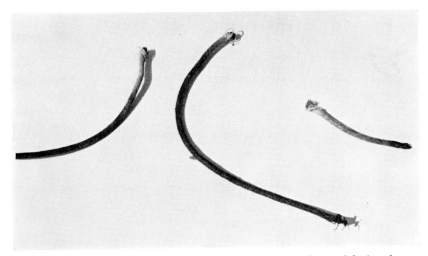

Figure 102. Evidence remaining after the explosion of a straight bomb.

Straight Bomb (Pipe Bomb)—Contained

In this instance a pipe bomb has been constructed consisting of a section of two-inch pipe, threaded and capped at each end and containing a stick of dynamite, a nonelectric blasting cap and a length of time fuse (Figs. 103 and 104). As can be seen in Figure 104, the evidence that remains after the explosion consists of threaded pieces of pipe, fragments of pipe end-caps, and shredded

Figure 103. Pipe bomb prior to its being detonated.

Figure 104. Evidence remaining after the explosion of a pipe bomb.

time fuse fibers (not shown). The fragments of the bomb container are thinned and jagged due to the swelling of the bomb case prior to its fragmentation. Fragments of virtually any container will be found after the explosion; however, diligent and thorough search is required.

Packaged Time Bomb—Clockwork Trigger— Electrically Initiated

This clockwork-triggered bomb incorporates an alarm clock, an electric blasting cap, two $1\frac{1}{2}$ volt batteries ("D" cells), and five sticks of dynamite plus packaging materials. The package consisted of a plywood frame inside a corrugated cardboard box, wrapped in common brown wrapping paper, tied with cord and labeled as shown in Figure 105. Figure 106 shows the interior packaging and contents. At a pre-set time the alarm goes off and the alarm winding key turns causing two metal contacts (cap wires) to touch and complete an electrical circuit. The $1\frac{1}{2}$ volt

Figure 105. Package time bomb, exterior view.

batteries produce enough current to fire the cap and explode the bomb. The evidence retrieved after the explosion of the bomb, see Figure 107, consisted of wood fragments, cardboard, wrapping paper, electric blasting cap lead wires, fragments of batteries and clockwork parts, respectively. The residue is blackened and torn from the force of the explosion, but laboratory analysis would determine the type of explosive used and that batteries were used indicating an electric firing train. Many pieces of clockwork gearing remain and other metal parts easily identifiable as having been part of a clock. Pieces of the batteries were located and a few small pieces of the electric blasting cap lead wires were found imbedded in wood fragments. If this homemade bomb had been

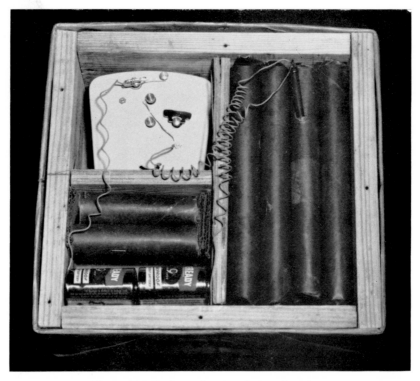

Figure 106. Package time bomb, interior view.

detonated inside of a building, the same evidence would be present imbedded in walls, mixed in the rubble, etc.

Evidence remains after an explosion to a greater or lesser degree than the examples illustrated by the author, but evidence does remain. The evidence shown in Figure 107 was gathered on the ground at or near the site of the explosion. Many small pieces of cardboard, wood and metal were left at the site, as the pieces depicted were enough for illustrative purposes. It is possible to gather virtually every piece of a homemade bomb container, and in a police investigation, every piece is important. If the bomb illustrated had contained a larger quantity of explosive, the evidence or fragments would still be present, just smaller and harder to gather as a result of the larger amount of explosive. The dis-

Figure 107. Evidence gathered after the explosion of a package bomb.

posal officer should never assume that the evidence of a home-made bomb is totally destroyed in an explosion; quite the opposite is true.

DETERMINING THE CAUSE OF AN EXPLOSION

Example No. 1

On a Sunday morning an explosion occurred at a meat-packing plant in Georgia. First reports and background information indicated that a homemade bomb had exploded. Careful investigation and analysis of visual evidence quickly determined that the effects of a heating gas explosion (mechanical) rather than an explosive (chemical), were present. Figure 108 is a photograph of the scene of the suspected bomb explosion. The photograph shows the various signs that an investigator-disposal officer must look for to determine the cause of an explosion. The building

Figure 108. General scene of the explosion. Evidence that indicated that this was an explosion of heating gas, rather than of an explosive bomb, is shown by numbered arrows: (1) Window frames; (2) Roofing; (3) Walk-in refrigerator; (4) Cinder block wall debris; (5) Ceiling boards; (6) Fluorescent light tubes unbroken.

construction consisted of cement block walls, cement floor, wood board ceiling and roll tarpaper roofing. The ceiling light fixtures were two tube fluorescent lights. The decision that this explosion was caused by a leak and subsequent explosion of heating gas, rather than the detonation of an explosive bomb, was arrived at after consideration of the following visual evidence:

1. Fluorescent lights near the point of origin of the blast were not broken, indicating a slow explosion rate. The lighting fixtures consisted of two tube fluorescent lights, several of which had dropped to the floor and contained unbroken tubes.

2. Window frames in the building had bulged and bent outward from the walls, yet the glass was unbroken. This is an indication of a gas explosion that exerts a relatively slow pushing effect, rather than the sharp shattering effect that a detonating explosive would have.

3. As can be seen in the photograph, the ceiling boards are hanging down. The roofing was rolled back and away from the originating point of the explosion, indicating that gas had seeped between the ceiling joists and exploded between the ceiling and roof. If a detonating explosion had occurred, the ceiling would probably have been blown up and back along with the roofing material.

4. The cement block walls have toppled outward with many cement blocks still held together with mortar. Dynamite would have pulverized the mortar and many broken pieces of cement block would have been present.

5. There was no evidence of scabbing of the cement floor, carbon blackening residue, or the smell of burnt explosives. No fragments of any bomb could be found.

6. A heating gas pipe was located near the entrance to a walk-in refrigerator. An electric motor and refrigeration unit was not enclosed. It was theorized that when the refrigeration unit cut on, a spark from the open commutator end of the motor had ignited the heating gas that had seeped from a loose connection.

Visual evidence coupled with common sense determined the cause of the explosion and quickly stopped rumor and conjecture in the community.

Example No. 2

In the investigation of an airline crash in which thirty-four persons were killed, investigators carefully fitted together pieces of the fuselage that had been scattered over a five-mile area. A section of fuselage on the right side was missing and could not be found. Fragments of the fuselage were not torn as from a natural crash. Residue on debris, when checked by the laboratory, was found to be nitrates (sodium and sulfur) from dynamite. Manganese dioxide residue indicated dry cell batteries. Portions of a bomb container and pieces of an alarm clock were found. It was decided that an electrically (battery) powered time (clockwork) bomb using dynamite as the explosive charge had detonated. In this instance the government investigation was painstakingly thorough and pinpointed the bomber.

It can be seen that careful, visual observation and search, coupled with common-sense reasoning, will enable the disposal officer-investigator to establish the cause of virtually every explosion.

Do include photographic coverage and laboratory analysis in any investigation where explosives are suspected to have been used.

Do Not forget the valuable assistance and experience that an arson investigator can provide in any explosion.

Do pass on the experience gained from any explosive incident to other members of the department by incorporating the incident into departmental training.

Passing on the experiences of your department to other officers in outside departments may be accomplished through reports to the International Association of Chiefs of Police, and many fine trade and police fraternal publications.

Questions

1. The three *primary* effects of an explosion are _____ _____, _____ and _____ _____.

2. A scabbed area and carbon blackening on a cement floor in-

dicates that a chemical explosion occurred at that point. True
_____ False _____.
3. Striation marks radiating outward from a scabbed area are indicative of a gas explosive. True _____ False _____.
4. Mortar, light bulbs and window glass are very apt to shatter in
a heating gas explosion, as they are very brittle substances.
True _____ False _____.
5. An explosion centered in the washroom of a building has occurred. A thorough search of the debris failed to turn up any
identifiable evidence, yet a clearly visible crater and effects indicated an explosive bomb was employed.
a. Describe the probable bomb that was used.

_____

_____

_____

_____

b. How could you go about determining what explosive was
used? _____.
c. Shattered washbowls and toilet bowls are indicative of the
detonation of a small, low-explosive bomb. True _____
False _____.
d. The only window in the washroom has been blown out;
plaster rubble is present; mirrors and lights are not shattered; one toilet bowl is shattered; striation marks and metal
fragments are seen on the tile floor. Put an "X" before that
which is *most* indicative of the probable bomb used?
_____ 1. Open dynamite bomb.
_____ 2. Pipe bomb with black-powder filler.
_____ 3. Disguised black-powder bomb.
_____ 4. Packaged bomb with dynamite filler.
6. After an explosion, several fragments identifiable as parts of a
wristwatch and several pieces of wire are found. Put an "X"
before the *most probable* type of bomb used?
_____ 1. Clockwork—pipe bomb—electric initiation.
_____ 2. Straight bomb—flame initiation.
_____ 3. Wristwatch time bomb—percussion initiation.
_____ 4. Time bomb—electric initiation.

Answers to Questions

1. Fragmentation, blast, and incendiary.
2. True
3. False
4. False
5. a. Straight bomb; explosive, nonelectric cay and fuse, open.
   b. Have residue analyzed in a laboratory.
   c. False (HE)
   d. Pipe bomb with black-powder filler.
6. Time bomb—electric initiation.

Chapter 11

FIREBOMBS

T HE CONSTRUCTION of an explosive bomb is not simple; it necessitates a basic knowledge of explosives and their use, a sometimes difficult-to-obtain source of explosive materials, and a certain amount of time for construction. In contrast, only the most rudimentary amount of intelligence is needed to construct a firebomb. The component materials are easily obtainable, virtually impossible to trace to the bomber, and quickly assembled. The low cost of materials and high destruction potential have made them a favorite tool of dissidents and rioters.

The mechanics of firebombs involve a source of heat (wick), a flammable filler, and a target of combustible material. The "Molotov Cocktail" that was widely used during World War II by partisan fighters, consisted of a frangible bottle that was filled to about two-thirds of its capacity with gasoline, and a wick consisting of strips of cloth inserted into the mouth of the bottle to a depth above the level of the gasoline filler. To use, the Molotov was turned upside down to saturate the cloth wick which was then ignited before the Molotov was thrown. The bottle shattered on impact with the target, and the burning wick ignited the gasoline filler and in turn, the combustible target material.

The term "firebomb" has replaced "Molotov Cocktail" and is more descriptive of the many variations of this incendiary that are currently employed by firebombers. The following describe the firebombs and firebomb components that have been used by firebombers.

Igniter (Wicks)

1. Strips of cloth inserted into the neck of the firebomb (Fig. 109).
2. Strips of cloth tied around the neck of the capped bottle. The cloth is saturated with lighter fluid immediately prior to use (Fig. 109).

Figure 109. Cloth wicks.

3. A sanitary napkin tied around the body of the capped bottle Saturated immediately prior to use (Fig. 110).

4. Rope tied around the body of the capped bottle. Saturated immediately prior to use. (Fig. 111).

5. A highway fusee (road flare) taped to the body of the capped bottle. Ignited prior to use (Fig. 111).

6. A cloth that is wrapped around the body of the bottle and saturated with a chemical that will cause ignition when it contacts the chemical filler—Hypergolic action (Fig. 110).

7. A nonelectric blasting cap with fuse is taped to the side of the bottle. The flash of the exploding cap ignites the filler. This firebomb is placed so that the length of the fuse gives the bomber time to get away (Fig. 112).

Figure 110. Cloth (hypergolic) wick and sanitary napkin.

8. A CO_2 cartridge or other container is filled with explosive powder, a fuse inserted, and is taped to the side of the bottle. This firebomb is also placed and permits getaway time (Fig. 112).

9. A clockwork timing mechanism is incorporated to allow getaway time (Fig. 113).

Fillers

1. Gasoline.
2. Gasoline mixed with motor oil. This mixture is less volatile than straight gasoline, burns longer, has good penetra-

Figure 111. Fusee and rope wick.

tion and is more effective than gasoline against all but the
most easily ignitable target material.

3. Gasoline and detergent. In this mixture, the detergent acts
as a thickener. The mixture is sometimes called homemade
Napalm. Thick fuel oil, diesel oil, grease, petroleum jelly,
paraffin, vaseline and egg white can also be used. The
thickened mixture burns longer, clings to the flammable
surface, and provides a long burning ignition source for
hard-to-ignite materials.

4. Gasoline and sulphuric acid. A cloth wick on the outside
of the firebomb body is saturated with a mixture of potassium chlorate and sugar, and does not have to be ignited.
When the bottle breaks and the mixture on the wick contacts the filler, a reaction takes place, and flame is produced—Hypergolic action.

Figure 112. *Right:* A nonelectric blasting cap and fuse. *Left:* A CO_2, powder filled cartridge and fuse. The length of the fuse determines the bombers getaway time.

Dry chemicals are preferable for extinguishing a burning firebomb. A CO_2 extinguisher may also be used and as a last resort, water. Water should not be aimed directly onto burning gasoline, but should be used to flush the gasoline or to cool surrounding combustible material.

Incendiary Bombs

There are many incendiary mixtures that may be employed. One type of incendiary that may be encountered consists of a container filled with a mixture of potassium chlorate and sugar. An inverted vial of sulphuric acid with a paper, plastic, or cork stopper is placed stopper down in a hole in the mixture. When the sulphuric acid eats through the stopper and contacts the mixture an intense fire results.

There are many other incendiary devices, and the local fire

Figure 113. The professional firebomber desires to be elsewhere when the fire occurs. Clockwork mechanism, electric blasting cap and battery allows for ample getaway time.

chief or the state fire marshal should be contacted for information on incendiary devices. Both law enforcement and fire service personnel should be informed on homemade bombs, firebombs and other incendiaries particularly as to precautions associated with unused firebombs and to evidence to look for, since both departments may be involved in any explosion and/or major fire investigation.

Questions

1. Basically, a firebomb consists of three components, a frangible container, _____ and _____.
2. List four substances that may be added to gasoline to produce a thickened fuel (Napalm).

   a. _____   c. _____
   b. _____   d. _____

3. Hypergolic action firebombs require a burning fuse for ignition. True _____ False _____.
4. The *best* extinguishing agent to use against burning firebombs is a _____ extinguisher.
5. A water extinguisher should be used to extinguish a burning napalm firebomb. True _____ False _____.

Answers to Questions

1. Wick and filler
2. Vaseline
   Detergent
   Thick fuel oil
   Grease
   Diesel oil
   Petroleum jelly
   Paraffin
   Egg white
3. False
4. Dry chemical
5. False

INSTRUCTOR INFORMATION

The question pages at the end of each chapter, taken together, constitute a written examination. If desired and the training officer has the time, the chapter questions may be used as a review of the text material prior to having the students take the practical exercise in the following chapter, Chapter 12.

Compared to a student exercise using model bombs and live explosives, the practical exercise represents the next most practical method of providing student application and/or means of measuring the student's ability and comprehension of explosives and homemade-bomb training.

The two factors that are most likely to influence the training officer's utilization of the practical exercise are the amount of training time available and the size of the class. The chapter is adaptable to various training considerations and may be employed several different ways:

1. If the individual students have the text in hand, they may write their answers directly in the text, or on answer sheets provided by the instructor.

2. The instructor may show 35MM color slides of the illustrations and use student answer sheets. (See Appendix F for available color slides)

3. If training time is restricted, the instructor may show the slides, ask the questions verbally and call for a verbal response from the students.

4. If the class is very large and time is limited, the instructor may show the slide, ask the question, pause and then answer the question himself.

5. If desired, the instructor may increase the practical exercise by the inclusion of slides of other bombs depicted in the text proper. Actual models of bombs, in lieu of slides, may be favored for a small class.

Answers to the practical exercise are located at the end of the practical exercise chapter.

Chapter 12

PRACTICAL EXERCISE

Initiating Source	*Triggering Method*
Flame—Heat	Pull
Percussion	Pressure
Electrical	Release of pressure
	Tension
	Time-delay (Mechanical-Chemical)
	Electrical—Miscellaneous

PROBLEM 1

1. Match the numbered explosives in Figure 114 to their explosive names.

   a. _____Black powder   d. _____Dynamite
   b. _____TNT   e. _____Smokeless powder
   c. _____C-4 (plastic)

2. Explosives are classified according to the speed of their chemical reaction as primary-initiating, high, or low explosives. Write the classification PI, H, or L, for the following explosives and components.

   a. _____Dynamite   f. _____TNT
   b. _____Black powder   g. _____Flex-X
   c. _____C-4   h. _____Safety fuse
   d. _____Electric cap   i. _____Astrolite
   e. _____Smokeless powder   j. _____Prima cord

3. Place an "X" in the column opposite those explosives that require a blasting cap to set them off.

   a. _____Black powder   d. _____C-4
   b. _____Dynamite   e. _____PETN
   c. _____Smokeless powder

4. What color is military FLEX-X explosive? _____

5. A vial of clear or yellow-tinted liquid is encountered at an interrupted safe cracking. What is the probable explosive? _____

6. Detonating cord may be identified by a _____ core and safety fuse by a _____ core.

7. By carefully observing a burning piece of time fuse, it can be determined where the burning action is taking place. True _____ False _____

8. An explosive item, such as the Jet-Axe, that focuses the explosive force is called a _____ charge.

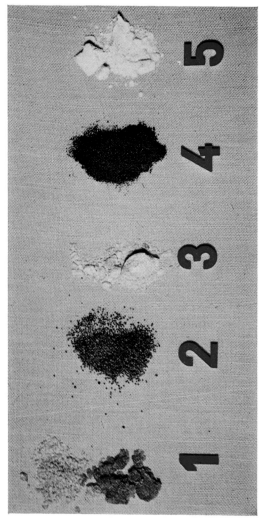

Figure 114. Problem No. 1.

PROBLEM 2

1. What is the triggering method for each of the examples shown in Figure 115?

   a. _____   e. _____

   b. _____   f. _____

   c. _____   g. _____

   d. _____   h. _____

2. Write in the *most probable* triggering method in the space opposite the description.

   a. _____Lifting a container lid.

   b. _____Stepping on an object.

   c. _____Cutting a taut wire.

   d. _____A bomb threat, 30 minutes given.

   e. _____Turning on an auto ignition switch.

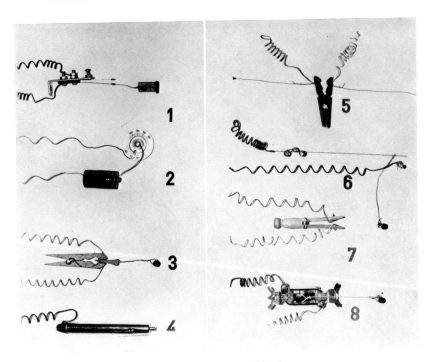

Figure 115. Problem No. 2.

PROBLEM 3

1. What is the initiating source of the bomb shown in Figure 116? _____

2. What evidence would you expect to find after the explosion of this bomb?

   a. _____ b. _____

3. If the explosive filler is dynamite, what other explosive components are necessary?

   a. _____ b. _____

4. If the fuse was burned and the bomb failed to explode, how long should you wait before assuming the fuse has failed? _____ minutes.

Figure 116. Problem No. 3.

PROBLEM 4

1. If the bomb shown in Figure 117 was closed, that is, with the end-cap in place, rank the following RSP's, 1, 2, etc., in order of *safety* preference:

   a. _____Place bomb by hand in carrier, remove remotely.

   b. _____Use a pole to place bomb in carrier, remove remotely.

   c. _____Pick up and carry away by hand.

   d. _____Unscrew end-cap, cut wire, carry away.

2. When tying a line to a pipe bomb for remote jarring, the line should be tied tightly to prevent slippage.

   True _____ False _____.

3. What are the three primary explosive effects of a pipe bomb?

   a. _____   c. _____

   b. _____

4. What is the initiating source of the bomb shown? _____
   _____

5. What is the triggering method? _____

6. How would you interrupt the firing train?
   _____

Figure 117. Problem No. 4.

PROBLEM 5

1. What is the initiating source? _____
2. What is the triggering method? _____
3. You *do not* have to take precautions to prevent a person from accidentally opening the door from the other side. True _____ False _____.
4. Why should the blasting cap be removed from the explosive, if possible, prior to commencing the RSP?

   _____
5. How would you render this bomb safe?

   _____
6. Should the blasting cap and the explosive be transported in the same container? Yes _____ No. _____.
7. When transporting an electric blasting cap, is it safe to use a radio receiver? Yes _____ No _____.
8. What are three nonsparking materials that could be used to slit open a dynamite stick prior to burning at a destruction site?

   a. _____ b. _____ c. _____

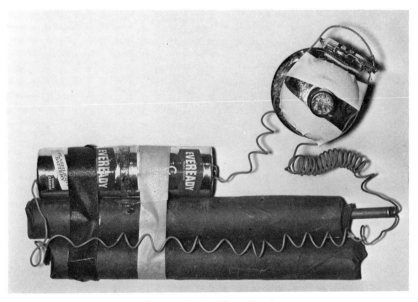

Figure 118. Problem No. 5.

PROBLEM 6

1. Why is it inadvisable to unscrew the end-cap of a pipe bomb by hand? _____

2. What is the initiating source? _____

3. What is the triggering method? _____

4. Which is the *most probable* explosive filler, a low or high explosive? _____

5. How would you render safe this open bomb?

_____

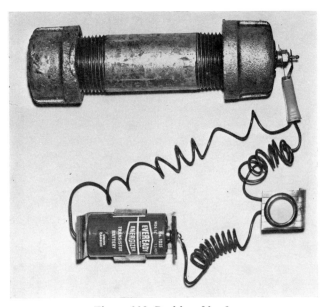

Figure 119. Problem No. 6.

PROBLEM 7

An unexploded pipe bomb is discovered. A small hole is noted in the body and a small piece of straight wire found nearby. A short while later when cutting into a suspected package bomb, the disposal officer discovers a small hole in the container. Answer the following:

1. Place an "X" opposite the *best choice of possible* initiating and triggering method.
   a. _____ Electrical—Clockwork time-delay
   b. _____ Flame—Release of pressure
   c. _____ Percussion—Release of Pressure
   d. _____ Electrical—Chemical time-delay.
2. If the pipe bomb did not explode when jarred, is it probably safe to transport? Yes _____ No _____.
3. If the pipe bomb is located in a building, What immediate protective measure could you take to reduce blast damage should the bomb explode? _____
4. Is it advisable to fire high velocity rifle bullets at a suspected bomb in an attempt to explode it?
   Yes _____ No _____.
5. There is a hole in both bomb containers, and the explosive filler is unknown. If you use an oil can to squirt water into the containers, can you be sure the main explosive charge is neutralized? Yes _____ No _____.

Figure 120. Problem No. 7.

PROBLEM 8

1. What is the initiating source? _____
2. What is the triggering method? _____
3. What will cause this grenade to function? _____
   _____

4. Place an "X" opposite the two *best* rendering-safe options.
   a. _____Insure the lever is secure, insert straight paper clip in the hole.
   b. _____Pull the grenade loose, throw out car window.
   c. _____Pull the grenade loose remotely with line.
   d. _____Do nothing; call the military.
5. What is the primary explosive effect of this grenade?
   _____.

6. How would you safe this grenade if there were no apparent trigger, but two wires extend from the open end of the grenade? _____
7. Is it advisable to check for a second bomb? Yes _____ No _____.

8. If you located a bomb under the driver's seat with wires running to the underside of a floormat, how would you render the bomb safe? _____
   _____

9. When breaking a bomb electrical circuit, is it advisable to cut one wire at a time as close to the cap as possible? Yes _____ No _____.
10. What could you do to prevent radio frequency energy from affecting a blasting cap during transit?
    _____

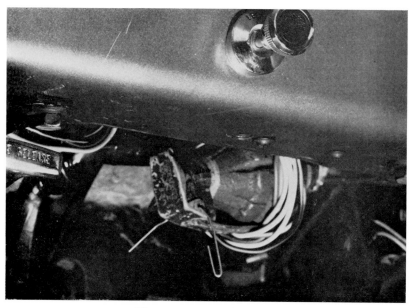

Figure 121. Problem No. 8.

PROBLEM 9

You have been called to a local theater where a bomb has been reported to have exploded. On arrival, you find that the theater has been evacuated and several patrons have injuries consisting of spot burns on their legs and holes in their clothing. There is no cratering or visible damage in the theater. A second bomb (Fig. 122) is found. Considering the construction of the bomb, answer the following:

1. List five pieces of evidence that you would expect to find in the explosion area.

    a. _____

    b. _____

    c. _____

    d. _____

    e. _____

2. What was the probable filler in the glass vial? _____

3. Check the RSP that you consider *most* correct.

    a. _____ Wait one hour.

    b. _____ Wait twelve hours.

    c. _____ Jar and remove remotely.

    d. _____ Wait twenty-four hours.

4. Could this bomb be removed by hand if complete rubberized clothing was secured from the fire department? Yes _____ No _____.

5. If you were confronted with the open container shown, what is the quickest RSP? _____

6. Number the following 1, 2 and so on in functioning sequence.

    a. _____ Vial shatters and contents are scattered.

    b. _____ Glo-plug heats up.

    c. _____ Firecrackers explode.

    d. _____ Fuse burns.

    e. _____ Current flow.

    f. _____ Clock completes circuit, triggers bomb.

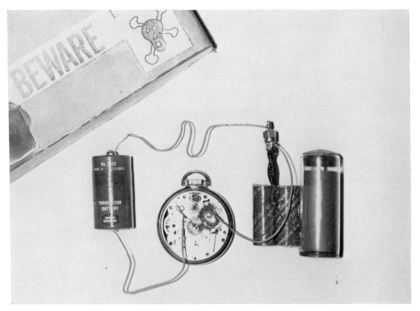

Figure 122. Problem No. 9.

PROBLEM 10

1. Assume the bomb depicted is located in a busy bus depot. Rank the following RSP's in order of preference as 1, 2, or 3.
   a. _____ Fluoroscope and RSP in situ.
   b. _____ Remove remotely and transport to a safe area.
   c. _____ Wait twelve hours and remove remotely.
2. If access is gained into a suspected bomb and dynamite is all that can be seen, remove the dynamite and work back along the firing train to the trigger. True _____ False _____.
3. A suspected clockwork time bomb should be dunked in oil in an attempt to stop the clock. True _____ False _____.
4. What is the initiating source? _____
5. What is the triggering method? _____
6. How would you interrupt the explosive train? _____

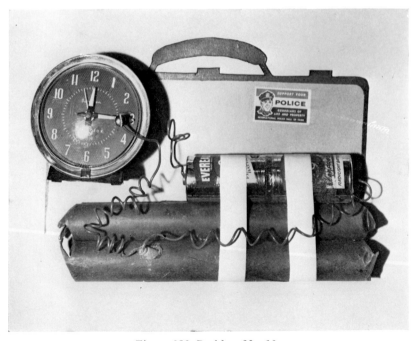

Figure 123. Problem No. 10.

PROBLEM 11

1. A telephone operator in a government building has a caller on the line stating, "A bomb is going to explode in the building in thirty minutes." List at least four things the operator should do while the caller is on the line.

   a. _____

   b. _____

   c. _____

   d. _____

2. Opening doors and windows will vent possible _____ _____ effects.

3. Complete evacuation of the building should be accomplished at least _____ minutes prior to any announced detonation time.

Figure 124. Problem No. 11.

4. One of the first areas that should be searched in a school or public building should be the _____ rooms.
5. If a bomb is located during a search, should the search be terminated? Yes _____ No _____.
6. An air gap should be left between a barricade and the bomb or the object to be protected. True _____ False _____.
7. It is always advisable to check the bindings on a package to prevent accidental opening during an RSP. True _____ False _____.
8. When cutting into a paper wrapped package, the cut should be made at a 90° angle to the surface. True _____ False _____.
9. What is the initiating source? _____
10. How would you interrupt the explosive train?
_____

PROBLEM 12

1. A suspected package bomb is reported in a campus ROTC building. Number the following actions 1, 2, 3, etc., in sequence:

   a. _____ Remove to a disposal area with sand-filled dump truck.

   b. _____ Use a length of cord and jar the bomb remotely.

   c. _____ Use the cord to pull the bomb from the truck remotely onto a bed of combustibles and burn.

   d. _____ Use the cord to pull the bomb from the building remotely.

2. What is the initiating source? _____

3. What is the triggering method? _____

4. How would you interrupt the firing train? _____
   _____

5. If you cut into the top of this container and the black powder was exposed, what could you do to safe the powder for transport? _____

Figure 125. Problem No. 12.

6. What could you do to preclude the possibility of static electricity from your body setting off the exposed black powder?

_____

7. When destroying a homemade bomb by burning, the disposal officer should *always* be prepared for a _____
_____.

8. Inhabited building distances listed in the American Table of Distances will not protect personnel from flying fragments. True _____ False _____.

9. In a burning operation, ignition of the bed or train should always be from the _____ end.

10. Never use less than a three-foot length of safety fuse when priming nonelectrically. True _____ False _____.

11. Both electrical and nonelectric caps should be secured to prevent accidental pull-out and preferably double primed charges should be set. True _____ False _____.

12. If a nonelectric misfire occurs, the disposal officer should wait _____ minutes before checking the charge.

13. An advantage of using an electrical hookup for destruction by detonation is that the explosion is under the control of the disposal officer. True _____ False _____.

14. Electrically primed demolition charges should not be placed if a thunderstorm is nearby. True _____ False _____.

15. The officer making the hookup should always secure the power source. True _____ False _____.

16. Chemical neutralization of nitroglycerin involves using a mixture of potassium nitrate and water. True _____ False
_____.

17. There should never be less than _____ officers present during any destruction operation.

PROBLEM 13

1. The evidence depicted in Figure 126 consists of a piece of
   _____.

2. Considering the evidence, describe the *most probable* type of
   bomb. _____

3. Write either *high* or *low* for the probable explosive involved,
   opposite the given evidence description.
   a. _____ Glass and light bulbs shattered over wide area.
   b. _____ Toppled sections of brick wall still held together by
      mortar.
   c. _____ Evident cratering on cement floor.
   d. _____ Brittle material shattered over a distance.
   e. _____ Evidence indicates a pushing force.

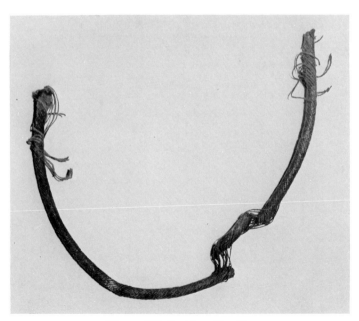

Figure 126. Problem No. 13.

PROBLEM 14

1. What is the evidence shown in Figure 127?
   a. _____   b. _____

2. List the four components of a high explosive filled bomb of this type.
   a. _____   c. _____
   b. _____   d. _____

3. Assume it is known that the bomb exploded sometime after being placed and that the *only* evidence consisted of pipe fragments, indicating that no holes existed in the nipple or endcaps. What is the most probable triggering method that was used? _____

4. Assume the evidence consists of pipe fragments and a small distorted battery and wire, and that criminalistics has indicated the presence of pulverized glass and mercury in the residue evidence. List the five components of the probable bomb.
   a. _____   d. _____
   b. _____   e. _____
   c. _____

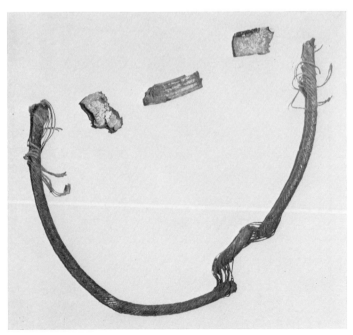

Figure 127. Problem No. 14.

PROBLEM 15

1. Based on the evidence, was this an open or disguised bomb? _____.

2. What type of bomb was involved? _____

3. What was the initiating source? _____

4. What was the triggering method? _____

5. Was a low or a high explosive used? _____

6. List the four components of the firing train.

    a. _____   c. _____

    b. _____   d. _____

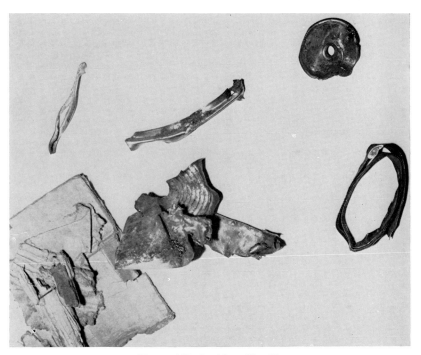

Figure 128. Problem No. 15.

ANSWERS TO PRACTICAL EXERCISE QUESTIONS

PROBLEM 1

1. a. 4, b. 3, c. 5, d. 1, e. 2.
2. a. H, b. L, c. H, d. PI, e. L, f. H, g. H, h. L, i. H, j. H.
3. b, d, e.
4. Green
5. Nitroglycerin
6. White, black.
7. False
8. Shaped

PROBLEM 2

1. a. Electrical—Miscellaneous
   b. Electrical—Miscellaneous
   c. Pull
   d. Pressure
   e. Tension
   f. Pull
   g. Pressure
   h. Pull
2. a. Release-of-pressure
   b. Pressure
   c. Tension
   d. Time-delay
   e. Electrical—Miscellaneous

PROBLEM 3

1. Flame
2. a. Burned safety fuse
   b. Can fragments
3. a. Safety fuse.
   b. Nonelectric blasting cap
4. 30 minutes

PROBLEM 4

1. a. 2, b. 1, c. 3, d. 4.
2. False
3. a. Fragmentation, b. Blast, c. Incendiary
4. Electrical
5. Time-delay
6. Break the electrical circuit (cut)

PROBLEM 5

1. Electrical
2. Electrical—Miscellaneous (twist)
3. False

4. The explosion would be minor in case of accidental initiation during an RSP.
5. Pull the blasting cap and break the electrical circuit
6. No
7. Yes (transmitter should not be used)
8. Glass, wood, plastic, hard rubber, formica, etc.

PROBLEM 6
1. There may be explosive pinched in the threads. Friction may cause an explosion.
2. Heat (glo-plug for model aircraft engine)
3. Pressure (on doorbell button)
4. Low (model aircraft glo-plug heats it does not detonate)
5. Break the electrical circuit

PROBLEM 7
1. c, Percussion—Release of pressure.
2. Yes
3. Open windows and doors
4. No
5. No

PROBLEM 8
1. Percussion
2. Release of pressure
3. Vibration from automobile movement
4. a, d.
5. Fragmentation
6. Cut the wires, one at a time
7. Yes
8. Pull the cap, if possible, break the electrical circuit
9. Yes
10. Twist bare lead wire ends together, fold wires.

PROBLEM 9
1. a. Pocket watch
   b. Wire and battery
   c. Glo-plug
   d. Pieces of container, firecracker and fuse
   e. Fragments of glass vial
2. Acid

3. a
4. Yes
5. Break the electrical circuit
6. a. 6, b. 3, c. 5, d. 4, e. 2, f. 1.

PROBLEM 10
1. a. 3, b. 1, c. 2.
2. False
3. False
4. Electrical
5. Time-delay
6. Pull the cap if possible, and break the electrical circuit.

PROBLEM 11
1. a. Attempt to determine sex
   b. Listen for tone of voice, accent
   c. Listen for background noise, sounds
   d. Ask the caller's name
   e. Ask for location of bomb
   f. Ask when the bomb is to explode
   g. Cut in a tape recorder if provided
2. Blast
3. Five minutes
4. Rest rooms
5. No
6. True
7. True
8. False
9. Electrical
10. Break the electrical circuit

PROBLEM 12
1. a. 3, b. 1, c. 4, d. 2.
2. Percussion
3. Release of pressure
4. Insert wedge between striker and shell primer
5. Wet it; tape the hole.
6. Ground yourself

7. Explosion or detonation
8. True
9. Downwind
10. True
11. True
12. 30 minutes
13. True
14. True
15. True
16. False
17. Two

PROBLEM 13
1. Burned safety fuse
2. Straight bomb consisting of safety fuse, nonelectric blasting cap, and high explosive
3. a. High b. Low c. High d. High e. Low

PROBLEM 14
1. a. Safety fuse
2. a. Pipe container
   b. Safety fuse
3. Chemical time-delay
4. a. Mercury switch trigger
   b. Battery and wire
   c. Electric cap

   b. Pipe fragments
   c. Nonelectric cap
   d. Explosive

   d. High explosive
   e. Pipe container

PROBLEM 15
1. Disguised
2. Package time bomb
3. Electrical
4. Clockwork time-delay
5. High (based on distortion of clock fragments)
6. a. Clock trigger
   b. Batteries and wire

   c. Electric cap
   d. High explosive

Chapter 13

MILITARY MUNITIONS AND
WAR SOUVENIRS

I̤т is соммоn кnowledge that a large number of youths have received detailed instructions on the assembly and employment of "field expedient" munitions, the homemade substitute for military munitions used in guerilla warfare. Underground publications have published detailed instructions and drawings of these field expedient munitions extracted from United States and foreign military publications. In addition, many thousands of ex-servicemen are acquainted with the techniques and use of field expedient munitions, and thousands of United States and foreign munitions have been brought home to our communities as so called "war souvenirs."

Pilferable munitions, such as hand grenades and demolition type explosives, have been stolen from military storage facilities, and mailed or carried home by servicemen despite the extensive precautions taken by the military. Pilfered military munitions have figured in bombings including such munitions as hand grenades, TNT, Composition C-4 (plastic) explosive, simulators, firing devices, and chemical munitions.

War souvenirs have included United States and foreign artillery ammunition, rockets, hand grenades, rifle grenades, small antipersonnel mines, pyrotechnics, small aerial bombs, mortars, etc.; some items date back to the American Civil War.

The fact that a particular explosive war souvenir may date back to the Civil War does not mean that the police officer can assume it is no longer dangerous. Black powder, TNT and other explosives do not become less effective with age; on the contrary, many explosives become more sensitive. Picric acid, the explosive filler in most World War II Japanese munitions, becomes more sensitive over a long period of time because of a chemical reaction with the metal munition body. A slight shock may cause detonation.

Dud-fired ammunition is always dangerous. The fuzes of certain munitions have cocked firing pins, that is, the firing pin is under spring tension similar to the firing pin in a hand gun. Strangely, many munitions can be fired, impact with the ground, and fail to explode, then a slight disturbance may cause detonation. Military range clearance personnel can give hair-raising accounts of dud ammunition on impact areas that suddenly explode during storms, minor ground vibration, and even due to the slight temperature change that occurs when a cloud passes between the sun and a dud munition. Dud-fired, unexploded munitions, removed from impact areas by military and civilian personel, account for a small but continuous number of deaths attributable to these very hazardous munitions. Note the following news accounts:

1. HARRISMITH, Orange Free State—A South African War shell (1899-1902) killed six people here when it exploded in a garden.

2. PLAINFIELD, New Jersey—New Jersey junkyard yields live World War I shells.

3. EL CENTRO, California—Scrap collector dies as bomb explodes.

4. EL PASO, Texas—Blast of souvenir shell kills 3 Texas children, injures 10—The father of one of the dead children explained the 90 MM artillery shell had been lying around the yard for a couple of months. He and his family had visited Fort Bliss and he may have picked up the shell there.

5. LONGWAY, France—Two Die, 18 Hurt in Blast of Mustard Gas Shell. . . . An Army medical team took over the Mont Saint Martin Hospital today to treat about 16 people, including doctors and nurses, who were burned while helping four school children wounded in the explosion of a World War I mustard gas shell.

6. DENVER, Colorado—Game of Catch Ends in Explosion for Boys. . . . A game of catch with a live five-pound bomb, played intermittently the past three months by two dozen Denver boys, ended in a blinding flash that injured three of them. The bomb exploded after the boys poured out some of the powder and removed the detonator. Police said the boys were taking it apart by pounding it with a rock and prying at it with an icepick and tablefork.

7. GOSHEN, New York—Dud Grenade Explodes on Stove, Kills Boy of 16. . . . A 16-year-old boy was killed by a hand grenade which exploded on a stove. The victim put the grenade on the stove to scare his 7-year old sister. Fifteen minutes later the grenade exploded.

8. JERUSALEM—A shell exploded in a field killing 14 school children. The shell from the 1948 Arab-Israeli War detonated when the children threw rocks at it.

9. YORK, Pa.—Four Playmates Killed by Bazooka Shell Found on Range. . . . Four farm children were killed in an explosion police said was apparently caused by an Army bazooka shell. Police said a bazooka shell, dropped from a tree by one of the boys, caused the explosion. One live and one practice bazooka round were found nearby. The father of one of the boys told police that about two weeks ago his family visited a son stationed at Fort Bragg, N. C., and while there the boys visited the firing range.

From the foregoing it can be seen that despite the age of military explosive munitions, they are always dangerous. A dud explosive item is always dangerous, despite the fact that it failed to fire as intended. It could suffer rough handling over a long period of time and then when least expected, detonate. *Do Not Touch.* Safeguard the item and report it to the nearest military installation immediately.

Ammunition does not have to be large or contain high explosive to be dangerous. Over a three year period in one locality where the author was living, one child was killed and three injured from exploding rifle ammunition. A boy firing a BB gun at the primer of a round of .30 caliber ammunition caused the round to explode. A fragment of the cartridge case cut the jugular vein in his throat and he bled to death before help could arrive. The ratio of children killed to adults by exploding ammunition is approximately eight to one. Some of the new items of military ammunition are very small in size, but they contain a very high explosive, more powerful than TNT.

A police officer with prior military service should never assume that he knows a particular munition because of his training and use of the munition while in service. While the munition may appear to be the same outwardly, the fuze may incorporate major changes, and applying previous knowledge may cause an explosion. The fragmentation hand grenade used during the Korean action represented a very radical change from the World War II grenades, and the Vietnam versions have included several fuze, body, and explosive filler changes.

What should the law enforcement officer do if a report is received, and he is confronted with a war souvenir munition? The following rules should be strictly adhered to:

1. Do not touch or disturb the munition in any way.
2. Safeguard the item, keep others away.
3. Report the munition to headquarters and/or to the nearest military installation.
4. Insure the munition is not disturbed until the arrival of military personnel, then assist them if requested.
5. Include discussion of the incident in the department in-service training program.

The purpose of this chapter is to acquaint law enforcement personnel with those pilferable munitions and war souvenirs that they are most likely to encounter and to assist them in making a visual identification for subsequent reporting to the nearest military installation.

COLOR IDENTIFICATION

The armies of all nations paint and mark their munitions in various color combinations to provide visual identification of the munition and to indicate the hazard. As an example, most United States high-explosive munitions are painted olive drab with markings in yellow, the yellow indicating high explosive is in the munition. Brown indicates a low explosive (propellant), blue a practice munition. Chemical munitions are painted gray with markings in various colors to denote a filler of toxic gas, riot, smoke, incendiary, etc. See Appendix F for a chart of United States color codes.

There is no standard color scheme used by various nations; a red color might indicate a high explosive in one country and incendiary in another. Because of the variety of color identification/hazard markings and the frequency of change, *it is recommended that all identifiable or suspected military munitions be left undisturbed and reported to the nearest military facility.*

PILFERABLE TYPES OF MILITARY MUNITIONS

The following are representative of the more easily pilfered military munitions and war souvenirs that are most likely to be encountered by law enforcement personnel. Several examples of field expedient substitute munitions are also included that have not been duplicated elsewhere in this text.

Simulators

To provide maximum realism in training and to reduce the costs of training with live ammunition, the services use simulators which are powerful firecrackers to simulate the sound, flash, and smoke which various munitions make when they explode. Two of these simulators are shown in Figure 129; however, there are others. All simulators are labeled by the military and should present no problem in identification in an unfired condition. *Caution:* Do not handle simulators roughly, as the powder is ex-

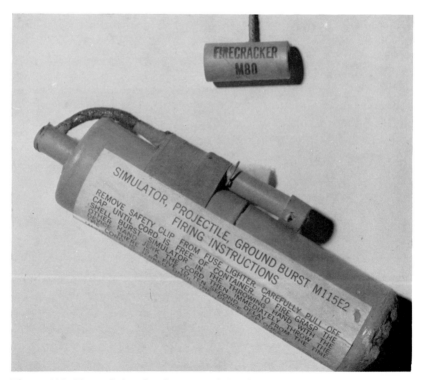

Figure 129. Two of the simulators used by the Armed Forces are the M-80 (firecracker) which is used to simulate small arms fire, and the artillery simulator.

tremely sensitive to friction, flame, and static spark. Cutting the container open with a knife will probably cause an explosion due to the friction.

Hand Grenades

Shown in Figure 130 are the United States hand grenades dating from World War II to the present.

Figure 130. High explosive, fragmentation hand grenades dating from WW II to the present. All may be found as war souvenirs and should be easily identified by the officer.

Figure 131 shows riot, white phosphorus smoke, and chemical grenade configurations. The grenade fuze of many riot and smoke grenades is not destroyed by the grenade action, and it is possible for militants to modify the used fuzes for reuse in a homemade bomb or munition. For this reason it is recommended that law enforcement and military personnel who employ riot and smoke grenades pick up the spent grenade bodies after use and destroy the fuzes. United States practice hand grenades, which normally contain only small black powder spotting charges, are desired by militants for reloading with high explosives.

A 40MM grenade cartridge, fired from a shoulder weapon, was developed for use in Vietnam. The small cartridges are a popular war souvenir and in several instances have been stolen from military storage sites (Fig. 132).

Figure 131. Chemical grenades—Smoke, riot and incendiary.

Figure 132. 40MM grenade cartridge. Some types have highly dangerous fuzes and fillers.

Military Demolition Explosives

DETONATING CORD (PRIMA CORD). Detonating cord has been stolen from storage sites or procured commercially, and has been used in several bombings. A field expedient use of detonating cord is to surround the cord with tightly wound wire, BB's, or metal washers as shown in Figure 133.

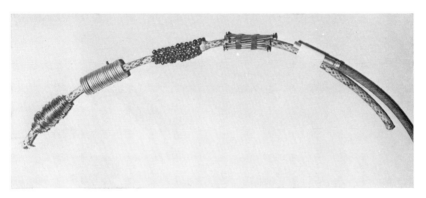

Figure 133. Field expedient application of detonating cord for antipersonnel use.

DEMOLITION EXPLOSIVES. Military demolition explosives have been covered elsewhere in this text; however, stolen military explosives have been employed by bombers with adaptations, such as a nail surround to make them more lethal.

Mines

In Figure 134, one of the smaller United States antipersonnel mines is shown, and Figure 8 in the text depicts a U. S. Army "Claymore" mine. Larger mines, such as antitank mines, are quite heavy and bulky, and are not popular pilferable items; however, substitutes for an antitank mine and other U. S. Army field expedients have been published in underground publications.

Figure 134. The M-19 antipersonnel mine.

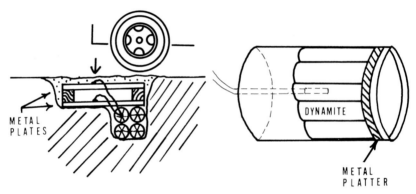

Figure 135. *Left:* Trigger details for an antivehicular mine. *Right:* "Platter" mine. Substitution of the steel platter with wood and the addition of nuts, bolts, stones, BB's, nails, scrap, etc., in the forward end makes this a substitute for the "Claymore" mine.

CIVIL WAR MUNITIONS

In the central and eastern sections of the United States, Civil War munitions, many of which are dangerous despite their age, are continuously being discovered. Many Civil War munitions in museums and personal collections are still loaded with black powder and represent a continuous threat to life and property.

In this instance also, the United States Army Explosive Disposal Detachments will check these items for the presence of explosives on request. In most instances, due to rust, prohibitive regulations and the hazard involved, it will not be feasible to inert or remove the explosive from the munition for historical purposes, and the best that can be done is to return fragments of the shell to the original owner. If it is considered vital to preserve a Civil War item for historical purposes, a letter giving details, accompanied by photographs if possible, will elicit free advice and information from the author. Some of these Civil War munitions were filled with black powder. The black powder explosive does not deteriorate with age and when dry is virtually as good as the day it was first manufactured.

Photographs in this section portray the most commonly used projectiles of the Civil War and no attempt has been made to show all of the various types and shapes of projectiles used. Artillery ammunition was undergoing changes during the Civil War period, mostly in design, in an attempt to secure rotation of the projectile in flight for greater stability and accuracy. Many rounds of ammunition incorporating new ideas were imported from Europe. The ammunition developed has a shape similar to modern artillery rounds, that is, a steel slug pointed at one end. All Civil War munitions should be considered dangerous until examined by qualified personnel.

Round Shot

This is the familiar "cannon ball" which was the most commonly used ammunition of the Civil War. It was used by both the Confederate and the Union Forces and manufactured in solid shot and explosive case shot. The size of the shot varied from $3\frac{1}{2}$ inches up to 20 inches in diameter. The larger diameter shot rounds were used primarily in mortar and seacoast guns.

The solid shot shown in Figure 136 represents no explosive hazard, being a solid metal ball with no openings or indentations. Explosive case shot as shown in Figure 137 contains a fuze, black powder bursting charge and steel or lead balls imbedded in a matrix binder of inert material. The explosive case shot shown is

Figure 136. Solid shot.

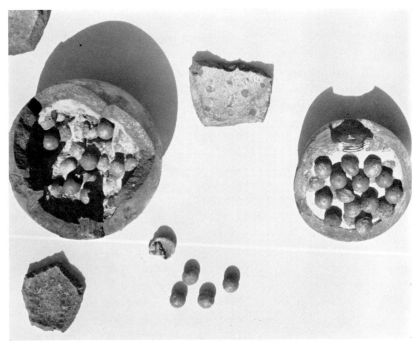

Figure 137. Explosive case shot.

fitted with a Boreman time fuze, with graduated time settings of from one to four seconds of delay prior to bursting. See Figure 138 for detailed photograph of Boreman time fuze. Some black powder paper-wrapped time fuzes were also used by Confederate and Union forces.

Figure 138. Boreman time fuse.

The following are but a few of the many types of ammunition that gradually succeeded the cannon ball and were used during the Civil War.

Studded Projectile

This projectile has lead studs in two rows around the outside body of the projectile which engage spiral grooves in the gun barrel to impart rotation. It had a time fuze in the nose and a black powder bursting charge (Fig. 139).

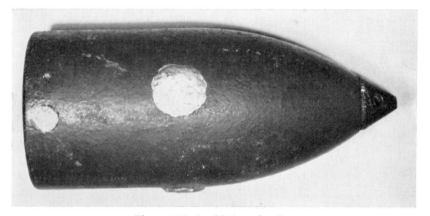

Figure 139. Studded projectile.

Confederate "Reed" Shell

This shell normally had a copper or lead band on the base. The band is missing on the shell shown in Figure 140. The fuze was either time or percussion; that is, it would explode after a delay or on impact, depending on the fuze that was used. The explosive filler was black powder. The Reed shell was probably the most commonly used projectile in Confederate rifled guns.

Figure 140. Confederate "Reed" shell.

U. S. Hotchkiss

The Hotchkiss round shown in Figure 141 was manufactured in both solid and case shot. The projectile base (missing) moves forward when the gun is fired, squeezing the lead band around the body, causing it to move forward and expand into the rifling of the gun. The case shot shown contained a black-powder bursting charge and had steel balls imbedded in an inert matrix binder.

Other rifled bore projectiles were used by both the Confederate and Union Forces, but all can be identified as military shells since their configuration is similar to the modern artillery shell, though the nose or pointed end of the shell was generally blunter.

Figure 141. U. S. "Hotchkiss" shell, case shot.

EXPLOSIVE DISPOSAL SERVICE

The discovery of an explosive item obviously not produced for civilian use is a problem that law enforcement agencies frequently have to cope with, and as previously mentioned, the military will provide disposal service. All Army areas have explosive dis-

Figure 142. The explosive disposal badge awarded to volunteers after successful completion of months of schooling and on-the-job training.

posal personnel assigned for this purpose. These Army disposal personnel are highly trained in the disposal of dangerous U. S. and foreign munitions including atomic loaded items.

While explosive disposal personnel are primarily intended for service in the event of an attack on this country, their peacetime functions include important services to communities, law enforcement and fire agencies. One form of this service is in training agencies in explosive ordnance reconnaissance and explosive sabotage devices which have application to the homemade-bomb problem also. Other services include the providing of assistance in any incident that occurs involving military munitions shipments, the pickup and disposal of war souvenirs and in most areas, assistance in the disposal of homemade bombs. Examples of the disposal assistance rendered are seen in the following news releases:

POLICE THINK FANATIC THREW SCHOOL BOMB. . .All available men of the police department were taking part. . .The FBI and Army disposal personnel entered the case on a cooperative basis. . . Atlanta, Georgia.

RAILROAD EXPLOSION. . .Army disposal personnel were at work today disposing of 105MM artillery shells littering the right-of-way, and the town of Lewis. . .Lewis, Indiana.

STUDENTS EVACUATE—BOMB THREAT. . .300 students were evacuated from Sacred Heart School. . .Officials called a bomb disposal squad from Fort Dix. . .Camden, New Jersey.

REP'S SOUVENIR OF CIVIL WAR—A LIVE CANNONBALL. . .the Armys 67th Ordnance Detachment (ED), Fort McNair, picked up the souvenir last week. . .the cannonball contained powder and a fuze . . .Washington, D. C.

ARMY CONDUCTS EXPLOSIVE SCHOOL FOR STATE POLICE . . .The Army conducted a course on explosives for Georgia State Police personnel at Fort Benning. . .Columbus, Georgia.

DYNAMITE BLAST KILLS FIVE, HURTS TWENTY SEVEN. . . Explosion of a truck laden with four hundred cases of dynamite. . . Army demolition crews from Fort McClellan scour area for unexploded blasting caps. . .Waco, Georgia.

The establishment of defensive missile sites in the United States, employing missiles with atomic warheads, and the carrying of atomic bombs by defensive aircraft have been responsible for the organization of air-transportable teams to cope with a transport or on-site accident involving nuclear weapons. These emergency teams are organized for rapid response to the scene of an accident and assume all responsibility for explosive and radiological safety, etc., at the accident scene. In addition to radiological and explosive cleanup, the team includes medical and legal assistance personnel to assist in filing claims for damages. A call to the nearest military facility will secure assistance from disposal personnel. Training assistance may be secured through letter of request to the nearest Army Area Headquarters.

Maximum safety to the community and to police officers will be assured by using the assistance of these skilled personnel for the disposal of identifiable military munitions. The fact that disposal personnel have access to range areas for the disposal of explosives and munitions relieves many police agencies of a major disposal problem.

Figure 143. A member of an explosive disposal detachment is suited-up in protective clothing and is prepared to take radiological readings in a contaminated area.

Chapter 14

TRAINING AIDS

Many very competent training officers have been placed in an awkward position when called upon to develop and conduct a training program on explosives and homemade bombs. The training officer is faced with gathering what little information and material is available, and painstakingly developing a course on an unfamiliar subject. To assist the training officer, the chapters in this text are grouped by subject, and provide a step-by-step basis for course and lesson plan development. The book may be used as a classroom text for individual student use.

However, lesson plans and the text alone will not result in the most effective instruction in a formal classroom situation without the use of visual aids to enhance student comprehension and learning. There is no questioning the fact that visual training aids will improve any presentation, as words alone are inadequate to carry understanding to the students. A slide, model, or both will involve the senses of sight and touch in addition to hearing. It is a fact that most individual students will see alike, but do not necessarily hear alike. Visual aids further serve to break the monotony of a verbal presentation.

A few aids are presently available for training use. As a public service, inert commercial explosive aids and pamphlets have been provided to official police-fire agencies by explosive manufacturer, through the Institute Makers of Explosives. The author has provided 35MM slide kits to hundreds of departments in the past, and concurrent with the publication of this text, will offer 35MM color slides that duplicate most of the illustrations in the text. *See Appendix F for listing of illustrations for which slides are available from the author.*

The author has received many requests from various police training agencies for inert model bombs for use in training programs and has advised the departments that models are not available from any source. The cost of manufactured aids would be quite high and the aids can be easily constructed at small cost by the individual department. The construction of model homemade explosives and bombs does not require particular expertise. The bombs depicted in the text were assembled by the author, using the most basic tools and with common materials obtained without cost or at low cost through numerous commercial sources.

An officer who assembles models as a hobby, or perhaps the son of an officer, is an ideal individual to call upon to assemble bomb aids, which are less difficult to construct than most other types of models.

INERT EXPLOSIVE AND BOMB TRAINING AIDS

The following outlines the materials and construction of representative inert bombs that are shown in the text. They represent the basic types of visual bomb aids for use in a training program. The construction techniques may be employed to construct models of any of the other bombs illustrated in the text.

While some inert blasting caps are obtained through official request from the Institute Makers of Explosives, if more than a few caps are needed for model bombs, it is suggested that training departments make their own as follows:

Nonelectric Blasting Caps and Fuse

Materials
1. Lengths of cotton clothes line and orange dye (dummy fuse).
2. Wood dowling, $\frac{1}{4}$-inch diameter.
3. Epoxy glue, five-minute setting time (available from hobby shops).
4. Copper or silver model paint.
5. Plastic tape.

Construction
1. Dye cotton clothes line orange.
2. Cut wood dowling into two-inch lengths and glue desired length of fuse to one end.

3. Wrap a narrow band of tape around the joint where the clothes line is glued to wood dowling.
4. Paint the dowling and tape copper or silver.

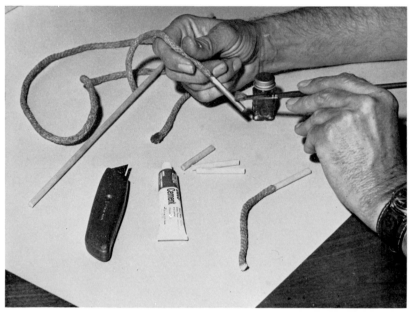

Figure 144. Inert model nonelectric blasting cap.

Electric Blasting Caps

Materials

1. Wood dowling, $\frac{1}{4}$-inch diameter.
2. Doorbell wire or equivalent.
3. Epoxy glue, five-minute setting time.
4. Copper or silver model paint.

Construction

1. Cut wood dowling into two-inch lengths.
2. Drill a small hole, the diameter of two bare wires into one end of the wood dowling. Place a drop of glue on the end and insert the bare wire ends into the hole.
3. Paint the wood dowel copper or silver.
4. Strip about $1\frac{1}{2}$ inch of insulation off of the other ends

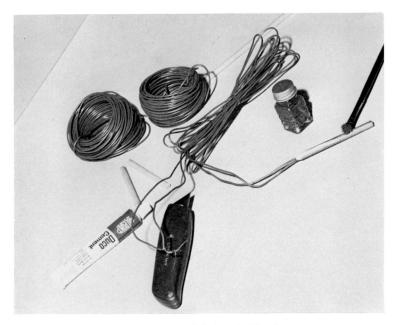

Figure 145. Inert model electric blasting cap.

of the wire leads and twist the wires together. The wire may be accordian folded if desired.

Note: The length of the wire leads is determined by the intended use, as a blasting cap alone, or as a bomb component.

Model Dynamite

Materials

1. Wood dowling, one inch diameter.
2. Brown postal wrapping paper.
3. Paraffin, or white candle wax, and a pan.
4. Inert electric or nonelectric blasting cap.
5. Paper or plastic tape.

Construction

1. Cut wood dowling into eight-inch lengths.
2. Cut the brown paper into pattern as shown in Figure 146.

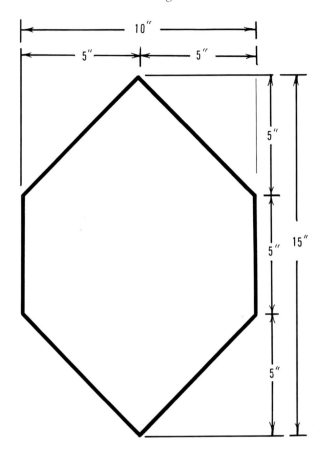

Figure 146. Wrapping paper pattern.

3. Roll the pattern onto a length of dowling, staple the end and fold ends onto the dowling ends (Fig. 147).
4. Drill $\frac{5}{16}$-inch hole in side of stick, at an angle, or into the end of the stick approximately one inch deep.
5. Place the stick into a tray of hot paraffin, roll and remove quickly.
6. Insert model electric or nonelectric cap.

Note: If more than one stick is desired for the model bomb, use tape to secure the sticks together.

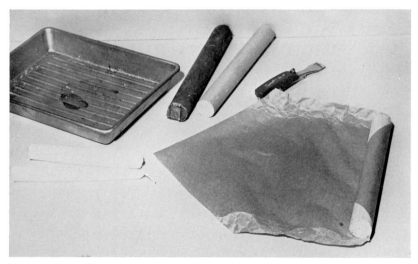

Figure 147. Roll paper around the wood dowling. Staple the tag end and fold the ends of the wrapper.

Model Pipe Bomb

The following models are representative of the various pipe bombs illustrated in the text. Other pipe bombs depicted in the text are easily constructed using the techniques outlined.

If desired, the pipe bomb body section (nipple) may be taken to a machine shop and cut lengthwise into two half-sections. Two bombs may then be constructed, each one using a half-section, which will enable the instructor to display the outer configuration and then turn the bomb over to display the inner workings.

The construction techniques that follow are for model pipe bombs that have not been half-sectioned. The end-cap is unscrewed by the instructor to show inner details. In general, half-sectioned bombs, as well as others in the text, follow the same construction procedure using the same materials.

Materials needed to construct representative model pipe bombs are as follows:

Materials

 1. Pipe bomb body section (nipple), $1\frac{1}{2}$-inch diameter. One per bomb.

2. Two end-caps per bomb.
3. Length of dummy fuse. One per bomb.
4. Plaster of paris and/or plastic wood.
5. Model electric and nonelectric blasting caps and wire.
6. Flat black paint.
7. Masking tape, BB's and liquid solder.

Construction

1. *Model-Straight Pipe Bomb*
   a. Drill a $\frac{1}{4}$-inch hole in the center of one end-cap.
   b. Pass one length of orange-dyed fuse through the hole and knot it on the underside of the end-cap.
   c. Screw the end-caps onto the body section (Fig. 148).

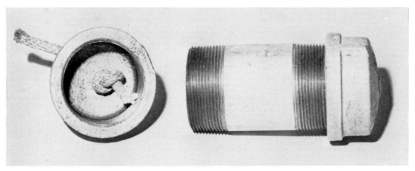

Figure 148. Dummy pipe bomb construction.

2. *Black-powder or Dynamite-Filled Pipe Bomb*
   a. Drill a $\frac{1}{4}$-inch hole in the center of one end-cap.
   b. Screw the second end-cap onto the nipple and fill the nipple to $\frac{1}{4}$-inch from the top with plaster of paris. Let dry overnight.
   c. Fill the remaining $\frac{1}{4}$-inch with plastic wood and let dry, then drill a $\frac{1}{4}$-inch hole in the center approximately one inch deep.
   d. If a black-powder filler is desired, paint the plastic wood flat black. Pass a length of dummy fuse through the drilled hole of one end-cap and into the drilled hole in the black powder and screw on the end-cap.

e. If a dynamite filler is desired, do not paint the plastic wood black. Insert a model nonelectric blasting cap and length of fuse. Pass the other end of the fuse through the hole in the end-cap.

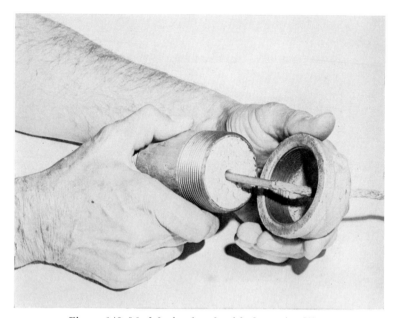

Figure 149. Model pipe bomb with dynamite filler.

3. *Improved Fragmentation Pipe Bomb*

If desired, any of the pipe bombs constructed as outlined in paragraph one or two above may be improved upon by the addition of BB's to the outer surface of the nipple (Fig. 150).

a. Wind masking tape around the nipple body with the sticky side out.

b. Arrange BB's on the tape, a small section at a time, and pour liquid solder over the BB's, a section at a time. Allow each section to dry before adding more BB's and solder.

Figure 150. Improved fragmentation pipe bomb.

Model Contained Bombs

Release-of-Pressure Bomb

Materials

1. Coffee can, one pound size.
2. Mousetraps, two each.
3. Inert (fired) 12 gauge shotgun shell.
4. Penlight battery, one each.
5. Glue, plaster of paris and plastic wood.
6. Doorbell wire and spool of thread.
7. Inert model electric blasting cap.
8. Flat black paint, $^1/_{16}$-inch by $\frac{3}{4}$-inch balsa wood.

Construction

1. *Percussion Initiated Bomb*

   a. Cut the one pound coffee can into two half-sections.
   b. Take one mousetrap and cut a round hole the diameter of the shotgun shell below the striker. Remove the striker retaining wire and the bait/tripper.
   c. Bend the striker wire to a point where it will hit the shell primer when released (Fig. 151).
   d. Cut the $^1/_{16} \times \frac{3}{4}$-inch balsa to fit the two ends and one side of the mousetrap.
   e. Cock the striker by hand and wind several turns of

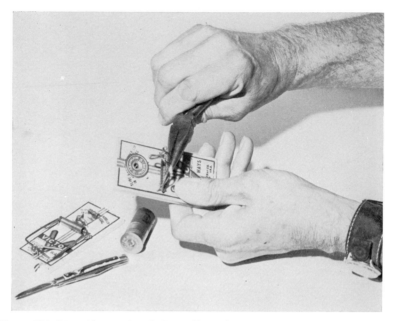

Figure 151. Use pliers to bend the striker wire so that the point will contact the 12 ga. primer when released.

    thread around the trap to retain the striker in a cocked position.

f. Secure the top of one half-section of can with tape and place the can on its side.

g. Pour in enough plaster of paris that when the mousetrap is placed in the container the open side will be flush with the cut top of the container.

h. Fill the remaining area with plaster of paris to a level where the shotgun shell is half covered. Allow to dry overnight.

i. Paint the plaster of paris black to simulate black powder. Cut and remove the visible portions of the thread holding the striker.

Note: The bomb may be displayed as constructed or placed in a package as shown in Figures 90 through 92 in the text.

2. *Electrical Initiated bomb*
   a. Take the other half-section of coffee can and secure the lid with tape.
   b. Remove the striker retainer and bait holder/tripper from the mousetrap.
   c. Cut and glue balsa wood strips to two ends and one side of mousetrap.
   d. Drill or use a nail to make a very small hole in the mousetrap at a location centered directly under the released striker wire. Insert one bare wire end of a blasting cap lead wire into the hole, so the striker wire and lead contact each other.
   e. Cut the second lead wire in half and solder the cut ends to opposing terminals of the battery.
   f. Solder the loose end of the lead wire to the striker spring hinge.
   g. Cock the striker and wind several turns of thread around the trap to secure the striker in a cocked position (Fig. 152).
   h. Lay the half-sectioned coffee can on its side and pour in enough plaster to support the mousetrap with the open side of the trap flush with the cut top of the container. Fill the remaining area with plaster. If desired, the wire and battery may be left loose or set into the plaster.
   i. Allow the plaster to harden overnight and cover with a layer of plastic wood to simulate a dynamite filler.

Package Time Bomb

Materials
   1. One cardboard box of desired size.
   2. Brown postal wrapping paper and twine or paper tape.
   3. Alarm clock.
   4. 9-volt transistor battery.
   5. Model dynamite sticks.
   6. Plywood, $\frac{1}{4}$-inch, for wood interior frame to secure the clock, model dynamite and battery.

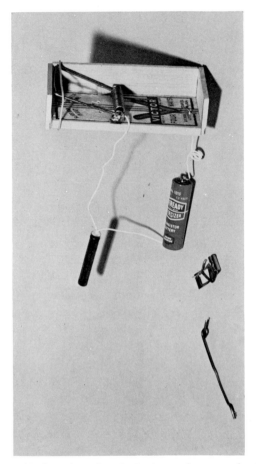

Figure 152. Complete electrical release-of-pressure hookup.

Construction

1. Drill a $\frac{5}{16}$-inch hole, at an angle, into the center of one stick of dynamite for later insertion of a blasting cap.

2. Use a heated pin to make a small hole in the plastic face of the alarm clock. Insert a bare wire cap lead wire end into the hole without contacting the metal face of the clock, but deep enough and in position for the clock hour-hand to contact the bare wire. Apply a drop of epoxy glue to secure the wire to the plastic clock face.

3. Cut the second cap lead wire in half and solder the cut ends to the battery terminals.

4. Attach the bare wire end of the second lead wire under one of the back-plate retaining nuts on the rear of the clock and insert the blasting cap into the stick of dynamite.

5. Layout the complete hookup, add additional sticks of dynamite, and construct a four-sided wood outer frame of $\frac{1}{4}$-inch plywood, to fit. Cut and insert wood spacers, as needed, to nail or wire clock, battery, and dynamite to the wood frame (Fig. 106).

6. Enclose five sides of the container with cardboard, postal wrapping paper, and paper tape or twine. Address the front face of the package and glue cancelled stamps on for realism (Figs. 105-107).

Note: If training time permits, and the class is small, the package bomb may be completely enclosed and the students called upon to cut into the package and perform an RSP. A photoflash bulb or flashlight bulb may be wired into the circuit and a mercury switch incorporated if desired. For best contact, take the face off of the alarm clock and break off the short hour-hand. Scrape the end of the long minute-hand of paint. The wire to the clock face should not be secured with glue, but with a small screw to permit replacement of the wire when necessary. Set the hand for the desired time and wind the clock.

Fake Bombs

From time to time, fake bombs have been encountered at airports and schools in particular. Figure 153 shows a typical fake bomb in which an automobile voltage regulator, distributor condenser, alarm clock, batteries, lengths of wire, and a can that supposedly contains the explosive are used. A good fake bomb to be used in training will include at least one clue for the student officer to discover, perhaps a wrong electrical connection. The instructor should stress that if the disposal officer has the slightest doubt as to a bomb's authenticity, he should treat the bomb as a valid, live homemade bomb.

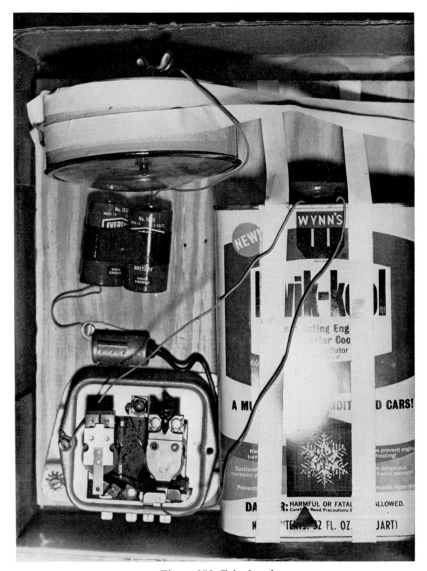

Figure 153. Fake bomb.

Flashlight Bomb

Materials

    1. Soft-bodied plastic flashlight.

2. Battery, 9-volt transister.
3. Model electric blasting cap.
4. Plastic wood-cardboard spacer.

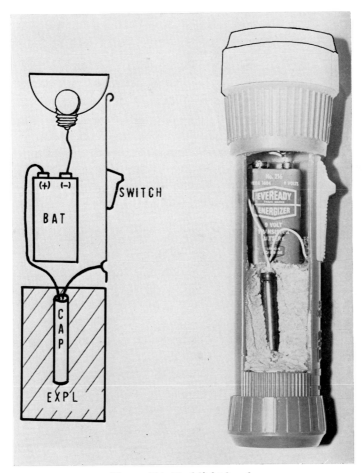

Figure 154. Flashlight bomb.

Construction

1. Use razor blade or sharp knife to cut out the side of the flashlight body as shown.
2. Solder a length of wire to the base of the bulb and to one terminal of the battery.

3. Solder one cap lead wire to the other terminal of the battery.
4. Solder other cap lead wire to the flashlight on-off switch.
5. Cut to fit and insert a cardboard spacer into the flashlight body. Fill this area with plastic wood and insert the blasting cap.

The flashlight bomb is very easy to construct and inexpensive. By connecting wires inside the blasting cap, the bulb will light when the on-off switch is on.

The officer who constructs the foregoing representative model bombs should have no difficulty constructing other bombs depicted in the text. A lesson plan, model bomb aids, and 35MM color slides represent the most effective instruction on explosives and homemade bombs available to most departments.

There is no secret to successful bomb disposal, beyond a requirement for knowledge of explosives and homemade bombs and the ability to apply this knowledge in a safe and practical manner on the job. *The most important single factor is common-sense reasoning at the scene of an incident by a knowledgeable officer.*

Appendix A

COMMON ROCKET, EXPLOSIVE AND INCENDIARY MATERIALS

The following is a list of materials that are easily obtained from commercial outlets and used in rocket, explosive and incendiary mixtures by bombers:

Ammonium nitrate
Ammonium perchlorate
Aluminum powder—sulfite
Barium peroxide
Charcoal, coal, coal dust.
Coffee, powdered
Calcium carbide
Calcium hyphochlorite
Cocoa
Corn starch
Cork dust
Carbon disulfide
Copper sulfate
Dinitrobenzine
"Duco" cement
Dye derivatives
Ferric oxide—sulfate
Fuel oil
Gasoline
Grease
Glycerin
Hydrochloric acid
Hydrogen peroxide
Kerosene
Liquid floor wax
Lead tetraethyl
Lead dioxide
Manganese dioxide
Mercury
Maganesium, powdered
Match heads
Nitrobenzine
Nitromethane

Nitric acid
Naptha
Photoflash powder
Phenol
Potassium permanganate
Potassium nitrate
Potassium chlorate
Petroleum jelly
Paraffin
Pitch
Potassium dichromate
Plaster of paris
Rosin
Rice powder
Resorcenal
Red phosphorus
Red lead
Sodium chlorate
Sugar
Soap powder
Sawdust
Sodium nitrate
Sulfur
Sulfuric acid
Stearic acid
Sodium peroxide
Shellac
Silver nitrate powder
Tapioca
Turpentine
White phosphorus
Wheat flour
Zinc powder

EVACUATION DISTANCES

Explosives (Pounds)	Safe Missile Distance (Feet)	Explosives (Pounds)	Safe Missile Distance (Feet)
1-27	900	250	1,890
30	930	300	2,008
40	1,020	350	2,114
50	1,104	400	2,210
60	1,170	450	2,299
70	1,230	500	2,381
80	1,290	550	2,458
90	1,344	600	2,530
100	1,392	650	2,599
150	1,593	700	2,664
200	1,754	750	2,725
		1000	3,000

This data concerns evacuation distances for persons in the open.

MEMBER COMPANIES OF INSTITUTE MAKERS OF EXPLOSIVES

420 Lexington Avenue
New York, N. Y. 10017

Explosives Manufacturers

Apache Powder Company
Box 700
Benson, Arizona 85602

Atlas Chemical Industries, Inc.
Concord Pike & New Murphy Road
Wilmington, Delaware 19899

Austin Powder Company
3735 Green Road
Cleveland, Ohio 44112

The Dow Chemical Company
2020 Abbott Road Center
Midland, Michigan 48640

E. I. Du Pont De Nemours & Co.
Nemours Building
Wilmington, Delaware 19898

Hercules Incorporated
910 Market Street
Wilmington, Delaware 19899

Ireco Chemicals
3000 West 8600 South
West Jordan, Utah 84084

Monsanto Company
800 N. Lindberg Blvd.
St. Louis, Missouri 63166

Trojan—U.S. Powder Division
Commerical Solvents Corp.
Allentown, Pennsylvania 18105

Explosive Accessories

Coast Fuse
Benson, Arizona 85602

The Ensign-Bickford Co.
660 Hopemeadow Street
Simsbury, Connecticut 06070

Appendix D

Copies of the following publications may be obtained by writing the Institute Makers of Explosives, 420 Lexington Avenue, New York, N. Y. 10017, on police department letterhead stationery. Only one set can be sent to a department.

Title	Safety Pamphlet No.
Standard Storage Magazines	1
American Table of Distances	2
Suggested Code of Regulations for the Manufacture, Transportation, Storage and Use of Explosives and Blasting Agents	3
Rules for Storing, Transporting and Shipping Explosives	5
Recommended Industry Safety Standards	6
Explosives in Agriculture	11
Safety in the Transportation, Storage, Handling and Use of Explosives	17
Radio Frequency Energy	20
How to Destroy Explosives	21

In addition to the above, posters on blasting cap safety suitable for school and other bulletin boards are available, and inert materials suitable for training purposes.

Blasting Handbook, $6.00, is available from:
Sales Development Section, Explosives Department,
E. I. Du Pont de Nemours & Co.
Wilmington, Del. 19898

Appendix E

TRAINING SLIDES AVAILABLE

In the past, the author has offered a training kit consisting of 58 ea., 35MM color slides, lesson, and practical exercise now used by hundreds of police and fire-service agencies. Concurrent with the publication of this text, the kit as such will no longer be offered; instead agencies may now order 35MM color slide duplicates of key illustrations in the text and use the text itself as the basis for development of a course peculiar to their own training needs.

The fifty-eight slides previously offered are identified by their number sequence next to the corresponding text figure number. If desired, the training officer may add individual slides to the basic set already in his possession, or order a selection of slides for the initial development of his own unique course.

Slides ordered will be shipped with the identifying text figure number written in pencil on each slide to permit the officer to erase and substitute his own sequencing number.

The charge for each slide ordered is 50¢. Because of the difficulty of duplicating, storing, and marking of large numbers of slides, the shipping time will vary from four to seven weeks. In general, all orders received by the first of the month will be shipped airmail-postpaid within four weeks.

Note: The position of the individual or the recipient agency must be identified. Shipments will not be made to a bookstore, library, or home address unless the position/agency is listed.

TITLE SLIDES

1. Explosives and Homemade Bombs
2. Firebombs
3. Practical Exercise
4. The End

Kit Slide No.	Text Figure No.	Kit Slide No.	Text Figure No.	Kit Slide No.	Text Figure No.	Kit Slide No.	Text Figure No.
	2	13	41	24	82		108
	11	14	42	25	83		109
	12	15	42	26	84		110
	13	16	44	27	85		111
	15	19	46		86		112
2	17		47		87		113
3	18	17	48		89	53	114
4	20	18	50	30	90		115
4	21 (1 slide)		51	31	91	50	116
5	25		52	32	92	47	117
8	27		54	33	93		118
	29		74		94	57	119
6	30		75 (lower view)	35	101	58	120
7	31		76	36	102		121
9	35		77	37	103		122
10	36	21	78	38	104	48	123
11	37		79	39	105	44	124
	38	22	80	40	106	45	125
12	40	23	81	41	107	54	126
						55	127
						56	128
							130
							131
							153
							154

Appendix F

U.S. AMMUNITION COLOR IDENTIFICATION CODES

SMALL ARMS
(Through .50 caliber)

Type	Tip Color
Ball	None
Armor piercing	Black
Armor piercing, incendiary	Aluminum (silver)
Incendiary	Blue
Tracer	Red
Duplex (Two bullets)	Green

(20MM and 30MM)

Type	Projectile Color
High explosive, incendiary	Red and Green—black markings
High explosive	Red and yellow—black markings
Training, Practice, Ball and Armor Piercing.	Black—white markings
High explosive dual purpose	Green—yellow markings

(40MM GRENADE CARTRIDGE

Type	Color of Projectile Nose
High explosive	Gold or yellow
Practice	Silver or aluminum

Note: Prior to the start of the Vietnam action, the United States changed its color coding system for identification of ammunition; however, most war souvenirs are painted under the old system. For this reason both the old and the new color systems are listed.

ARTILLERY AND GRENADES

Type Projectile	Old Code	New Code
High explosive (HE)	Olive drab-yellow marking	Olive drab—yellow marking
Armor defeating with HE.	Olive drab-yellow marking or black-yellow marking	Black—yellow marking
Antipersonnel	Black-white marking	Olive drab—white marking & yellow band
Practice	Blue-white marking	Blue—white marking. Brown band/low expl. Yellow band/high expl.

CHEMICAL AMMUNITION

Toxic chemical (Casualty)	Gray-green marking and band or bands	Gray—green marking and band or bands. Yellow band if HE present
Irritant agents (Riot control)	Gray-red markings	Gray—red markings. Yellow band if HE present
Smoke	Gray-yellow markings	Light green—light red markings. Yellow band if HE present
Incendiary	Gray-purple markings	Light red—black markings

INDEX